Astroball

Astroball

THE NEW WAY TO WIN IT ALL

//////////

BEN REITER

CROWN
ARCHETYPE
NEW YORK

For Alice, Madeleine, and Celia

the best team there is

The most merciful thing in the world, I think, is the inability of the human mind to correlate all its contents. We live on a placid island of ignorance in the midst of black seas of infinity, and it was not meant that we should voyage far. The sciences, each straining in its own direction, have hitherto harmed us little; but some day the piecing together of dissociated knowledge will open up such terrifying vistas of reality, and of our frightful position therein, that we shall either go mad from the revelation or flee from the deadly light into the peace and safety of a new dark age.

—H. P. LOVECRAFT, 1928

///////////

A mix isn't done 'til I feel it in my gut.

—DR. DRE, 2014

CONTENTS

THANK YOU
FOR THE LAUGH

In June 2014, when I walked into the Houston Astros' offices, located in the shell of the city's old Union Station, to begin reporting a story about the team for *Sports Illustrated,* one fact overshadowed everything else I knew about them, as it did for most everyone in the sporting world.

They were ludicrously bad.

The Astros were the worst baseball team in half a century. They lost 106 games in 2011, 107 games in 2012, and 111 games in 2013, the poorest performance over a three-year span since that of the expansion New York Mets in the early 1960s. Now they were on pace for another dreadful, last-place finish. They had received local television ratings of 0.0 for several of their games, meaning that Nielsen couldn't verify that a single Houstonian had tuned in. A more appreciable audience watched Alex Trebek make fun of the club with a $1,000 question on the November 18, 2013, episode of *Jeopardy!*:

THE LARGE VALVE
USED TO CONTROL
WELLBORE FLUIDS
ON OIL RIGS IS THIS
"PREVENTER";
THE ASTROS COULD
HAVE USED ONE

"What is a blowout preventer?" answered a fifth-grade teacher from Cincinnati, correctly.

From the outside, the Astros appeared to be a run-of-the-mill, cheap, tanking team, albeit one unusually committed to both the cheapness and the tanking. While it might have been entertaining to explore the depths of their degradation, the truth was that *Sports Illustrated* and its editor, Chris Stone, would not have paid for my plane ticket to Houston, let alone published a feature about its terrible baseball club, without a good reason. I had convinced Stone that something about the losing didn't add up.

The Astros were run by executives who were said to be prodigiously intelligent and who had previously successfully led the scouting department of the St. Louis Cardinals. And yet in Houston all they did was lose, season after season, in the process becoming not just the laughingstock of baseball but of all of sports. After nearly a year of discussions, the organization promised me virtually unprecedented access to its inner workings, for a period that encompassed the first rounds of the 2014 amateur draft and a home series against the Los Angeles Angels.

They had to have a plan. I wanted to discover what it was.

What I found surprised me on several levels. No, the members of the Astros' front office did not anticipate that the club would win in 2014, as it hadn't in 2013 or 2012. They weren't exactly tanking, either, as least in the traditionally understood manner: losing in order to secure high picks in the following year's draft. High picks came anyway. The week I was embedded with them, they would make their third No. 1 overall selection in a row.

But that was only part of a grand, unified strategy in which they would not make one decision or spend a single dollar that might delay the creation of a team that could be not just a champion but a dynasty. Struggling sports teams had played for the future many times before, but never with such a purity, as the Astros called it, and they'd never been so open about their intentions. This began before the NBA's Philadelphia 76ers initiated "The Process," and before the NFL's Cleveland Browns started whatever they did in the mid-2010s. This was new.

Even more intriguing was the manner by which the Astros' executives were making their decisions. Baseball was more than a decade into its data revolution, and many of the men now running the Astros had begun their careers in tech industries. One of them had even been a rocket scientist for NASA. So they understood Big Data, and they had built a department to parse it and harness its power.

Crucially, they also recognized its shortcomings, with which the world at large had only begun to wrestle. In a way, that's the subject of this book.

But I'm getting ahead of myself.

Just two years before, *The New York Times* had heralded the Age of Big Data, extolling the limitless potential of computers to scour and analyze what had previously been incomprehensibly enormous, or simply nonexistent, troves of information to, among many other things, curtail crime, stifle outbreaks of disease, link romantic partners, and make investors buckets of money. Big Data would uncover hidden patterns in the way the world worked, allowing us to solve its mysteries and, by projecting those patterns forward, even predict the future.

By the next year, it had become a hackneyed corporate buzzword. One blog combed through transcripts and determined that the phrase had been used 43 percent more often in Wall Street conference calls and investor presentations in 2013 than 2012. The term sounded cool in a TED Talk, but in reality it was only as good as the data itself and the algorithms used to process it, and more often than not, those were incomplete and flawed. As it had begun to turn out, an overreliance on it as a decision-making engine could lead to increased racial bias in the criminal justice system, flash stock market crashes, and the mass firing of talented teachers, as well as, the Astros believed, middling and one-dimensional baseball teams. One day, a presidential campaign would rely on what it proclaimed to be the most advanced data operation in the history of politics to determine that its candidate hardly needed to campaign in several battleground states, like Michigan and Wisconsin, so certain was her chance of capturing their electoral votes.

The Astros, though, had developed a method of integrating a recently overlooked source of information back into their decision-making: humans. They synthesized human observations into their probabilistic models, and made humans responsible for triaging—and sometimes rejecting—the results. And they realized those results were rarely indisputable, relating, as they did, to human beings, with their mutability and unpredictability. They sought to identify players who were unsatisfied with their lot, who possessed an uncommon drive and ability to improve. A growth mindset, they called it.

By the time I left Houston, I had started to think there was more than win totals riding on the Astros' approach. If it worked, it might function as proof of concept for a new way of thinking not just about how to build a baseball team, but how humans and computers can bring the most out of each other. In an age in which we are deluged by data, with the specter of job-killing artificial intelligence on the horizon, positive results for the Astros could demonstrate that success is not a matter of man or machine, but of man *plus* machine—as long as man remains in charge.

Or they could become the most disastrous sustained loser in the history of not just sports, but any industry. One of the two.

///////////

CHRIS STONE BECAME the ninth managing editor of *Sports Illustrated* 20 years after he had gone to work for the magazine as a hockey reporter. Publishing was in his blood. His father was the longtime deputy editorial page editor of one of the country's last independent newspapers, Connecticut's *The Day*. From the moment Stone, fresh out of Columbia's School of Journalism, joined *SI*, he hoped to one day run it, which would mean, among other things, that he would help set the agenda for each week's national sports discussion. In 2012, he got there.

Two years later, near the end of June 2014, Stone faced a problem that for many other magazine editors represented a regular headache: The issue's close was approaching, and he did not have a cover.

Stone hadn't expected it to be that kind of week. Early summer was a fertile period on the sports calendar, bringing with it the Stanley Cup finals, the NBA finals, and, in 2014, the World Cup. That year, though, the best-of-seven series that decided the hockey and basketball champions had ended early. The Los Angeles Kings needed only five games to beat the New York Rangers, on June 13, and the San Antonio Spurs required the same number of contests to put away the Miami Heat, on June 15. Both of those championships happened too quickly to be honored on an *SI* cover that would close on June 23 and officially be dated June 30.

The US men's soccer team seemed a strong cover contender until the final seconds of stoppage time in its World Cup group stage game against Portugal on June 22. Then Cristiano Ronaldo curled a cross into the box in Brazil, which a diving Silvestre Varela headed past US goalkeeper Tim Howard to turn what had promised to be a stunning American win into a draw. The cover of *Sports Illustrated* didn't memorialize ties.

A fourth possibility emerged that same Sunday. The American golfer Michelle Wie, a six-foot-tall former phenom who turned pro a week before her 16th birthday in 2005, had, after years of promise, finally broken through to win her first major—the US Women's Open.

Alan Shipnuck, *SI*'s senior golf writer, was on the scene at North Carolina's Pinehurst No. 2 and pulled an all-nighter to produce a sensitively observed 3,000 words about how Wie, into whom he'd invested a decade of reporting, had overcome the pressures of having been a failed child prodigy to achieve her long-awaited victory. He filed in the certain expectation that it would make the cover, a rarity for a golf story that was not about Tiger Woods.

Stone, though, had begun to consider a fifth option. He genuinely bought into the Astros' potential as I described it in the piece I submitted. "I came away from the story convinced that the Astros had a really interesting plan," he said. "And I believed in it."

The Monday the issue was to close—June 23, 2014—Stone asked me a question: By when, realistically, would this thing work? That is, by when would the nucleus of players the Astros had in place be old enough to become stars, and by when would the front office have had enough time to make enough decisions to put the winning product it envisioned on the field? Was it 2020? 2019?

2017, I told him.

A few days later, Shipnuck walked the 50 yards from his house to his mailbox in Carmel, California, with a smile on his face. He opened the mailbox's rusty door and fished around until he felt *SI*'s smooth pages. He couldn't wait to see the photograph of a triumphant Wie that Stone had selected. He looked down, and his mouth fell open. "Imagine my utter shock and despair to find that waiting for me instead was the garish uniform of the crappiest team in baseball," Shipnuck recounted. "Was this a prank being pulled by my mailman? Sadly, no."

The cover photo wasn't of Michelle Wie—it was of George Springer, the Astros' rookie outfielder. Not only had Stone chosen to honor the worst professional club there was—one that didn't even seem to be trying to win—instead of a newly minted champion, but he blessed it with an absurd prediction about its future success. YOUR 2017 WORLD SERIES CHAMPS, read the cover line, printed in capital letters to the right of the swinging Springer.

The June 30, 2014, cover of Sports Illustrated.

It was the longest of shots. During spring training, Vegas usually assigns a given year's favorite less than a 20 percent chance of actually winning that fall's title. *Sports Illustrated*'s baseball preview issue, in fact, hadn't accurately predicted a season's champion in a decade and a half, since the Yankees in 1999, and Derek Jeter's defending champions were no dark horse. The magazine still got letters about a cover from 1987 headlined—regrettably, for several reasons—INDIAN UPRISING, on which it anointed Cleveland's club the American League's best, six months before it finished 61–101. Now *SI* was telling three million subscribers that baseball's worst team in half a century was just three and a half years away from winning the World Series.

Stone had just joined Twitter, and soon he had his first troll. It is exceedingly unusual for any staffer, at any publication, to publicly question a top editor for a cover choice, but Alan Shipnuck was so incensed that he couldn't help himself. He pulled out his phone and tweeted, "My @themichellewie feature is in this week's SI.

The one with the, uh, last-place Astros on the cover. #KillMeNow #Please."

Stone accepted Shipnuck's insolence with good humor. His was just one voice in the chorus of disbelief and rage that greeted the Astros cover, rising even from the club's hometown. Especially there, actually. It was "more of an attention-grabbing, perhaps even tongue-in-cheek projection than a prediction," sniffed the *Houston Chronicle*.

"Thank you for the laugh!!!" tweeted one representative fan. "I haven't had a healthy laugh like that in a long time . . . 2017 champs bahahahhaha."

You know how this turns out. On November 1, 2017, the Houston Astros won the World Series. George Springer was named the series' Most Valuable Player. It was a result that thrilled almost everyone in sports, especially Astros fans and gamblers, who saddled Las Vegas sportsbooks with a record $11.4 million loss on baseball that month, many of their bets inspired by what had once appeared a preposterous prediction.

There was at least one notable exception. "Bite me, Reiter," wrote Alan Shipnuck.

The Houston Astros were one of the worst teams in baseball history, and decided to become one of the best. This is how they did it.

THE JUDGE

THE HOUSTON ASTROS, CONCEIVED AT BOTH THE DAWN AND LOCUS OF the space age, were an innovative organization from the start. Their founder, a spindly armed, potbellied impresario named Roy Mark Hofheinz, knew no other way to operate. His first and greatest project was himself.

Hofheinz was born in 1912 in Beaumont, Texas, 85 miles northeast of Houston. While some of the city's families grew rich from the oil that had begun to gush from the nearby soil, Hofheinz's didn't. His father drove a laundry truck until he died behind its wheel when Roy was 15.

Roy envisioned a longer and more successful future for himself. Four years later, when he was 19, he passed the state bar exam. He became a state legislator at 22 and the youngest-ever US county judge at 24. He was a millionaire at 35, in oil but also radio, television, real estate, and slag, which is a by-product of steelmaking used to make concrete. In 1953, when he was 41, he became Houston's mayor, and over two terms he curtailed the city's gambling and prostitution industries and successfully fought off the city council's efforts to impeach him.

Hofheinz was by then known, well beyond Houston's city limits, simply as the Judge. He began looking for his life's second great work. He believed he had found it in a 260-acre swamp seven miles south of downtown. Where most everyone saw varmint-hunting land, suitable only for alligators, ducks, mosquitoes, and those who stalked or were stalked by them, Hofheinz imagined something else. He saw the future site of what the Reverend Billy Graham would one day deem the Eighth Wonder of the World.

The Judge did everything big, even by the standards of his home state. His waistline, in inches, matched his age, in years, through his late 50s. He liked to say his diet encompassed "anything that won't bite me back." His idea of moderation was to mix his Jack Daniel's with Diet Dr Pepper and to give away at least a few cigars from the box of 25 Sans Souci Perfectos he burned through each day.

Hofheinz wanted Houston to eat just as big, to transform its national reputation from hinterland jerkwater, as even he called it, to gleaming boomtown. During Hofheinz's lifetime, oil and shipping had multiplied the city's population by a factor of 12—from under 80,000 in 1910, when it was the country's 68th-largest city, to more than a million, meaning it trailed just New York, Chicago, Los Angeles, Philadelphia, and Detroit. It was time everyone knew about Houston's rise, and to Hofheinz that required luring a Major League Baseball team to Houston. A serviceable ballpark wouldn't do. Announced Hofheinz, "We'll build a stadium that will make Emperor Titus's playhouse look like an abandoned brickyard."

One feature of Titus's playhouse, which is better known as the Colosseum of Rome, served as a particular inspiration to Hofheinz. This was its velarium, an awning that the enslaved could pull over the stands to ensure that patrons could enjoy the sight of lions devouring convicts without suffering sunburns or damp tunics. The weather in

Houston was rarely clement, with 46 inches of annual rainfall and average summertime highs in the mid-90s. That was one reason the big leagues hadn't already expanded to the subtropical, crude-soaked metropolis. After an Italian tour, Hofheinz returned to Texas with a plan for how not only to eliminate the threat of bad weather, but to ensure that his stadium's events could be conducted in an ideal, and perfectly predictable, climate every day of the year. That, as Hofheinz told it, anyway, was how he conceived of what was officially called the Harris County Domed Stadium. Hofheinz, with his showman's ear, quickly renamed the facility, tapping into the excitement surrounding Houston's recent awarding of NASA's Manned Spacecraft Center. It would be known as the Astrodome.

A welder works inside the Astrodome in 1964, a year before its grand opening.

When the Astrodome was completed in 1965, after the swamp had been drained and then filled with $31.6 million in taxpayer money, it was in most ways everything that Hofheinz had dreamed. "The only sight this wandering reporter ever saw that surpasses it is the exquisite Taj Mahal at Agra in India," gushed *The New York Times* columnist Arthur Daley. It was the world's first fully domed stadium; the roof awed even NASA's engineers. It rose 208 feet at its apex, meaning an 18-story building could have been constructed at second base with air rights to spare, and it spanned 642 feet, twice as many as any other roof in existence. It was made of an intricate latticework of 4,596 panes of clear Lucite to allow sunlight to stream in to nurture the three and a half acres of Tifway, a Bermuda grass hybrid, that covered the field.

Hofheinz ensured that the 45,000 fans he imagined flocking to baseball games beneath his great dome would be cultivated, too. The cheapest ticket, $1.50, would buy a seat comfortably upholstered with foam rubber in an environment cooled to 74 degrees by a constantly humming $4.5 million air-conditioning system. Fans would be tended to by 2,091 game-day employees who wore 53 different kinds of uniforms; the grounds crew would do their raking and watering wearing space suits. In center field was the world's first animated scoreboard, the 474-foot-wide, 50,000-bulb Astrolite, which would tell them when to cheer and when to charge. When a Houston player hit a home run, the board would erupt into a light show of soaring rockets, gun-slinging cowboys, and snorting bulls. High rollers were in for even better treatment. They had their choice of three restaurants and a private club, in which they could order roast prime eye of beef for $5.50 per king-size slab. "After examining the way baseball's business has been conducted in the past, I figure this gives me a marked advantage over the rest," Hofheinz said.

No fan would enjoy the Astrodome as much as the Judge. Beyond the fence in right field, he installed a two-story penthouse for himself, 26 feet deep and 200 feet wide on each level, and decorated it with selections from the 26,000 pounds of art he'd acquired during a six-day tour of Hong Kong, Thailand, and the Middle East. A golden faucet filled his pink marble bathtub and a golden telephone rested next to his 12-foot-by-12-foot bed, which sat on a golden carpet. He stubbed out his Sans Soucis in one of seven golden ashtrays shaped like baseball mitts placed around the penthouse.

Judge Roy Hofheinz in the ornate boardroom of the Astrodome.

"Nobody can ever see this," Hofheinz boasted on the eve of the dome's opening, "and go back to Kalamazoo, Chicago, New York, you name it, and think this town is still bush league, that this town is Indian territory."

Hofheinz rarely slept, which was how he had enough time to choke down so many daily cigars. He spent a week testing the lighting in the stadium's most expensive boxes to ensure it flattered his female patrons' makeup and clothing. He thought of every detail.

Every detail, that is, except one: baseball.

"Hofheinz has been more interested in the peripheral things that attract the general public," said one of his architects. "In fact, the ball team was the last thing on the Judge's mind while we sweated building this thing."

The trouble started with the first pop fly. The promise of the Astrodome had induced the National League to award one of two 1962 expansion teams to Houston—the other was the New York Mets—and the members of the Colt .45s, as they were initially called, had suffered for three years in a humid, buggy, hastily constructed,

33,000-seat torture chamber. "I don't care what ballpark they ever talk about as being the hottest place on the face of the earth—Colt Stadium was it," said Rusty Staub, who joined the Colts as a 19-year-old outfielder in 1963. One night in the outdoor park, a pitcher looked down and saw that his ankles were covered with dozens of mosquitoes. He swatted at them, and his white socks turned red.

So the players welcomed the dome as enthusiastically as anyone, as well as a name change to the Astros, for which the Judge had secured the endorsement of the astronaut Alan Shepard. During their first scrimmage in their new home, against their minor league club from Oklahoma City, the players realized the old place had at least one advantage: It allowed them to see balls that were hit in the air. "Unable to follow the flight of the ball against the jigsaw pattern of the roof, the players staggered about like asphyxiated cockroaches as fly ball after fly ball dropped at their feet," reported *Time* magazine.

The issue was worst when the sun was bright, so a heavy cloud cover permitted the outfielders to eschew helmets for the official exhibition opener, against the Yankees on April 9, 1965, the day the country observed the 100th anniversary of the end of the Civil War. From Hofheinz's box, the Judge's old friend and fellow Texan Lyndon B. Johnson—who, two days prior, had explained in a nationally televised speech from Johns Hopkins University the necessity of escalating the American presence in Vietnam—watched Mickey Mantle hit the stadium's first home run.

Still, the troublesome roof revealed flaws in the vision of Hofheinz, Houston's self-fashioned Kubla Khan. One paper had already dubbed his symmetrical Xanadu "the Biggest Blister in Texas," and to fix it Hofheinz solicited 1,000 suggestions from around the country: brightly colored baseballs, different types of glasses, a smoke screen. The Judge's solution was to have the roof's Lucite panels glazed with 700 gallons of off-white acrylic paint, which did solve the problem, only to cause another one. His special strain of Bermuda grass, now deprived of sunlight, started dying.

The Judge pitched that calamity as another opportunity to innovate. He replaced the infield with zippered-together, 14-foot-wide strips of synthetic grass developed by the Chemstrand division of Monsanto—called, naturally, Astroturf. "Even bad bounces will be eliminated," Hofheinz boasted, and the surface would also hold up better under the stress of the many events besides baseball he would host in the stadium: football games, and religious revivals, and livestock shows, and the Ringling Bros. and Barnum & Bailey Circus, with its copiously urinating elephants, a show in which Hofheinz, of course, had an ownership stake. Not everyone was as enthused. "Under the worn soles of a sportswriter," wrote the columnist Red Smith, "it feels like the carpeting in a funeral home." A funeral home, Smith failed to note, with a roof that had begun to leak.

Even so, Houstonians did just what Hofheinz had promised they would: They came. While the Colt .45s drew just 725,000 fans in 1964, the Astros pulled in more than 2.1 million in '65, part of a total of 4.5 million who passed through the Astrodome's doors for all events during its first year. Three years after it opened, nearly half a million people spent a dollar each to tour the dome during the rare days on which nothing was going on inside, just to have the experience of standing in what their guides pointed out was the biggest room on earth.

Hofheinz, who as a judge had integrated Harris County's golf courses and buses, accepted patrons of all types. "My policy then as now is an all-green policy," he explained. "If you've got the green you can buy a seat, wherever you want to sit, whether you're white, black or polka-dotted." Soon, he gave visitors more places than just the Astrodome to spend their money in the former swamp. The dome became the centerpiece of Astrodomain, a complex that grew to include four hotels as well as Astroworld, an $18 million amusement park covering 57 acres, all cooled by an outdoor air-conditioning system. The complex also contained Astrohall, a 500,000-square-foot exhibition space in which the Judge rang in 1969 with a public New Year's party for thousands that featured a performance by Duke Ellington. Hofheinz called the extravaganza the Astroball.

The former swamp that came to hold an amusement park and the first-ever fully domed stadium.

The Judge suffered a stroke in 1970 that left him wheelchair-bound, but, the ember on his stogie still burning, he continued to bring in internationally covered events: a six-show run by Elvis Presley in 1970; Evel Knievel's 13-car motorcycle jumps on two nights in 1971; Billie Jean King's three-set victory over Bobby Riggs in 1973's Battle of the Sexes. The show he belatedly realized he needed most was the one he couldn't book: a winning baseball team.

The Astros, *Sports Illustrated* noted, were "born at the same time as the New York Mets, but not as funny." While Elvis or Knievel or King might fill the dome a few nights a year, the Astros were supposed to do it 81 times, at minimum. Soon, the novelty of the roof and of the scoreboard wore off, and young stars like Staub, Joe Morgan, and, later, César Cedeño couldn't help the club prosper in its strange environs. Even the laughable Mets won a World Series, in 1969, but the Astros couldn't come close. By 1975, after 14 years without a single playoff game, the club bottomed out. Attendance at their games plummeted to less than 860,000. The year brought an even bigger shock. Roy Hofheinz—Giltfinger himself, the Astrobrain, the man with a mind that was said to be as quick as a cash register and who was touted as knowing as much about money as Richard Burton knew about girls—had run up $38 million in debt. The Judge lost control of the Astrodome to his creditors, and then of the Astros.

Over the next quarter century, domed and Astroturfed imitations of Hofheinz's weatherproof stadium sprouted across the continent: the Kingdome in Seattle, Olympic Stadium in Montreal, the Metrodome in Minneapolis, SkyDome in Toronto. None of those similarly symmetrical, multipurpose facilities had the Judge's gilded, aspirational touches. Hofheinz died in 1982, six years before his penthouse was demolished.

The Astros, their home field no longer quite as much of a competitively disadvantageous outlier, began to experience modest and periodic success. Behind stars like the ageless Texan pitcher Nolan Ryan, they even made the playoffs six times. But they never gave the Astrodome a single World Series game.

"Many people resist change, are afraid to move," Hofheinz once said. "You have to grow. Take baseball, for instance. You've got to understand why most baseball owners resist change. The clubs are owned by people not in day-to-day contact with the hour-to-hour operation. The owners, for the most part, are successful in another business but they know little about baseball and depend for advice on recommendations from the ranks. And the philosophy in the ranks goes right back to Tinker to Evers to Chance." That celebrated Cubs trio had turned its last double play in 1912.

"You've got to do one of two things," Hofheinz continued. "Get more customers or more money per ticket, and if you get more money per ticket you price yourself out of the market."

Hofheinz's ultimate miscalculation related to the best way to draw more customers. It wasn't about where the games were played.

It was, even more, about *how* they were played. Still, in the spring of 2000, the Astros left the Astrodome for a sleek new ballpark downtown, with a retractable roof and naming rights purchased by a corporation whose ascendant fortunes they were certain would soon mirror their own. Their new home was called Enron Field.

1

GUT FEELS

In the late 1980s, when people got too drunk and were kicked out of the other casinos in Lake Tahoe, they ended up at Del Webb's High Sierra, a place where there was no such thing as too drunk. Sometimes they staggered by indifferent security guards who were costumed as Wild West deputies, past stages adorned with fake tumbleweeds, and over to a blackjack table manned by a tall, thin young dealer with thick black hair.

"Sig?" they would say, squinting at the tag pinned to his chest. "What kind of name is that?"

Sig Mejdal was an undergraduate at the University of California, Davis, studying mechanical engineering and aeronautical engineering. During the summers he'd head 120 miles east, clip an oversize bow tie to his collar, and sling cards at Tahoe's seediest betting house. He thought the tie made him look more like someone with a dead cat draped around his neck than a Dodge City barman—or like a Dodge City barman who hunted house pets, best case—but he loved the job anyway. It was more fun than the internships his classmates at Davis pursued, and more lucrative, too. He would spend the day at the beach, deal all night, fling the hundred bucks he'd made in tips onto the steadily accumulating pile on his dresser in the morning, and head back to the beach.

At the High Sierra, he learned things he knew he couldn't have in a lab. The best way to get someone to stop smoking at his table, for example. When a gambler rested his cigarette on the edge of his ashtray, Sig would subtly put a little extra on the next card he dealt to him, so that it hit the cigarette and knocked it onto the felt or the ground in a shower of sparks. The player, embarrassed and believing it to have been an accident, usually didn't light up again.

Sig also learned something that he would use more frequently during his future professional career. He learned that human beings do not always make decisions that serve their own long-term self-interest, even when they are equipped with a wealth of experience and knowledge of the mathematical probabilities that ought to guide their choices.

Blackjack is a probabilistic game. For any combination of cards, the player's and the dealer's, there is an optimal action for the player to take in order to increase his chances of winning—or, generally, of losing less. Sometimes, the action is both easy and obvious. You hit a 10, against anything. Often, though, players know what they ought to do from a probabilistic perspective, but they do something else, because their intuition tells them to.

Even the sober patrons of the High Sierra usually declined to hit on a 16 against a dealer's 7, because it sucked to bust, especially with a big bet on the table. The mathematically sound move was to take another card, though. It was a bad hand no matter what, but standing led to a loss rate of 74 percent—the chances were that the dealer would pull a 17, at minimum—while hitting decreased that to 67.5 percent, even factoring in the busts, a big difference in the long run. Sometimes, even other dealers, who saw more than 100,000 hands a year, with immediate feedback, advised players to stand.

This, to Sig, illustrated the limitations of human judgment. "Just because it feels right," he told himself, "doesn't mean it *is* right." Human beings tended to trust the combination of experience, intuition, and emotion that comprised their gut. Their gut certainly had value. Sometimes their gut was wrong.

When he wasn't spending his free time at the beach, Sig spread his wrinkled tip money onto the blackjack table himself. He rarely won. The house's advantage was the house's advantage. Playing the right way, though, he lost slowly, and when he factored in the complimentary drinks he consumed in the process, he considered it a financial wash.

Sig and the other dealers marveled at the way gamblers they had wiped out would unquestioningly follow the custom of tossing their last few chips to them for the trouble, sparing the casino the burden of paying them more than minimum wage. A hundred bucks a day was good money, and many dealers decided to make a career out of their summer gig. Sig did not.

He graduated from Davis and went on to earn two master's degrees, in operations research and cognitive psychology, from San Jose State. He took a job at Lockheed Martin, where he helped launch satellites into orbit. Then he performed research for NASA's Fatigue Countermeasures Group, where, among other things, he revealed the relative uselessness of napping. Even though tired subjects believed that naps fully restored their ability to perform, that turned out to be empirically untrue unless they had gone through a full night's sleep cycle.

Sig was initially inspired to undertake that study not by astronauts, but by a different type of American hero: baseball players. He had wondered how the performance of major leaguers from the East Coast was affected when they traveled to play in different time zones, interrupting their circadian rhythms. In fact, the entirety of Sig's mathematically driven career had stemmed from his passion for our most mathematically driven sport.

Unlike many American boys, Sig did not inherit his love of

baseball from his parents. His father, Svend, came from Denmark, and his mother, Norma, grew up in Colombia. They each arrived in the United States in their 20s, and met in the US Army, an officer and a nurse. Sig's older brother, Svend Jr., was born in France, while his parents were stationed there. Norma gave birth to Sig—Sigurd, actually—in California in 1965, when Svend Sr. was in Vietnam.

Nobody could ever pronounce the family's last name, Mejdal, until a friend of Sig's came up with a mnemonic chant. "Whose dell?" the friend asked. "My dell!" Sig shouted. If some of his peers still stumbled on his surname, Sig had little trouble connecting with them via a pastime neither of his parents much understood.

He spent great swaths of his childhood flicking the spinners of All-Star Baseball, a board game that allowed players to simulate major league contests. Each year the game's maker, Cadaco-Ellis, released a new set of circular, insertable cards representing players both current and past. Each card was divided into fourteen zones, sized to correspond with the player's statistics, on which the spinner might land. A slugger's card might have had large zones for No. 1 (Home Run) and No. 10 (Strikeout), while slap hitters' cards featured more room for the spinner to end up on No. 7 (Single) or No. 11 (Double). Sig favored the latter. He loved the 1894 Baltimore Orioles of Dan Brouthers and Wee Willie Keeler.

He began subscribing to newsletters produced by the Society for American Baseball Research, or SABR. When he was in sixth grade, he read a paper that included a formula that could predict how many runs and runs batted in a given player should amass based on the number and type of hits he had. The analyst had worked backward from real run totals to determine how much each constituent part contributed to them. This was called regression analysis.

Sig wrote a rudimentary program on his Atari 800 computer that allowed him to project those results for his All-Star Baseball players, like Brouthers and Keeler, and he recorded his players' stats in reams of notebooks. "It seemed magical," he said. "It was why I liked math."

He played simulated season after simulated season, competing against not only his buddy from across the street but, after responding to an ad in a newsletter, retirees across the country by mail on the honor system. In his imagination, his living room became the site of nerve-rattling championships won by legendary players under his control. "These heroic actions would be taking place whenever you wanted, in your living room," he said. "You'd keep track of the statistics and get excited by the drama, as if this was important."

To the even deeper mystification of his parents, Sig also played six years of Little League, from the fourth grade through the ninth. He was so skinny that he could rarely lift the ball out of the infield. His mother inadvertently sat in the wrong bleachers and cheered whenever the umpire called him out, which was almost always.

Sig loved it anyway, especially after he began reading the annual *Baseball Abstract* self-published by Bill James, the godfather of sabermetrics—the statistical analysis of baseball data. When he wasn't in right field—where the coaches always played him, hoping that a ball wouldn't be squibbed his way—he calculated James's pioneering statistics, designed to capture a player's value better than batting average or home run totals could, for each one of his teammates. Every member of the 1981 Papagallos of San Jose's Union Little League had a Runs Created, whether he knew it or not.

Even so, as a teenager there was only one career path Sig could imagine following. "I have immigrant parents," he said. "They wanted their son to make it in this country. I was brainwashed since grade school to be an engineer, and I don't think I ever rethought it." His one minor rebellion, the summers he'd spent at the High Sierra rather than buttressing his résumé with internships, turned out to be his best piece of luck: The hiring manager at Lockheed loved blackjack.

"I wanted a job," Sig said. "This was fine." In fact, it was undeniably cool to become an expert in subsystems that controlled a rocket, and to be responsible for averting mistakes that could cost hundreds of millions of dollars. Still, to Sig it felt remote, bloodless. The rockets and satellites were thousands of miles away, and success meant they stayed on course. They always did.

For most engineers, a well-paid job like that would have been enough. It wasn't for Sig. The trouble was that, unlike many of those with his quantitative background, Sig was a people person, too—a humanist. "The stereotype of the introverted analyst? I guess I don't fit it so well," he said.

In the early 1990s, he realized that he was spending much of every weekend standing in line at Macy's, waiting to get another gift wrapped to tote to the weddings to which he kept being invited. He began to keep track of them. A quarter century later he had attended 96. That he knew the precise number was itself remarkable—only someone who quantifies everything would keep count—but so is the number itself. How many of us are so invested in people and relationships that 96 couples couldn't imagine observing their happiest of days without us there? His greatest regret, as he got older, was that the frequency of invitations slowed down.

His tasks at NASA, like the sleep cycle research, were more satisfying than his previous jobs. He had studied cognitive psychology in graduate school because he was fascinated not by dry engineering problems like how to keep a rocket on course, but by how math and science intersected with people, how they could help humans understand and overcome their natural limitations. Still, NASA was just a job, too. He had always maxed out his vacation days at Lockheed, and at NASA he insisted on working on short-term contracts so that for a month or two each year he could pursue another passion: travel. He called it "high-concentrate living," in his value-focused way.

Seeking out adventure, he met people throughout Europe and South America. In 2001, he published an article in the *Los Angeles Times*, headlined CLIMBING THE STAIRWAY TO HEAVEN, in which he chronicled his experiences as the novice member of an expedition that ascended Mount Chimborazo. Sig mischievously asserted that, factoring in Earth's ellipsoid shape, the Ecuadorean peak was actually its highest, 7,000 feet farther from the planet's center than Everest's. "To the south I could see the mountains of Peru; to the west, the blues of the Pacific Ocean; and to the north, snowcapped

Cotopaxi," he wrote of the vista from the hypoxemic summit. "I was overwhelmed by the magnitude of what my eyes could take in. Exhaustion and emotion are a volatile combination for an oxygen-starved brain. Some climbers collapsed in the snow. Some cried. Others hugged. I did a little of each before turning my attention to the view before me, the view from the top of the world."

After that, it was back down to the lab, where he continued to dream of a job that would unite his mathematical expertise with his passion for figuring out what made humans their best selves, a job in which he wouldn't feel as if each year amounted to working for 11 months in order to live for one.

Two years after Chimborazo, he thought he'd found it.

///////////

SIG WAS 37 WHEN, in 2003, he read Michael Lewis's *Moneyball*, a book that described how people with his skill set in the Oakland Athletics' front office were reimagining the underpinnings of baseball by harnessing the power of data to take advantage of inefficiencies in the evaluation of players. They were, in other words, making a living by using math to get better at the thing Sig had always loved most. While he had remained an engaged fan and a member of SABR, he now realized there might be a place inside the game for someone like him. "I thought, hey, that job would be better than NASA," he said.

Soon, Sig was spending two days a week sending out résumés and proposals in an attempt to land the dream job he hadn't known until recently was even a job. His pitch was that by applying statistical techniques he had developed to the amateur draft, a club could instantly double its success rate on its picks. Part of his package was specific to the club he was contacting. He'd pick one of the club's best players and demonstrate how back testing could reveal the player's future performance and therefore value. Part of it was general: how to evaluate a player's college performance controlling for the level of competition against which he played and the idiosyncrasies of the ballparks in which he hit or pitched, and then how to project those numbers into the pros. A player who hit 15 home runs in a college season, but did so in a strong conference and in big stadiums, could be far superior to one who slugged 25 against worse pitching in bandboxes.

Sig traveled to baseball's 2003 Winter Meetings, in New Orleans, hoping to catch an executive's ear. He stayed in a dump, but that didn't matter because he spent most of those three days on his feet in the lobby of the Marriott, thrusting his materials into the hands of anyone whose face appeared on the grid of headshots of executives he'd printed out from the website of *Baseball America*.

Although he knew most of his pamphlets ended up in the Marriott's trash bins, he kept at it. He mailed proposals to every team. He heard back from almost no one. A terse "no thank you" was a rare gesture of politeness. Most clubs, run by longtime baseball men, weren't yet inclined to consider hiring a nerdy fan, especially one who was respectfully suggesting that the way they'd always operated was wrong.

Then, in the summer of 2004, he got an email from someone with the Cardinals whose name he'd never heard before and whose headshot hadn't appeared on his *Baseball America* grid. His name was Jeff Luhnow.

Sig Mejdal, the former NASA rocket scientist turned baseball data guru.

Sig had a conference to attend in Florida that summer for NASA, and he spent much of it ruminating in his hotel's pool. He arranged for his flight back to California to connect through St. Louis. He landed and took the train to Busch Stadium, and soon sat in a room with Cardinals general manager Walt Jocketty and John Mozeliak—Jocketty's assistant—as well as Luhnow, who did most of the talking.

The meeting ran long. Afterward, Sig rode the train back to the airport and convinced the ticketing agent that he had slept through his connection. She put him on the next flight with no penalty. That wasn't the only reason his three hours in St. Louis had felt so good. For the entirety of the interview, Luhnow had clutched Sig's brochure and one of his reports in his hands.

///////////

JEFF LUHNOW, A TRIM MAN WITH NEAT, graying hair, never slung cards at a place like the High Sierra, but he also knew gambling. He had worked as a management consultant at McKinsey & Company, the longtime industry leader, for five years, and he believed that one project there had best prepared him for a job in baseball. The project involved the advising of one of the world's largest casino operators.

"I learned a lot about how the gaming industry works, and probabilities," Luhnow said. "How if you have a large number of occurrences, even though luck is involved, you can still make things pretty predictable. For the player, when you do start to follow your gut or you've had a couple of drinks and think you've seen a lot of tens, you're just basically giving the house back some money. The odds are the odds."

Like Sig, Luhnow also had several diplomas—two undergraduate degrees, in chemical engineering and economics, from Penn, and an MBA from Northwestern—and a varied, searching professional career. Before McKinsey, he had an engineering job with W. L. Gore, the makers of Gore-Tex, in which he designed suits intended to protect troops from nuclear, biological, and chemical warfare. Later, he helped start an internet business called PetStore.com, and another that brought customized apparel to the masses.

Luhnow felt that one of his strengths as an executive was an ability to build a bridge between two cultures. Though his parents were American, he was born in Mexico City in 1966, and spent the first fifteen years of his life there. He had two passports and spoke two languages. On many childhood weekends, he traveled to Mexico's resort towns, where his parents researched the guide books they produced as part of their publishing business. One of his two brothers, David, would grow up to become the Latin America editor for *The Wall Street Journal*. Sometimes, the family took trips to the States, where they watched baseball. The first major league game Luhnow ever attended was in the stadium located closest to Mexico City, the Astrodome. Later, he would go to Dodger Stadium to join the manic crowd as the Mexican ace Fernando Valenzuela cast his left-handed spells.

Luhnow was not the type of person to waste a summer, let alone several of them, in Tahoe. At Penn, he enrolled in the prestigious Management & Technology program. Split between the engineering school and Wharton, the program took five years to complete and was so intensive that it allowed its students just one elective. Luhnow chose a class that was as different from the rest of his load as it could be: the philosophy of existentialism, focusing on writers like Camus. There was logic behind the choice, of course. In his economics and engineering and science courses, he learned the world's rulebook. There was always a right answer. But true success would also mean peering beyond that which was already known. Luhnow wanted to be exposed to thinkers for whom there was never a right answer, at least never an easy one, which was usually the case when humans became involved.

Like Sig, Luhnow always dreamed of baseball. During business school, he often sat in the bleachers at Wrigley Field. He wrote a paper for one of his classes about how he would turn around the

Cubs, who hadn't lifted a World Series trophy in nine decades and remained also-rans in the mid-1990s despite Sammy Sosa's homers. He played fantasy baseball and he knew not just every player but every prospect, even in the pre-internet days when information about them was hard to find. He usually won.

Baseball combined so much of what he was good at—blending cultures, crunching numbers, solving problems, even speaking fluent Spanish. But there was no place in the majors for an MBA, not even a point of entry, except maybe in ticketing or merchandising. So instead, he went into business. At McKinsey, he worked with the country's top CEOs, helping them solve their most pressing problems. Later, at the tech companies he helped build in Silicon Valley, he solved them himself.

The apparel company, called Archetype Solutions, allowed customers of brands like J.Crew, Lands' End, and Tommy Hilfiger to design clothing fitted to them, based on measurements they took of themselves and typed into the brands' websites. Here he learned what Sig had discovered at the blackjack table: His customers often did not behave in ways that would ultimately benefit them. The problem was that the measurements they reported were often wrong—too small, usually—and the customers ended up with supposedly custom jeans that pinched at the waist. So Luhnow's company designed algorithms to correct those reported measurements, counteracting the cognitive biases customers had about the sizes of their own bodies.

In August 2003, he received an email from someone he had recruited to McKinsey from the University of Chicago. The man knew that Luhnow was an expert in business and technology but also ran roughshod over the competition in his fantasy baseball leagues. "My father-in-law wants to talk to you," the email said.

The father-in-law was a man named Bill DeWitt Jr., the principal owner of the St. Louis Cardinals. DeWitt was a second generation baseball man—his father had been a Branch Rickey protégé who went on to run several teams during a 65-year career—and a successful investor who had owned stakes in the Cincinnati Reds, Baltimore Orioles, and Texas Rangers before taking control of the Cardinals in 1996. Seven years later, in 2003, the *Moneyball* era had begun, and DeWitt thought there might be a way to blend his life's animating passions, baseball and business, in a way that could improve his organization's fortunes in what was any successful club's lifeblood: the amateur draft.

If there was one club in baseball that didn't appear to require an overhaul, it was the Cardinals. Only the Yankees had won more World Series than the Cardinals' nine. Since 1960, they'd had consecutive losing seasons just once, in 1994 and '95, and no St. Louisan born since 1902 had reached the age of 25 without having lived through at least one victory parade. They had just made their third straight playoff appearance, the last two driven by one of the greatest finds in the history of the draft. Their 13th rounder in 1999, the 402nd player selected, was a hitter from Maple Woods, an obscure community college in Kansas City that had never before produced a big leaguer. His name was Albert Pujols, and just four years later he seemed destined for the Hall of Fame. If there was anyone who demonstrated that the so-called Cardinals Way—led by baseball lifers, executives and scouts who generally did things the same way they had always been done—still worked, particularly in the draft, it was Pujols.

As DeWitt saw it, though, Pujols was an anomaly. Since 1996, St. Louis's scouting department had selected only a handful of other stars, like the outfielder J.D. Drew in 1998, the catcher Yadier Molina in 2000, and the pitcher Dan Haren in 2001. Of their 323 picks since then, just 47 reached the big leagues at all, where most of them made only marginal contributions. To DeWitt, four stars in seven drafts wasn't nearly good enough.

The draft was important because it could continually infuse an organization with talented players who were not just young but cheap. Though every draftee received an initial one-time bonus based on where he was picked, those who made it through the minors were controlled by their clubs for the first six years of their major league careers at an artificially depressed salary, only after which did they become free agents available to the highest bidder. For each of their first three seasons in the majors, their clubs were required to pay them the league minimum of around $300,000, sometimes 50 times less than the annual wage of a top free agent who might not necessarily be any more productive than a great young player. DeWitt knew that unearthing more stars in the draft was essential, and the Oakland A's, overseen by general manager Billy Beane, provided a model for the type of data-driven thinking that could help the Cardinals do it. He needed to find the right guy to lead that effort, someone even smarter than he was.

Jeff Luhnow, named the Cardinals' scouting director in 2005.

In mid-September 2003, not long after meeting Jeff Luhnow, DeWitt issued a memorandum, titled "Proposed Organizational Change," to his front office. "I think he presents a unique opportunity for us to bring to the Cardinals a high level McKinsey talent at a below market price to fill a very challenging and important position," he wrote of Luhnow. It was not in DeWitt's nature to be confrontational. Despite his extreme financial success, he was a Midwesterner. But the change was more than just a proposal. He was the owner, which meant it was happening. Jeff Luhnow was the club's new vice president of baseball development.

Luhnow viewed his first season in St. Louis as a consulting gig. He stayed in the background and analyzed the organization's operations, figuring out what could be improved by the introduction of analytics. If he'd been able to use data to deliver correctly fitting jeans to his customers, he could use it to deliver better draft picks to DeWitt. The 2004 draft, which Luhnow only observed, was a disaster. Ultimately, the 47 players the Cardinals selected combined for a grand total of 55 major league games and a single home run. For the next year, 2005, DeWitt promoted Luhnow to scouting director, which meant he would now be responsible for running the draft. Luhnow set out to complete the formidable task of hiring someone who could find, process, and analyze the enormous body of information that he knew the Cardinals could be applying to player procurement but weren't yet. He looked at the brochure and proposal that sat on his desk, and thought of the blackjack dealer turned rocket scientist who had produced it.

//////////

AFTER LUHNOW HIRED HIM, Sig worked remotely for a few months as he prepared to move away from California for the first time in his life. He was to report to St. Louis on Opening Day of the 2005 season. That gave him time to do something he hadn't since he was a kid: attend a ballgame without a beer in his hand, which he figured he'd be doing a lot more of going forward. The number one collegiate player in the country, according to his projection system, was a second baseman with a great baseball name, Jed Lowrie. Though most top college infielders played shortstop, Lowrie's numbers suggested that he could rake. He led his team in home runs, RBIs, and on-base-plus-slugging percentage in both his sophomore and junior seasons, and he did it in one of the most competitive conferences in the country, the Pac-10. Lowrie attended Stanford. Palo Alto happened to be a 20-minute drive from Sig's house.

Sig discovered that Stanford didn't stitch its players' last names on the backs of their jerseys, only their numbers, so during warm-ups he had fun trying to figure out which of their muscled behemoths was his prize, whom he'd imagined to resemble Paul Bunyan. Was it No. 25, who looked about six foot five, 230? That turned out to be John Mayberry Jr. Then it must be No. 30, who was even bigger— maybe six foot six, 235? No, someone told him, that was Michael Taylor. He noticed a little guy, a full head shorter and at least 50 pounds lighter than many of his teammates, trotting out at the back of the pack, wearing No. 4. Must be a chemical engineer they'd allowed onto the team after they'd run out of scholarships, Sig surmised. Then he went and got a team roster. No. 4 was Jed Lowrie.

Sig thought he was going to throw up. He was going to go to St. Louis to start his dream job, and he was going to say that *this* was the best player in the country, *this* was who they needed to draft. They were going to laugh him out of the room and redeposit him in California. He'd already quit NASA. Maybe they'd have him back. Maybe he needed a beer after all.

Jed Lowrie during his final season at Stanford, in 2005.

Then his intellect took over. *OK, so Jed Lowrie is short. He doesn't look like a major league player. He doesn't even look like a college player. But he wasn't taller last year, nor the year before, and he's outperformed every one of these guys. Mayberry Jr. was the first baseman, the athletic son of a big leaguer. They played 30 feet apart for three years, and Lowrie outhit him. If he's outhit that guy, there must be something invisible that makes him good, but reveals itself in the performance numbers.* Sig resolved to stick to his data. If he didn't vouch for Lowrie as his number one dude, he didn't deserve his job in the first place. The beer could wait, for now.

Three months later, as the 2005 draft approached, Sig had convinced Luhnow to believe in Jed Lowrie, too, even though Lowrie was no taller than Luhnow himself. "The scouts are saying that this second baseman is not going to be hitting more homers than John Mayberry in the big leagues, that it's just not possible," Sig told his new boss. "But it is, and he will."

Luhnow believed in Sig, but he also believed in something he had learned at McKinsey: the benefits of introducing cultural change gradually, especially into a successful organization like the Cardinals. This was just the first of what he hoped would be many drafts he would oversee, and his scouts, whose qualitative evaluations of amateurs had always guided the Cardinals' picks, liked another college infielder, a shortstop, far more than they did Stanford's Lilliputian: Tyler Greene of Georgia Tech. Greene looked better than Lowrie—he was six foot two and a solid 200 pounds—and he ran better, though he didn't hit better and struck out a lot more.

Winning a war often meant losing a few early battles. Luhnow picked Greene at No. 30 overall. The Red Sox—analytics pioneers under their 31-year-old, third-year GM, Theo Epstein—snapped up Lowrie at No. 45, one slot before the Cardinals would have had another crack at him. Sig was nauseated by something involving Lowrie for the second time. He was also right. In 2017, Lowrie completed his tenth year as a major league infielder. Greene washed out in 2013.

///////////

THOUGH LUHNOW GAVE THE TRADITIONALISTS GREENE, his strategy of gradually integrating analytics into St. Louis's operations didn't go entirely well. They were the Cardinals, after all. They had made their latest World Series just the year before, in 2004, though they had been swept by Epstein's Red Sox, and they had gotten that far thanks largely to Pujols, whom *they* had found in the 13th round. And the organization needed help with the draft from someone who had only played fantasy? The new guy—the owner's pet—was trying to fix something that wasn't broken.

If they hadn't yet invited Sig to any of their weddings, everyone was nice to him, because they didn't think he had much power, and because he was Sig. Sig, quite obviously, wasn't hiding anything. He ran as hot as his whirring hard drives, and always told you what he thought. Luhnow was quieter, more calculating, and he did have power, including a line to DeWitt. Some members of the Cardinals' front office refused to talk to him. Others called him Harry Potter, perhaps overlooking the fact that Harry's magic seemed to work pretty well.

But DeWitt let it be known, politely, that Luhnow would be the exec who lived. If you refused to work with him, you would no longer be working for the Cardinals. Some bought in. Some didn't. The mild-mannered Mozeliak, who accepted the organization's evolution, replaced Walt Jocketty in 2007, even though the Cardinals had won their tenth World Series the year before. Not all transitions were as smooth. On the day of one firing, DeWitt had Luhnow work off-site, so that if the axed executive came after him, he wouldn't be around.

At McKinsey, and even as a young American boy in Mexico City, Luhnow had developed something besides what he believed to be an ability to meld distinct cultures: a thick skin. He would need it as he sought to modernize the Cardinals' ossified ways while retaining the qualities that had made the franchise successful to begin with. When he scanned the baseball landscape at the end of 2005, he identified one organization that was most similar to the Cardinals.

The Houston Astros also played in the National League Central, and they had a similar market size and payroll. The clubs had just faced each other in consecutive National League Championship Series, with the Astros winning the second. Luhnow sat in the visitors' seats in Houston for both series, and he had seen how, when the city's fan base had a winner to cheer, it could be just as energized as St. Louis's famously supportive one.

His goal, for however long he was in St. Louis, was to beat the Astros, and then everyone else, and he would do it his way, even if some of his coworkers froze him out and condescendingly compared him to a fictional wizard. Though DeWitt would over the years ramp up his responsibilities to include oversight of the Cardinals' international scouting and its player development, Luhnow knew that everything would spring from the tense days each June in which he ran the draft.

///////////

OVER THE NEXT SEVERAL YEARS, even as Luhnow brought a new approach to the Cardinals' drafts, he never tried to eradicate their old one. He sought to invent a method of combining Sig's advanced, performance-based data analysis with the evaluative contributions of his scouts, who, no matter the names they called him, had discovered Albert Pujols. In *Moneyball*, scouts were largely portrayed as the story's antagonists, the dimwitted Luddites who stood in the way of progress. "I think for all the wonders that the book did, the portrayal was a dichotomous one," Sig said. "It's either the scouts or the nerd, in the corner of the room. But from the very beginning in St. Louis, Jeff framed it as an *and* question. It's the scouting information *and* the performance information." A systemic rejection of all potentially predictive information the scouts provided, based on their experience and observations, meant discarding potentially talented babies along with the bathwater. The scouts might be flawed—they were, after all, human—but they still had value. It was for this reason that in 2006, Sig had developed the first iteration of a metric that sought to incorporate the reports of the club's scouts with his own performance-based algorithms, to integrate quantitative and qualitative evaluations. He called it STOUT—half stats, half scouts.

When the men emerged from the Cardinals draft room on June 11, 2009, after 10 days of arguing and celebrating and grumbling, the recycling bin was overflowing with the empty bottles—some of them now repurposed into dip spit receptacles—of the water and Diet Coke that had fueled them, and they couldn't be sure as to exactly what they had just done. The draft hadn't felt particularly different from any of the previous four to the 30 or so minds that had collectively shaped it.

Luhnow had as usual spent a week and a half on his feet at the front of the conference room on the third floor of Busch Stadium, shuffling around some 1,200 magnets, each of which bore the name of a draft-eligible amateur: high school seniors and collegians who had completed at least their junior years. "Every time you move one," said Luhnow, "half the room is cringing, and half is clapping."

The room was the size of a high school classroom, and most of those reactions came from the men who sat at desks arranged as those of AP History students might have been: in a U-shape, facing Luhnow's magnet board. These were Luhnow's scouts, 16 area scouts and a half dozen more cross-checkers who were responsible for supporting or undercutting the reports the area scouts had delivered. Among them they had over the past several years gotten to know the person connected to virtually every one of those 1,200 names, and their opinions about them—voiced in an orderly, but often passionate, manner—would affect not only the organization's future, but the course of their own careers.

Behind the scouts, tapping away at their computers, were the analysts. Sig led the three-man team, which also included a new hire named Chris Correa. Correa had an academic background in cognitive science, psychology, and education, and had recently abandoned a doctoral program at the University of Michigan to join the

Cardinals. Luhnow and Sig had been impressed by his internet writings, which demonstrated an ability to find and analyze certain data that they hadn't yet been able to. In the back were chairs for the leaders of the Cardinals' front office. DeWitt and Mozeliak came in and out to observe the proceedings when they were not handling the club's other business.

After the 1,521st player had been selected, and when the men looked back at the 50 whose rights were now theirs, they felt as they usually did: weary yet energized, and optimistic. "We always talk about how it's sort of Christmas morning in a sense, in that you have no idea what you're going to unwrap—and it takes a while to find out," said Mozeliak. Luhnow used a similar analogy. "It just so happens that my birthday is on June eighth, so every year the draft's right around it," he said. He had just turned 43. "Always feels like I got fifty presents."

Years later, Luhnow would come to view the 2009 draft as something else. It showed that the culture war he and Bill DeWitt had ignited a half decade earlier burned on. But he would also consider it an ultimate, and generally successful, beta test for the decision-making philosophy he would install in his next stop.

///////////

IF, AS MOZELIAK SAID, each draft is like Christmas for a baseball team, then the vast majority of the gifts it receives will prove to be scratchy sweaters. Not even 10 percent of amateurs who are drafted will ever aerate a major league field with their spikes, even for a single inning. In 2013, one of the Cardinals' rival scouting departments commissioned a study that examined draft outcomes more deeply still. The study, which extended back to 1990, found that if a club's draft produces nine players who appear in the majors for even a single game, it ranks in the 95th percentile. The 95th percentile for number of everyday players—defined as those who go on to accumulate 1,500 big league plate appearances or batters faced—is four. The

95th percentile for number of firmly above-average players—that is, those who produce a cumulative Wins Above Replacement above 6.0 in their six cost-controlled, pre–free agency seasons—is three. The Cardinals, before Luhnow arrived, had fared poorly by all those measurements, particularly the last.

Luhnow, with Sig's help, had only conducted four drafts by 2009. Though they had yet to have a selection higher than 13th overall, due to the big league club's ongoing success and to the draft's structure, which rewarded bad teams with high picks, they had demonstrated an ability to blow up the curve. Ten of their picks had already reached the majors, including outfielder Colby Rasmus—whom they'd taken two spots ahead of Tyler Greene in 2005—as well as starter Jaime García and reliever Chris Perez. At least five others—like first baseman Allen Craig, outfielder Jon Jay, and starter Lance Lynn—waited on the doorstep at Triple-A.

"Every draft class is a portfolio," said Luhnow. "You've got to mix up some big bets with some fliers. You're going to have some hits and failures." In 2009, with his first pick at No. 19, his goal was no different than it always was: to produce enough hits to ensure the perpetual health of the Cardinals, and to demonstrate the ever-improving efficacy of his system.

////////////

SHELBY MILLER WAS AT HOME in Brownwood, Texas, surrounded by his friends and family, when his name was read on the MLB Network and he found out he was now property of the St. Louis Cardinals.

Matt Carpenter sat by himself in the three-bedroom house he rented with his Texas Christian University teammates in Fort Worth, constantly refreshing the draft results page on his computer, when he received a congratulatory text message from his aunt. He refreshed once more and saw where he was headed.

Trevor Rosenthal perspired in the parking lot of a Price Chopper supermarket in Lee's Summit, Missouri, spreading mulch with the landscaping crew on which he worked that summer. His phone rang. "I was drafted by the Cardinals!" he announced to his fellow mulchers. "That's great!" they said. "You missed a spot."

In Philipsburg, Pennsylvania, Matt Adams and his family had long before turned off their computer when he got the call. He had thought it would come many hours earlier. He was, mostly, relieved.

The different ways in which each of the four discovered that he had been drafted, and by whom, reflected the divergent manners by which Jeff Luhnow, back in the conference room in St. Louis, had come to zero in upon their names.

Everybody in baseball knew that Miller, an 18-year-old senior at Brownwood High, was a top-ten talent. Since he had become scouting director, Luhnow had shied away from taking high school pitchers, with their proven risk of injury and failure, in the first round. His first four top picks had been three hitters—Rasmus, shortstop Pete Kozma in 2007, and first baseman Brett Wallace in 2008—and a collegiate pitcher, Adam Ottavino in 2006.

Miller was different. "Of all the pitchers I had seen in my years as scouting director, I never felt quite as comfortable as I did with Shelby," Luhnow said. "He exemplified everything I was looking for, body-wise, stuff-wise, everything about his makeup and athleticism." Miller fell through the top ten and all the way down to the Cardinals because his young agent had let it be known that he was after Porcello money. That meant a deal commensurate with the record-setting four years and $7.285 million that New Jersey high school pitcher Rick Porcello had received from the Tigers two years earlier. Nobody was certain if this was a negotiating tactic to try to get Miller to his preferred club, which was located five hours southeast of his hometown and was picking two spots after St. Louis: the Astros.

The Cardinals scout who had covered Miller thought the agent was bluffing, and convinced the draft room of that. Miller was shocked when his name was announced, but a month later he agreed to a $2.875 million signing bonus. "I didn't really want to go to this organization, to be honest," he admitted. Four years later, after he had watched the team for which he had rooted in childhood badly decline, he had changed his view. "I'm glad I'm not with Houston," he said.

Everyone in the Cardinals' draft room, the scouts and the stats guys, had agreed on Miller. By the draft's second day, which begins with the fourth round, such concurrence was unusual, as all the players without either a glaring quantitative or qualitative flaw had already been taken. It was particularly rare in the 13th round, which is where the Cardinals were considering selecting Matt Carpenter. Carpenter was a fifth-year senior at Texas Christian, after a difficult tenure there that had included a temporary weight gain to 240 pounds and a Tommy John surgery. As such, he was closer to his 24th birthday than his 23rd and among the oldest players in the draft, too grizzled for seasoned scouts to take much of an interest in him. Sig's team, though, was intrigued. Their metrics suggested that his statistics as a senior—a .333 batting average, 11 home runs, an OPS of 1.134—made him well worth the pick and the $1,000 signing bonus he would have to accept without the leverage of a potential return to school. Luhnow plucked his name from the board.

Trevor Rosenthal, who remained available in the 21st round, did not have enough of a track record for Sig to analyze with any certainty. As a converted shortstop, he had more experience as a mulcher than a pitcher. In his one season at Cowley College, in Kansas, he had thrown $4\frac{2}{3}$ innings from the mound. A 32-year-old named Aaron Looper happened to be in the community college's stands for $1\frac{1}{3}$ of those innings. Looper knew pitching; six years earlier he had worked seven frames for the Seattle Mariners, and his cousin Braden was wrapping up a dozen years as a big league pitcher, four of them with the Cardinals. Looper was now an area scout for St. Louis, and he liked Rosenthal's arm.

As of 2009, about two-thirds of clubs did not invite their area scouts into the draft room, in order to minimize the cacophony of voices. Luhnow did. He did insist upon certain rules, to maintain some order during sessions that could stretch to 13 hours: no food, no phone calls. He had 30 guys between the ages of 30 and 60, most of them former athletes, in a single room, and he had to keep the environment tolerable. But he encouraged open, honest debate from the men who knew the players best, right up until each pick was made. "Human nature is to tell us what you think we want to hear, and that's not what we're looking for," Luhnow always told his scouts. The day before the draft began, Looper stood up and delivered an impassioned speech about Rosenthal's talents, and affixed a gold star to his magnet to affirm his belief in him. Luhnow gave each scout five of the stars, which he called gut feels. After Looper had applied one of his stickers to Rosenthal, he sat down next to another Cardinals scout named Mike Elias.

"All I saw was one fuckin' inning," he whispered to Elias, shaking his head. "That was it."

"That's really what those gut stickers are all about," Luhnow said. "You maybe don't have the best information on the guy, but you feel he's going to be better than what you might see looking at his scouting report. Looper, being a pitcher, making the big leagues? I really trusted his ability to evaluate arms." Looper's gut feel gave the Cardinals their 21st rounder.

Matt Adams's problem was not experience. He had set his college's all-time record for batting average, at .473. But he did have knocks against him, which caused him to plummet from the 10th or 12th round, where he thought he might be selected, all the way to the 23rd. One was that his school was Pennsylvania's Slippery Rock, which plays in Division II and had never produced a major leaguer. The second was that he was chubby, to put it kindly. That was why he flunked most scouts' eyeball tests when he strapped a chest protector over his bulk and squatted behind home plate to play his usual collegiate position, which nobody believed he could handle as a pro. "It's quite a leap to expect a kid in D-2 with that kind of body to be able to hit enough to be a big league first baseman," said one scout.

As the rounds progressed, though, Brian Hopkins, the area scout who covered Pennsylvania, stayed in Luhnow's ear. Don't worry about the body, Hopkins said. Think about the light show he put on during his pre-draft workout at Busch, and his numbers. One of Chris Correa's early contributions to the analytics department had been the ability to find the statistics of Division II and Division III players, which weren't centralized anywhere. He was fluent in the programming language Python, which he used to scrape performance data from the individual websites of hundreds of tiny schools whose players almost always ended their baseball careers on their campuses. It was a difficult and labor-intensive exercise that had seemed unlikely to bear much fruit.

In the 23rd round, though? Sig and Correa stared into their laptops and nodded.

///////////

THE FACTIONS IN the Cardinals' draft room agreed on their 23rd-round selection much more easily than they had on their third rounder, the 2009 draft's 98th overall. That player had awaited the news at Oggi's Pizza in his hometown of Corona, California, the site of a party that had been planned to celebrate both his drafting and his 21st birthday. He proved to be the most internally contentious pick that Luhnow had ever made.

Sig wanted Angelo Songco, a prototypical power-hitting outfielder from Loyola Marymount. The scouts pounded the table, in their patois, for Joe Kelly, a reliever from another California college, UC Riverside. Songco's college numbers lit up Sig's screen. He had hit consistently since he was a freshman, and by his just completed junior season he had displayed an ideal mix of contact, patience, and power. Songco batted a robust .360, he reached base on nearly half his at-bats, and he slugged 15 homers, with 17 doubles and three triples, in 59 games. "Had a track record of performance, had done well in our workout, raw power, safe bet to make the big leagues," said Luhnow.

Kelly's tenure at Riverside, meanwhile, was unpromising. During a junior year in which he'd done his best to lose his role as the team's closer, he had an ERA of 5.65, and his underlying statistics were no better. On average he'd struck out less than one batter per inning, while yielding more than a hit per inning. Additionally, his biological markers, as Sig called them, were inferior to Songco's. Both were barely six feet tall and weighed around 170 pounds, an acceptable size for a third-round hitter, but tiny for a pitcher. Nearly a quarter of big league hitters in 2009 stood under six feet, but eight percent of pitchers were that small.

This is unusual, Sig thought. *He's not a big, imposing pitcher. The coach has taken him from the closer role. He's had almost no good games at all. It surprises me the scouts like him so much.*

Kelly had one thing going for him: his stuff, which included a fastball that reached the upper 90s. His arm was of a quality usually attached to the body of a first rounder, no matter his size, and the scouts loved it. So did Luhnow, who had been in the stands for one of Kelly's 28⅔ generally unsuccessful innings as a junior. "Gave up a home run, but I saw the stuff and couldn't get it out of my mind," he said.

When the time came to make the 98th pick of the 2009 draft, 30 pairs of eyes watched as Luhnow raised his hand to the magnet board. His fingers might have hovered over Angelo Songco's name for a moment, but they grasped the strip printed with Joe Kelly's. As Luhnow turned around, he peered past the scouts who cheered at the front of the room, to the back. His gaze caught Sig's. He'd seen his data man look deflated before, like four years earlier when he had passed on Jed Lowrie in favor of Tyler Greene, but perhaps never so deeply as he did now. Since then, Sig had designed a system that incorporated the scouts' evaluations, and STOUT still liked Songco over Kelly. But Luhnow went with Kelly anyway. As he did it, a part of Luhnow felt dejected, too.

It was never about the pick itself. If Luhnow hadn't believed that Kelly was the right choice, he wouldn't have reached for his magnet instead of Angelo Songco's. It was about the process. "There wasn't a way to rationalize the decision that I could defend to Sig," Luhnow said.

In the end, he'd had to perform a mental coin flip, weighing his and the scouts' gut feels about Kelly's stuff against Sig's analysis of Kelly's track record. He knew there had to be a more systematic way of synthesizing all that information, so that everyone in the room, himself included, could at least understand the rationale for every decision, even if they didn't all agree with it. "I didn't want to always be the guy that takes the Songcos of the world, but I didn't want to be the guy that always takes the Joe Kellys of the world, either," he said. "After that, Sig and I really said, 'How do we bridge this gap?'"

In other words, he longed for a system that better allowed him to settle disagreements between his scouts and his analysts—which usually existed, although never quite as clearly as with Songco and Kelly—in a way that didn't rely on custom, or habit, or his own intuition, the foundations of which even he didn't understand. The scouts obviously had value, but if he could, Luhnow wanted to avoid ever again having to stand in front of a room at a crucial moment in which the scouts were still pulling one way, and the analysts another entirely, and in which he would have to settle the argument because neither side trusted the other.

Sig agreed. You couldn't both accept and reject a player, but those moments in which the different methods of evaluating him clashed represented not a bug in the system, but a feature—a potential opportunity to spot a star that others missed. "If you say the world is round and I say it's flat, we don't agree to disagree," he said. This wasn't Camus's *The Myth of Sisyphus*. There was always a right answer. The trick was becoming as good as possible at finding it, which required every member of the organization to buy into the process. Perhaps that would never happen as long as Luhnow and Sig remained in charge of just one piece of a club, the scouting department, and not the entire thing.

What Luhnow really wanted was to run a start-up again, but in baseball. As he had done in Silicon Valley, he wanted the chance to create something nobody had ever seen before, from nothing.

/////////

WHEN THE CARDINALS' RIVAL conducted its 2013 study of the preceding 23 major league drafts, it did more than compute their best theoretical outcomes. It also ranked their specific results. The 99th percentile of draft classes included the one the Montreal Expos had assembled in 2000, which produced the outfielders Grady Sizemore and Jason Bay and the starting pitcher Cliff Lee. It included the Tampa Bay Devil Rays' 2006 class: third baseman Evan Longoria, starter Alex Cobb, outfielder Desmond Jennings. It also included the St. Louis Cardinals' draft class of 2009.

Though the rival club had applied rigorous data analysis to the study, and had factored in its own proprietary projections through the remainder of players' pre–free agency years, it was obvious to everyone by 2013 that the Cardinals' 2009 draft had proven a masterpiece. Shelby Miller went 15–9 with a 3.06 ERA that season, finishing third in the Rookie of the Year voting behind a pair of phenoms, Marlins starter José Fernández and Dodgers outfielder Yasiel Puig. Matt Carpenter led the majors in runs scored, hits, and doubles, and wound up the fourth-leading vote-getter for the National League MVP award. Trevor Rosenthal regularly threw his fastball at 102 miles per hour, and used it to strike out an astonishing 13 batters per nine innings; by September, he had become the club's closer. Matt Adams—now slimmed down to a mere 260 pounds—slugged 17 home runs in just 108 games. The only member of the '09 draft's 23rd round who would ever go on to spend significant time in the majors was already, on many nights, hitting cleanup for the Cardinals.

And Joe Kelly? While Angelo Songco's development with the Dodgers had stalled out at Double-A, where he hit .214, Kelly started Game 3 of that October's World Series against the Red Sox, for which the Cardinals fielded a 25-man roster that was 20 percent composed of players they had picked in a single draft. It came two years after Luhnow draftees like Allen Craig, Jaime García, Jon Jay, and Lance Lynn had been central contributors to St. Louis's 11th title. Early in 2013, a *Baseball America* writer named Conor Glassey determined that Luhnow was responsible for drafting 21 players who had been on that season's Opening Day rosters, more than any of the league's other scouting directors, several of whom had overseen many more drafts than Luhnow's seven. Clearly, his and Sig's commitment to using the power of data to guide the draft had worked. By then, though, they were no longer in St. Louis. And they had already begun to figure out an even better way of determining when their scouts' gut feels were wrong, as they had been with Tyler Greene, and when, as with Joe Kelly, they were right.

2

THE NERD CAVE

LIKE JUDGE ROY HOFHEINZ, JIM CRANE SUBSCRIBED TO A RIGOROUS all-green policy. When he graduated from Central Missouri State with a bachelor's degree in industrial safety in 1976, his mother, a grocery store clerk, handed him an envelope. As he later told *PaperCity Magazine*, inside was a card and a bill for $220.85. Though he had attended school on a baseball scholarship—as a sophomore he struck out 18 batters in the opening game of the Division II College World Series—the bill was for the spending money she had given him over the past four years, at four percent interest.

Crane arrived in Houston, in a U-Haul, in 1982. In 1984, when he was 30, he used a $10,000 loan from his sister to start his first business, called Eagle USA Airfreight. His first clients didn't have to know that Eagle had just two employees, a receptionist and Crane himself, as long as their shipments arrived on time and at a competitive price. By 2006, 10,000 people worked for him, and *Fortune* magazine ranked his company—now called EGL, for Eagle Global Logistics—the 599th largest in the country, with annual revenues of more than $3 billion.

Over the next five years, Crane lost control of EGL but expanded his portfolio to include the Crane Capital Group, Crane Freight & Cartage, Crane Worldwide Logistics, and Champion Energy. *Golf Digest* named him the best CEO golfer in the country, with a handicap of 0.8. He often hit the links with Barack Obama, and bought his own course, Floridian National in Palm City. Yet for a man who rarely worked in his office without juggling a baseball in his hand, the asset he most coveted remained out of his grasp. He tried without success to buy the Astros in 2008, the Cubs in 2009, and the Rangers in 2010. Then, in November 2010, Drayton McLane, the billionaire entrepreneur who had purchased the Astros in 1992, announced that the team was for sale again.

As rivals like the Cardinals knew well, the Astros had put together some good years under McLane, especially once their new stadium had been renamed Minute Maid Park following Enron's spectacular implosion in 2001. They particularly prospered in the middle of that decade, behind Jeff Bagwell, Lance Berkman, and Craig Biggio—the slugging Killer B's—as well as a pitching staff led by Roy Oswalt and a couple of former Yankees who had grown up in Texas, Roger Clemens and Andy Pettitte. But a World Series sweep by the White Sox in 2005 left the franchise still without a single victory in the Fall Classic.

Then, while the Cardinals' newly rocketing drafts enabled them to continue to reach the playoffs almost every year, the Astros experienced a jarring fall back to earth.

In 2010, the Astros had their third season in four of finishing 10 or more games below .500. In 2011, with the franchise on the auction block, they were on their way to a 56–106 mark, a record at which Roy Hofheinz's worst teams would have scoffed. Their core was gone. Berkman and Oswalt had been traded. Pettitte was back with the Yankees. Bagwell, Biggio, and Clemens had long ago retired. The Astros were in essentially as dire a condition as a baseball team could be, paying a lot of money—nearly $71 million, as of Opening Day of 2011—to a collection of players who couldn't win, while losing tens of millions of dollars a year. Their minor leagues promised no quick replenishments. Prior to the 2010 season, *Baseball America* ranked Houston's farm system as the game's worst.

At that point, the Astros could have been purchased by one of two types of owners. The first was a rich guy who viewed them as a plaything and didn't mind plowing hundreds of millions into free agents to try to make them a winner, balance sheet be damned. In other words, a guy who wanted something to impress his friends that was even cooler than another yacht. The second was a rich guy who wanted to transform them into a sustainably profitable business.

Jim Crane was not the first type of rich guy. "I can tell you right now that my partners aren't going to be excited to keep writing check after check," Crane said at the May 2011 press conference at which it was announced that he and several minority stakeholders had agreed to buy the club for $680 million.

Central Missouri State pitcher Jim Crane, 35 years before he bought the Astros.

The club's sale officially went through on November 22. Crane fired its incumbent general manager, Ed Wade, the next day. He had no intention of taking over the team and maintaining business as usual, since business as usual had resulted in an ever-worsening six-year slide. If there was an Astros Way, it had never led anywhere.

Crane wanted someone who could give him a new type of competitive advantage. One candidate happened to work in the front office of a National League Central rival. The industry viewed Jeff Luhnow as a long shot to become the Astros' GM, primarily because the leap from one team's scouting director to another's top executive position was both large and rarely made. Crane asked for permission from the Cardinals to interview Luhnow anyway. He soon discovered that Luhnow was no ordinary scouting director.

Several aspects of the 23-page proposal that Luhnow brought along to his job interview appealed to Crane. One was that Luhnow had, with one day's notice, produced it in time for a 10 a.m. meeting. In truth, Luhnow had been working on such a proposal for years, even back to his days in business school, in the unlikely event that he ever received a chance like this. More persuasive still, to Crane, was Luhnow's message that the Astros' days of spending big for losing players should be over.

Luhnow outlined his vision to Crane. Unlike other rebuilding teams, their Astros would not make cosmetic decisions, wasting money on a free agent or hanging on to old and expensive fan favorites in an effort to keep up appearances, particularly when those players might instead be immediately converted into future assets. He described a decision tree, with a 56-win team at its roots and a perennial contender at its tip. His only goal was to reach the top as quickly as possible, but in a fiscally responsible way, one in which they wouldn't spend money until, thanks to their winning team, they had it. That meant that every decision he made, no matter how painful, would be based on the probability that it would prove helpful in the long term. He would hit a 16 against a 7 every time. Even if it sucked.

"You look at how other organizations have done it, they've tried to maintain a .500-level team as they prepare to be good in the future," Luhnow said. "That path is probably necessary in some markets. There would be ramifications if you didn't do that. But it takes ten years. Our fans have already been on the decline, from 2006 to 2011. It's not like we're starting fresh. How do we get things on the upswing as soon as possible so that we can get to the point where we're consistently competitive?

"Would it be the right strategy for somebody else, who had a great farm system, younger up-and-coming players already at the big league level?" Luhnow continued. "No. But for us, it was. At the end of the day, when you're in 2017, you don't really care that much about whether we lost 98 or 107 in 2012. You care about how close we are to winning a championship in 2017."

The meat of Luhnow's proposal, the part that really sold Crane, centered on how they would reach that championship. It was one thing to commit to only making decisions with a long-term goal in mind, but another to figure out how to make those decisions.

Data was key to the shipping and logistics business, in which Crane had made his fortune. "If you have better information, faster than your competitors, you can run 'em ragged," Crane told *Bloomberg Businessweek*. The Astros, under Luhnow, would be driven by data in a way that represented a quantum leap from anything that Billy Beane had been doing in *Moneyball*.

Jim Crane hired Jeff Luhnow on the night of December 7, 2011, during baseball's annual Winter Meetings, which that year were held in Dallas. Luhnow walked across the corridor from the Cardinals' suite on the sixth floor of the Hilton Anatole and into the Astros'. Then he called Sig.

///////////

IT WASN'T LONG AFTER THE 2009 DRAFT that Luhnow began to look back at the mechanics behind a decision he had made that now seemed far more consequential than the one to pick Joe Kelly. So did 22 of the league's other 29 scouting directors. They had all declined to draft a high school outfielder who had fallen to the Angels at No. 25 overall—the Diamondbacks had passed on him twice—and who, just a year and a half later, already looked as if he had the potential to become his generation's best player.

That Luhnow and his team had still assembled one of the top draft classes ever softened the blow of missing on the outfielder, Mike Trout, but didn't erase it. "There has to be some regret there," said Luhnow. "Thank goodness we got Shelby Miller. Makes it a lot less painful." Still, Luhnow spent a lot of time reflecting on why he hadn't selected Trout, whose magnet had been directly below Miller's on his draft board and who had ultimately represented the only other contender for the pick. Perhaps it had been overly emotional. Everyone was so thrilled when Miller was still available at No. 19. Perhaps it had been a result of biases, particularly against players from Trout's home state. Those biases could even be embedded in Sig's algorithms, which relied on past examples of success to predict future ones. High school hitters from New Jersey played so much less—maybe 16 games a season, three of them snowed out—than their counterparts from warmer states like Miller's Texas, and they rarely overcame that early developmental deficit to amount to anything. Of the 10 who had been first-round picks since the draft began in 1965, only Willie Wilson, of the town of Summit, had become any sort of star.

Even so, just because there hadn't been many successful high school hitters from New Jersey didn't mean there couldn't be any. At the same time, just because one of them had become Mike Trout didn't mean a single future outfielder from the Garden State would do the same. Those were the types of biases that Luhnow resolved to eradicate from his decision-making when he was finally in charge.

A week after Luhnow took over the Astros, he made his first trade. He sent his new club's young closer, Mark Melancon, to the Red Sox in exchange for the pitcher Kyle Weiland and an undersized, 27-year-old infielder. The infielder's name was Jed Lowrie.

////////////

SIG KNEW HE'D FOLLOW LUHNOW ANYWHERE. He was the best boss Sig had ever had, in the only job he'd ever loved. When Luhnow had an 8.94 ERA in 15 outings for the Mets and Rockies in 2012 and 2013.

The Astros picked him up off waivers anyway, because Sig and his analytics team—including Mike Fast, a former semiconductor engineer and *Baseball Prospectus* writer who was an expert in PITCHf/x—noticed that McHugh had at least one extraordinary skill: a curveball that revolved more than 2,000 times per minute, putting him in the company of the league's great breaking-ball artists, like Félix Hernández and Adam Wainwright. Perhaps his results could approach theirs if he just threw the pitch more frequently.

An exploitation of performance data was just one element of the strategy that Luhnow proposed to win over Jim Crane. It was, in some ways, the easy part. Luhnow also promised that he would re-integrate information from another source into his decision-making process: humans, specifically scouts.

Luhnow set about building a front office team largely composed of modern thinkers like him, who could bring a new perspective to the game. The new special assistant to the GM for scouting was Mike Elias, the 29-year-old from Yale who had worked in the Cardinals' scouting department for five years and to whom Aaron Looper had once confided the limited basis for his gut feel about Trevor Rosenthal. Eventually, Luhnow would add a new assistant GM—David Stearns, a young Harvard graduate who had most recently worked for the Cleveland Indians—and a new pro scouting coordinator named Kevin Goldstein, who had long been a respected writer for *Baseball Prospectus* but who had never before been employed in pro baseball.

Luhnow also created a position with a title that no one in baseball had heard before, and which was therefore roundly mocked around baseball: Director of Decision Sciences. That was Sig.

One reason Luhnow named the position that, as opposed to something like Director of Analytics, was that he wanted to send a message to the members of his organization that he and Sig would value their work as they made the decisions that would return the asked him to leave St. Louis for Houston, Sig only had time to ship a couple of boxes of clothes south. An old Theta Xi brother of his from Davis happened to live in Houston and had a room available above his garage, rent-free. Sig thought he might store his clothes there for a few days. He never left. It was a nice garage.

"That's Sig," the man's children told their friends, when they asked why the garage's lights stayed on at all hours. "He's trying to win the World Series."

With the Astros, Sig and Luhnow faced a more difficult task than they had in St. Louis. There, they had been responsible for finding new ways to keep a healthy organization healthy. In Houston, they were asked to figure out how to defibrillate a club that was dying.

By 2012, baseball's landscape had changed from when Sig first went to work for Luhnow, when, outside Oakland, there were few other people like him in the game. *Moneyball*'s lessons had been absorbed by most of baseball's front offices and no longer represented much of a competitive advantage. On-base percentage was better than batting average. Wins were a poor indicator of a pitcher's value because, unlike strikeouts, for instance, they were so dependent on the play of the pitcher's teammates.

These were performance metrics, and they were relatively straightforward, even if there were many more of them than there had been a decade before. Starting in 2006, Major League Baseball had installed a system called PITCHf/x in its stadiums. By triangulating between three stationary cameras, PITCHf/x could detect not only the velocity of a given pitch but also its precise release point, its horizontal and vertical break, and its location as it crossed the plate, and could be used to extrapolate the rate at which it spun, in revolutions per minute.

By traditional measures, a 26-year-old pitcher named C McHugh appeared to be one of the league's worst. McHugh had been a particularly heralded prospect. He had been an 18th selection out of Georgia's tiny Berry College in 2008, and th made the major leagues four years later, he experienced no su

Astros to contention. Though he had often disagreed with the scouts in St. Louis, Sig didn't look down on them for their flaws, just as he didn't the gamblers who made bad decisions at the High Sierra—or anyone, for that matter.

Sig had studied the work of the Israeli psychologists Daniel Kahneman and Amos Tversky. In the mid-1970s, around the same time Bill James began publicly writing, Kahneman and Tversky introduced the concept of cognitive biases, which they argued lead humans to make irrational choices, particularly when faced with deeply complicated, multiattribute decisions such as, say, how to evaluate a baseball player or plan a wedding. Humans rely on heuristics, mental shortcuts that lead them to arrive at judgments based on only a thin slice of the overall problem—such as the memory of one emotionally satisfying and often recent event, called availability—because their brains can't cognitively assess the problem's full scope. Kahneman won the Nobel Prize in Economics in 2002, six years after his colleague Tversky had died. "Certainly, we would have gotten this together," he said. "There is that shadow over the joy I feel."

Kahneman and Tversky essentially invented a new field, modern behavioral economics, and Sig applied it to baseball. "I don't want to minimize the scout's gut whatsoever," he said, though he didn't really like that term, because the gut was nowhere near the organ actually responsible for forming judgments. "That's their expertise speaking to them. It's tremendously important. But he has observed all sorts of signals that never point in the same direction, and he has to make sense of them. And most are in different languages. How do you make sense of it? You could do it in your head. You could have some rules of thumb. Or you could really dive in to try to make a decision aid that could perhaps do something a little better than what you could do in your head."

Scouts gathered many types of information about players. Some of it was hard, similar to on-base percentage or PITCHf/x data: how fast he can throw a fastball, how quickly he can reach first base. Much of it was soft, based on the scout's own judgment: how hard he wants to work, how his power stroke might develop, how likely he is to become injured. Most of it was both useful and predictive, if analyzed properly.

Sig oversaw an analytics team that over the next couple of years grew to four and occupied an office they named the Nerd Cave, which they decorated with a doctored image of scientists examining the slugger Vladimir Guerrero mid-swing. The poster was a joke. Sort of. In the Nerd Cave, they built upon the evaluation system Sig had developed in St. Louis, boiling down every piece of information the Astros had about every prospect and every player into a single language, and even a single number.

The inputs included not only a player's statistics, but also information—much of it collected and evaluated by scouts—about his health and family history, his pitching mechanics or the shape of his swing, his personality. The system then ran regressions against all the information that had been fed into it against a database that stretched back to at least 1997, when stats for college players had just begun to be digitized.

The idea was, essentially, to systematically scout the scouts in order to determine which of their judgments had real predictive value and which were the product of cognitive biases—and then to properly weight them along with the performance data by comparing that universe of attributes against those of players who had once performed or been judged similarly. Scouts had long graded players in all sorts of categories on a scale that ran from 20 to 80. If a scout gave a 70 grade to the work ethic of 99 past players, and had a 70 on a current prospect, how did those past players turn out—and how might the prospect? If a scout reported that a young pitcher's trunk rotated a bit earlier than was ideal when he threw and gave his mechanics a low grade, how likely were past pitchers about whom that scout had reported the same thing to get injured? "If a human being can sense it, a human being can quantify it," said Sig. "If he can quantify it, he can learn about it."

The end result was expressed as a numerical projection that

roughly translated into how many runs a player could be expected to produce measured against the salary he was likely to command. Draft prospects received a similarly scaled score that combined all information provided by the organization's computers and its people to produce a metric that rendered a decision on a player as simple as one in blackjack: hit or stand. "It's not rocket science," said Sig, at least on the scale of a former rocket scientist.

Conceptually, it wasn't so different from what Sig had done when he was 11, when he had written his computer program to predict the outputs of his All-Star Baseball players based on the formula he'd read about. Now he was the one who had to come up with the proper algorithm. That meant determining which of dozens of potential variables didn't matter and which did, and then figuring out how much each mattered—including those perceived by his scouts' guts, which were far less consistent than a radar gun's reading or a slugging percentage but just as valuable. Probably more valuable, because every other club knew how to read a radar gun.

"They're not trying to ask us to be sabermetricians," said Ralph Bratton, a Texan with a thick white mustache who became an Astros scout in 1990. "They're asking us to do what we've always done." The trick was that Luhnow's front office would process that information differently and make its decisions largely based on the result, even when the result, like hitting on a 16, felt wrong.

For the first two years of Crane's ownership, and Luhnow and Sig's stewardship, it felt very wrong.

////////////

THE ASTROS WERE NOT A RESTAURANT THAT, faced with withering reviews and dwindling returns, could shut down, renovate, hire a new chef, reimagine its menu, and relaunch. They had to stay open for business. Business was bad. Members of the Astros' quickly dwindling fan base made T-shirts silk-screened with the new nicknames they had bestowed upon their once beloved, if perennially frustrating, club. They were now the LASTROS or, alternatively, the DISASTROS. Attendance fell to 1.6 million, barely half of what the Killer B's drew less than a decade before, and catastrophically lower than league average.

Jeff Luhnow followed through on his promise to Jim Crane to rid the club of high-priced, underperforming veterans, in order to squirrel away the savings to spend in a future in which they could realistically hope to compete. In July 2012 alone he traded away his top slugger, Carlos Lee; his most reliable starter, Wandy Rodriguez; and his closer, Brett Myers—who were between them earning around $40 million that year—for prospects.

The team went 21–43 the rest of the way. Then things got worse.

It was one thing to plan not to devote resources to a club that was going to lose anyway, but another entirely to live with the ramifications of that plan. Major League Baseball had offered to knock $65 million off Crane's purchase price if he agreed to move from the National League Central to the American League West at the outset of the 2013 season in order to balance the leagues at 15 clubs apiece. Crane was not the type of man to turn down $65 million, but the move meant his team had to play against even tougher competition with an Opening Day payroll of about $26 million, roughly half that of any other club's and just over 10 percent of the Yankees'. What type of players could the Astros pay so little? Those who were, by and large, not ready for any league above Triple-A. It was not a formula for winning.

The season is best remembered, by those who care to remember it at all, for the Butt Slide. In the bottom of the first inning of the Astros' game against the Reds on September 17, with his club already trailing 4–0, leadoff man Jonathan Villar attempted to stretch a single into a double. By the time Villar approached second base, the Reds' Brandon Phillips had already received the throw from left center field. Without deigning to turn around, Phillips squatted and thrust his glove between his legs, in the process tagging Villar, who was sliding in headfirst, and allowing Villar's face to crash into his posterior. The Astros clinched their third straight 100-loss season that night, but all anyone wanted to ask about was the slide, videos of which were posted on blogs from every available angle. You could almost hear the Looney Tunes *splat*.

The infamous Butt Slide on September 17, 2013.

It was the beginning of the nadir for the Astros, whose only innovation seemed to be finding previously unimaginable ways of losing. Two nights later, they lost an extra-innings game to the Indians in which they'd gotten a leadoff double in the top of the tenth, only to have the pinch runner picked off second base by Cleveland's catcher. Nine days after that, they fell after their catcher attempted to fake a throw to second but lost his grip and spiked the ball off home plate to allow the winning run to score. The Astros reached the last game of the season, on September 29, riding a 14-game losing streak, but with a chance to enter the off-season on a positive note. They even extended the Yankees to the 14th inning. Then New York scored four runs in the top of the frame. The Astros lost that game, too. It was their 111th defeat of the season, against 51 wins, to tie for the league's worst record in a decade. "It was," said David Stearns, Luhnow's assistant GM, "the season that wouldn't end."

Luhnow wouldn't let it end, either, even when it had. The vanity license plate on his Audi soon read GM111, part of his commitment to radical honesty. He had consistently explained his plan, in detail, not just within baseball but to his new hometown. "Nothing's more frustrating than being told one thing, and all the actions suggest something else," he said. "We thought from the beginning we'd be the most transparent front office in baseball. Is there a risk we end up giving away some company secrets? Possibly. But we felt the benefit of having fans feel like they're involved in the process is important."

While Luhnow tended to sit eerily still during games, in part because he didn't want TV cameras to catch an emotional reaction to a player or play, he lived to celebrate wins. "There's nothing I love more than walking down to a winning clubhouse, hearing the music, saying hi to the coaches," said Luhnow. Those nights were rare in Houston. "You never get hardened to the point where you don't feel every loss. It's hard for fans to understand that we suffer just as much as they do. I've watched every inning of every game for every year I've been here. I'm convinced this is the right way to go. While it's painful to watch the team lose, ultimately the rewards are going to be there. They're going to be there for the entire city, and anyone who watches the team." In the moment, the Astros were worse than a laughingstock, one that irked the players' union with its parsimonious payroll, was mocked by Alex Trebek, and was watched on television by, quite literally at times as far as anyone could tell, no one. They were a circus, though one that Roy Hofheinz would have never booked to play the Astrodome.

///////////

BY THE EARLY PORTION OF 2014, the Astros' act was wearing thin in other ways. In an article published in the *Houston Chronicle* on May 23, beat writer Evan Drellich detailed the manner in which, as the headline read, RADICAL METHODS PAINT ASTROS AS "OUTCAST."

"They are definitely the outcast of Major League Baseball right now, and it's kind of frustrating for everyone else to have to watch it," said Bud Norris, a starting pitcher who had been traded to the Orioles the previous July. "When you talk to agents, when you talk to other players and you talk amongst the league, yeah, there's going to be some opinions about it, and they're not always pretty."

The criticisms fell into two categories. One related to the Astros' deployment of new competitive tactics, such as extreme defensive shifts. The club's proprietary database—built by an initial Nerd Cave hire named Ryan Hallahan and christened Ground Control by Mike Elias's wife, Alexandra—contained not just projections of the future value of every player, but spray charts for every hitter on every count against every type of pitch thrown by every type of pitcher, as well as a suggestion as to the probabilistically optimal way to position defenders in each scenario. This sometimes led to defensive alignments called shifts, in which, say, the Astros' shortstop played on the first-base side of second against a pull-happy left-handed hitter, in violation of baseball norms.

A problem: baseball players, who do the same thing 162 times every year, like norms. "The front office is not going to not shift, so if I did have a problem with it, there's nothing I can do about it, as a lot of the older players have told us," a 24-year-old Astros starter named Jarred Cosart grumbled to Drellich.

That sort of complaint reminded Sig of another author he'd once studied: Thomas Kuhn, who, in *The Structure of Scientific Revolutions*, had written that scientific advancement is not gradual but instead a "series of peaceful interludes punctuated by intellectually violent revolutions." Sig noted that in 2014, more than half the league's teams shifted as frequently as the Astros had the year before, in which they hadn't even led the majors in the use of the tactic. According to the stats service Inside Edge, the Rays, Orioles, Pirates, and Brewers had all shifted more than the Astros in 2013, though no one was talking about those other teams, as they weren't both shifting and losing a drastic number of games. "Innovation, by definition, suggests change will be taking place," Sig said. "If there's change taking place, it's not likely going to feel right. If it felt right, it would have been done a long time ago."

The other criticism was that the Astros' analytics-centered approach dehumanized players by reducing each to a fungible number. That one bothered Luhnow, and especially bothered Sig. "We realize these are human beings, not widgets," Sig said. "As far as assigning a number to a person—well, I assume you get a salary? Do you feel dehumanized because your boss has put a number on you? Baseball players, they get released in harsh terms. What a horrible industry, in some ways. The constraint of the system we have means that we must let some of the most skilled people on the planet go." Wasn't it better, Sig wondered, if players whose dreams are crushed know that it happened as a result of hard, unbiased evidence and not just someone's whim?

Arguably, the real backlash was against the corporatization of baseball—against bringing the strategies of shipping and logistics and management consulting to the sandlot, by men who were still viewed, and might always be viewed, as outsiders. In some ways, it was no different than the pushback Luhnow had received within the Cardinals' front office, only now that he was one of the 30 men who had the dream job of running a major league team, it came from the entire baseball world.

But the backlash was also against the losing. There was so, so much losing.

/////////

WHILE LUHNOW AND SIG believed in their plan, and gradually surrounded themselves with a front office that bought into it, too, they fought off the notion that they fundamentally knew how to operate better than anyone else. All they knew was what they believed to represent best long-term practices, based on the information they acquired and processed, in an attempt to get more things right than wrong. "We're far from perfect—in everything," Sig said. Even what they believed to be the best decisions often didn't work out. Sometimes a left-handed pull hitter went the other way. Sometimes players the Astros discarded, or declined to draft, turned into stars. "Sometimes, you hit on a sixteen," said Sig, "and if you stayed, you would have won."

In his mind's eye, Sig often saw a poster his aunt had on her wall. IF YOU WANT TO MAKE GOD LAUGH, TELL HIM YOUR PLANS, it read. It was a Woody Allen quote. He also thought of an old proverb from Denmark—he was half Danish, after all—that had over the years been misattributed to people like Yogi Berra, Niels Bohr, and Mark Twain: "It is difficult to predict, especially the future." Even a long string of correct, intricately considered decisions might not turn out favorably.

Luck: Sig reflected upon that concept move than anything. His parents had come to the United States searching for the American dream, and though his mother sat in the wrong stands and cheered his outs, he had already enjoyed a near-decade-long career in the American pastime because he had been fortunate enough to live in an era in which baseball had begun to value people with his worldview and intellectual gifts. If he'd been born 10 years earlier, he'd have likely lived out his days in a windowless lab instead of watching each night as his childhood fantasies, his pointer finger's flicks of the board game spinner, came to life.

By the beginning of 2014, Roy Hofheinz's Astrodome sat empty and derelict, its only patrons the maintenance workers who ensured it didn't collapse and the security guards who kept out urban adventurers. Modern impresarios had presented plans to turn what was once the Eighth Wonder of the World into a hotel, a production studio, an indoor park, a parking garage, or a convention center. They all failed. Astroworld's last roller coaster had completed its final run nine years earlier. Meanwhile, the fate of the baseball team around which it had all once been built, and the responsibility for its first World Series victory, rested in the hands of a new set of innovators.

"What if we don't have good results?" Sig said. "I love my job in baseball. It would be terribly disappointing. But all we can control is the process, and I'm confident we're creating good processes and making good decisions.

"The rest," Sig said, "is hope."

3

GRACEFUL BEAST

In the mid-2000s, the residents of Santa Isabel, Puerto Rico, had two nicknames for Carlos. One was 24/7. The other was Hitler.

The first was for the way he worked to support his family, which, like many in the town of 23,000 on the island's southern coast, needed every dollar. His first construction job began at 4:30 each morning. Then, for six hours beneath a midday sun that permanently scorched his forearms, he worked maintenance for Santa Isabel's parks and recreation department. After that, another construction job.

The second, less-admiring nickname came from what he did at night. From 8:30 until 10:30 every evening, starting when his son was seven years old, he took him out to a local diamond to run him through baseball drills. Carlos's son shared a name with him, but the family called the boy by his middle name, Javier. They drilled six days a week, and sometimes on Sundays, too. Neighbors reprimanded Carlos through their car windows as they watched Javier field hundreds of grounders and take hundreds of swings. "That's too much for a little kid!" they shouted.

Javier, though, wanted to be out there as badly as his father. He started playing baseball as a five-year-old, ceaselessly flinging a ball at a concrete wall in front of his grandmother's house even though bad caroms off tree roots blacked his eyes. "Did you get in a fight?" teachers asked him in school. Many nights, Carlos would be lying on his bed, nearly passed out after three shifts of hard labor, when Javier shook him awake to go to the field.

Javier's father certainly pushed him. Baseball provided the glimmer of a type of life that had always been beyond Carlos or anyone he knew. Nearly 50 percent of Santa Isabel's families subsisted below the poverty line, Carlos's included. Carlos had gone to work when he was 13. Just three years later, at 16, he'd married his 14-year-old girlfriend, Sandybel. Their futures were already determined, so they saw no point in waiting, despite their families' objections. He was going to work construction, and he was going to support her.

Sandybel gave birth to Javier, who was the first of their three children, in September 1994, when she was 16 and her husband was 18. Where Carlos had only had one option, he wanted Javier to have at least three. He could go into construction, but the father often took his young son along on his jobs to show him the grueling work it took to make, maybe, 50 bucks. During one sweltering summer, father and son even built an extension onto the modest house into which the government had moved them after their old one had flooded, the two of them endlessly laying concrete block after concrete block.

Option two: Javier would certainly take school more seriously than Carlos had, perhaps even go to college.

The third option became obvious after it turned out that Javier was bigger and stronger and more coordinated—and more driven— than the other boys.

"My parents taught me about the mistakes that they made," Javier said, years later. "At the end of the day, it worked out pretty good for them, but it doesn't work out for most people. The way that they talked to me about life and stuff, it was like I was a man already. My dad never treated me like a little boy. He wanted me to be like him: a man, at a young age, who could go out and work for his family." His work, ideally, would not be in construction.

//////////

PUERTO RICO WAS ONCE A 110-by-40-mile hotbed of major league talent. Hall of Famers Roberto Clemente, Orlando Cepeda, Roberto Alomar, and Pudge Rodríguez grew up on the island, along with other stars like Juan González and Edgar Martínez. As recently as 2005, there were 46 Puerto Ricans on big league rosters.

By 2012, there were just 18, and only Carlos Beltrán and Yadier Molina had ever counted as genuine stars. Several theories attempted to explain the decline. One was that Puerto Rican children had an increasing number of options: basketball, soccer, and even volleyball had all grown popular, and, as US citizens, they could perhaps pursue traditional professions more easily. For lots of boys in somewhere like the nearby Dominican Republic, which produced 128 members of major league rosters in 2012, there was only baseball.

Another scapegoat was the draft, with its strict age requirements and compensation structure, for which Major League Baseball made Puerto Ricans eligible in 1990. The rigid system eliminated the incentive of signing a big-money deal at 16, as well as the motivation for independent local scouts to discover young talent for a cut of the proceeds. However, the average Puerto Rican draft prospect had less high-level competitive experience and less leverage than his mainland counterparts.

Carlos believed his son Javier had the talent to overcome those trends, and he resolved to help him do it however he could. It would not be easy.

One early problem with that plan was that Carlos knew next to nothing about baseball. He attended three practices when he was young—in the mid-1980s, when the Rio Piedras–born Ruben Sierra was emerging as a young superstar for the Texas Rangers—but he did not know how to field a ground ball. He had worked as a fisherman as a boy and tried to pick up grounders the same way he plucked crabs out of riverbeds: with his palm down. The coaches hit him balls in order to laugh at his awkward stabs, so he quit.

When his son first played Little League, which is called Pampers League in Puerto Rico, Carlos listened closely to the coaches' instructions, and repeated them during his nightly one-on-ones with Javier. He also studied the techniques of major leaguers on TV, particularly of the era's great shortstops, Derek Jeter

A young Javier in Pampers League in Puerto Rico.

and Alex Rodriguez. Starting when Javier was eight, Carlos had him practice Jeter's famous jump throw from the hole again and again, thousands of times.

Javier wanted to emulate those players in other ways. When he was eight, he asked his parents, neither of whom spoke English, to enroll him in a bilingual Baptist school. While Jeter and Rodriguez were always so composed in their postgame interviews, many of the Latin players seemed stilted and flustered no matter the nature of the heroics they were trying to explain, especially when they had to do so through a translator. "Dad, I don't want to be one of those guys," Javier said. "I want to speak for myself." The tuition was $250 a month, but Carlos and Sandybel went to the pastor and asked for a break. A scholarship knocked it down to $150. To afford that, Sandybel took on a job at a water-bottling plant to supplement Carlos's three shifts and also started a small business in which she took photos of Javier's Pampers League teammates and sold prints to their parents.

Once, driving his family home after one of Javier's games, an exhausted Carlos fell asleep behind the wheel and ran off the road. Only Carlos sustained any injuries. "He had a couple of days' rest," Javier said. "After that, he went back at it."

By the time Javier reached high school in 2008, he had become one of the island's best young players, tall and lean and powerful. He earned a more considerable scholarship to the Puerto Rico Baseball Academy and High School, which had been founded in Gurabo in 2001. His working hours began to rival those of his father. He woke up at five. He waited in a McDonald's parking lot to catch a ride to the school, an hour away from Santa Isabel, at six. He took academic classes from eight to noon. He worked on baseball from one to four. He went home and studied. At night, without fail, he went to the ballpark to drill with his father.

People still came out to watch him through their car windows. Now, instead of lobbing insults at Carlos, they cheered when Javier crushed ball after ball and made throws across the diamond that reached 97 miles per hour. Professional scouts watched, too, more of them each year, but still Javier had doubters, even at the baseball academy. His fellow students invited him to parties. He never went.

"You're crazy," they told him. "You won't go that high in the draft."

"I'm going to be a first rounder," Javier replied. "While you party, I'll be working."

"They thought what they did at school was enough," he said later. "It was not enough."

His family had deprived itself of so much—sleep and social opportunities were just the start of it—to give Javier the best possible shot at living a different sort of life. Still, as he entered his senior year of high school, there remained a real chance that pro baseball wouldn't take much notice of Carlos Javier Correa Jr.

///////////

MIKE ELIAS HAD A BACKGROUND that suggested it was unlikely he would ever become a major league scout. The life of a scout was a hard one. A scout spent eight or nine lonely months a year on the road, during which he observed hundreds of games that few other people cared about, for a salary of perhaps $50,000 a year. A scout endured that lifestyle because he loved baseball, and because he yearned to discover a player who might become a star, and most of all because he couldn't imagine doing anything else. It was a frustrating job, too; almost all the amateurs with whom a scout fell in love would end up being drafted by one of the 29 other clubs. Elias always had other options, as did most of his classmates at Yale, who, by and large, hoped to spend their evenings in their 20s with their friends in major cities on considerable expense accounts, not alone in far-flung motels.

Elias grew up in the Washington, DC, suburb of Alexandria, Virginia. Alexandria has a median household income of around $90,000, nearly six times that of Santa Isabel's. Elias's childhood was comfortable, if not luxurious: His father was a Secret Service agent who protected Ronald Reagan and Bill Clinton, and his mother was a court reporter. He went to Yale for the education but also because, by his freshman season in 2002, it had become a crucible not just for lawyers and bankers but professional pitchers, too.

Yale's baseball coach, John Stuper, had twirled a complete game as a rookie for the Cardinals in Game 6 of the 1982 World Series. The year before Elias arrived in New Haven, Stuper's ace was a junior named Jon Steitz, who had a 94-mile-per-hour fastball and a diving, 85-mile-per-hour slider that his teammates called the Nodball, because scouts would look at one another and nod every time he threw it. Steitz's parents, Joan and Tom, were both longtime Yale professors of molecular biophysics and biochemistry. Tom would win the 2009 Nobel Prize in Chemistry for his work on the structure and function of the ribosome. The rumor around campus was that the Steitzes had designed their only child in one of their labs. He left school a year early after the Milwaukee Brewers made him a third-round draft pick.

When Elias was a freshman, he joined a rotation led by two of Steitz's former classmates, Matt McCarthy and Craig Breslow. Both were considered potential pros, too, though they were not as coveted as Steitz had been. Elias always watched the men who sat in the bleachers with radar guns and notebooks, scribbling observations about his teammates. They were the scouts. At night, McCarthy and Breslow descended into Yale's subterranean Cross Campus Library to comb through scouting message boards on the internet,

Mike Elias pitches for Yale in 2006.

in an attempt to assess their rising and falling prospects. Elias went with them. I was a classmate of McCarthy's and Breslow's, and I knew the quiet, observant freshman who often tagged along with them by the nickname his baseball teammates had given him. They called him the Protégé.

Soon, as a joke, Elias began to adopt the scouts' mannerisms and lingo. He bought a pair of the Ray-Ban aviators they all wore. "Kid's got a pro body," he would say, as he watched a student lug his cello across the quad. After Yale suffered yet another defeat to a Dartmouth soft-tosser—a regular occurrence that year, as the team went 12–27 despite its pitching talent—Elias would break the tension on the long bus ride back from New Hampshire by referring to a scout all the players knew. "You think that junk is going to impress Anup Sinha?" he said of the Dartmouth kid's alleged fastball, which came in at 82 miles per hour.

It was a freshman's way of amusing the upperclassmen, but like most running jokes among guys in college, it was built on a foundation of truth. Elias really was fascinated by the scouts: how they talked, how they processed what they saw, their power to grant or crush dreams, their ability to make a living in baseball, however modest, long after they could no longer play. That only increased after the Anaheim Angels selected McCarthy in the 21st round that June, and the Brewers took Breslow five rounds later. McCarthy and Breslow were lefties, like Elias, and as a senior McCarthy just barely outpitched his freshman rotation mate: He had a 4.04 ERA to Elias's 4.18. Elias stood several inches taller than both McCarthy and Breslow. At six foot three, he had the makings of a pro body of his own, and he still had three years left to improve his draft stock. Then his shoulder started to hurt.

Elias tried to pitch through his torn labrum. He took four Tylenol before starts and became familiar with the long, thick needles that delivered cortisone shots, but even those didn't help. As a sophomore, his ERA spiked by a run and a half. He knew he had to have surgery. At another school, he could have taken a redshirt season, remaining enrolled while retaining both of his two remaining years of baseball eligibility, the last of which he might have completed as a graduate student. But the Ivy League does not allow redshirt seasons. Elias had to withdraw while his shoulder healed. He decided to use the time off to lay the groundwork for what was now not a joke at all, but a future career.

Stuper used his old connections to help Elias get an internship with the Philadelphia Phillies. He sold tickets and cleaned out rat-infested storage rooms in the bowels of the old Veterans Stadium, in advance of the club's move to the newly constructed Citizens Bank Park. "Encountered some wildlife," he said, but when he wasn't doing that he also got something more by hanging around the executive suite: a window into how a front office operated, and an impressive line on his résumé.

For the second half of the year, he interned in San Diego with Tom House, the former major league reliever and a PhD in sports psychology who founded the National Pitching Association, which trained pitchers to throw with optimal mechanics. Elias rehabbed under House, but also helped him evaluate and coach the other pitchers who flocked to the program, including major leaguers like Randy Johnson and Mark Prior.

House used regression analysis to identify the mechanical characteristics that healthy and successful major league pitchers shared, like a front arm and a pitching arm that mirrored each other as they moved through space. "It was the first time I'd seen somebody base their baseball philosophies off of an observed data set, rather than arbitrarily posit things and hope they worked out," Elias said. Major league executives came to visit House, too. Elias particularly bonded with one named Dan Kantrovitz, with whom he had a similar background and hoped to share a similar future. Kantrovitz had played shortstop for four years at Brown and then joined the baseball operations department of the St. Louis Cardinals.

Though Elias returned to New Haven with ideal mechanics, his damaged shoulder never healed enough to allow him to make effective use of them. The Anup Sinhas of the world took little notice of an Ivy League pitcher whose best season came when he was a freshman. An extended career as a pro had always been a long shot, anyway. By 2006, Elias's senior season, Jon Steitz had enrolled at Yale Law School, and was soon to become a consultant with McKinsey. Matt McCarthy was at Harvard Medical School. Only the lowest picked of the three, Craig Breslow, had, improbably, reached the majors. He had two major league seasons under his belt and would go on to pitch 10 more, winning two World Series rings with the Red Sox. Elias knew he would have to follow a different path to pro ball.

At the time of Elias's graduation, *Moneyball* was three years old, and front office slush piles were becoming littered with applications from Ivy Leaguers who aspired to be Theo Epstein, who had graduated from Yale 11 years before Elias. They were mostly data experts adept at exploiting statistical inefficiencies. Elias was an American Studies major. For his senior thesis, he had written a history of Tommy John surgery.

If he couldn't compete with their hard quantitative skills, he felt he had a couple of advantages that might differentiate him: on-field experience and, thanks to his spring with Tom House, an idea of how to systematically evaluate baseball players that almost no other 23-year-old could have possessed.

By the fall of 2006, Kantrovitz's boss with the Cardinals had begun looking for a new type of scout, one who knew how to subjectively evaluate players but was young, open-minded, and computer literate, and who wouldn't mind chasing down some of the obscure prospects that Sig's analytical system identified. Jeff Luhnow hired then 23-year-old Elias as an area scout over 800 other applicants. He joined a scouting staff that by then included someone he recognized: Anup Sinha.

As his Yale classmates worked their way through graduate school or lucratively shuffled spreadsheets for investment houses, Elias spent the next five years on the road, mostly in the mid-Atlantic region. He got a head start on what, for scouts, represented almost as great an achievement as discovering the next Albert Pujols: lifetime platinum status with Marriott hotels. Luhnow came to trust his precociously clear-eyed analysis and sent him ever farther afield. In early 2010, the scouting director dispatched Elias on a trip to Puerto Rico. That was the first time he saw a 15-year-old shortstop who immediately stood out, even in a game against players much older than he was. The shortstop was Carlos Correa Jr.

////////////

WHEN CORREA ENTERED THE DRAFT in 2012, it had been three years since any club had picked a first rounder out of Puerto Rico. While the island-born infielders Francisco Lindor and Javier Báez had been selected back-to-back at eighth and ninth overall in 2011, both had previously moved to Florida. Prior to his senior year, Correa received offers to do the same, to improve his exposure and his draft stock. He declined. "I want to come out of Puerto Rico," he said. "I want to show people it can be done from here."

Jeff Luhnow stationed Mike Elias in West Palm Beach in 2011, and also made him the Cardinals' cross-checker responsible for Puerto Rico, a recently futile assignment. The young Elias, though, had no biases against Puerto Rican players, either intellectual or experiential, and he had been keeping tabs on Correa's development. In October of that year, his interest began to pique. Correa had traveled to Jupiter, Florida, to play in a tournament at the Cardinals' and Marlins' shared spring training facility there. It was the type of cattle call that has 12 fields going at once, with scouts zipping between them on golf carts.

Elias was one of them, and happened to see Correa hit an opposite field line drive that never rose more than 10 feet off the ground, but that carried down the right-field line and struck the foul pole for a home run. *I can't remember ever seeing anyone do that on a baseball field*, Elias told himself. *Not just a 17-year-old. Anyone.* He powered down his cart and watched for what Correa might do next.

Luhnow crossed the Hilton hallway to join the Astros a couple of months later. His first new hire was Sig, but his second was Elias, his new special assistant. That winter, Elias couldn't get the foul pole's clang out of his ears. He saw Correa as often as he could and checked in frequently with Joey Sola, the Astros' Puerto Rico–based scout, who put 25,000 miles on his car's odometer each year trying, mostly in vain, to find the island's next star. Every time Elias or Sola watched Correa, he seemed to do something spectacular: a long home run, a laser throw from the hole. "I've never seen a kid coming out of the island like this," Sola reported. Elias had never seen anyone like him, either—not in the DC suburbs, not at Yale, not in the mid-Atlantic region. To Elias, he resembled Manny Machado, the Orioles' soaring shortstop prospect. *This is what guys like Machado must look like when they're seventeen,* he thought. "It became one of those gut feelings scouts talk about," he said. "One of the strongest I've ever had."

In May 2012, a month before the draft, Elias filed his final scouting report on Correa. At 450 words, it was twice as long as the standard report, which embarrassed Elias. Scouts' evaluations were supposed to be concise and digestible, particularly as they were to be coded into Sig's database. But he had a lot to say. He assigned Correa a 55 grade, on the 20-to-80 scale, as far as his ability to hit for contact, which projected to a .272 to .287 average in the majors. He gave him a 70 for power, which projected to 35 to 40 home runs. He graded his throwing arm an 80, the best it could be. And Correa, at 17, had more than just an acceptable pro body.

"Graceful beast with large, rangy frame," Elias wrote. "Physical presence along the lines of A-Rod or Cal Ripken Jr." The key question, as Elias saw it, was whether Correa would quickly grow too big and unwieldy for shortstop—as Miguel Cabrera and Alex Rodriguez had—and move to third, where his hitting ability wouldn't represent quite as much surplus value. Plenty of sluggers could handle third base, while few possessed the combination of athletic gifts necessary to hit home runs while passably playing the more demanding position of shortstop. Elias thought Correa could stay at short. The bottom line, he wrote: "Upside play with chance to be top talent out of this draft class."

Elias's report convinced Luhnow that he had better do the one thing his young scout hadn't: meet Correa and his family in person. Elias had only evaluated Correa's personality from afar, as he had once judged Yale Symphony Orchestra cellists from across the quad. "There was a way he carried himself, his posture, the way he managed his teammates," said Elias. "I remembered that an article I'd read about how the Braves had scouted Chipper Jones described the same thing. His presence. This kid had that, to me." But he'd never actually spoken to Correa.

Luhnow brought along another special assistant, one he had inherited from the previous regime. The 62-year-old Enos Cabell was everything someone like Sig Mejdal was not. He had played in the majors for 15 years, and though he accepted the advanced analytical methods that had begun to take over the game, he wasn't necessarily a student of them. In fact, Cabell had been a target of Bill James in an early *Abstract*, after Detroit Tigers manager Sparky Anderson insisted on playing him at first base nearly every day. "Sparky is so focused on all that attitude stuff that he looks at an Enos Cabell and he doesn't even see that the man can't play baseball," James wrote in 1983, a season in which Cabell hit five home runs in 121 games and stole four bases on 12 attempts. "This ballplayer, Sparky, can't play first, can't play third, can't hit, can't run and can't throw. So who cares what his attitude is?"

James softened his stance on Cabell in the next year's book, based in part on feedback he'd received from Cabell's agent, Tom Reich. "Everybody tells me that Enos is a hell of a good guy, and you know, you can tell he is," James wrote. "His abilities being what they are, would he be in the major leagues if he wasn't? Tom Reich insists that if the Tigers don't re-sign Enos, it will cost them 10 games next year because they'll lose Enos's steadying influence on some of the other players. I don't deny it; I just don't have any way of knowing about it. I'm an outsider. And I find that the closer I get to becoming an insider, the harder it is to resist their distortions and misjudgments. So I spray a little acid around, make a few enemies. It helps keep me honest."

Nearly 20 years later, Cabell still sometimes mispronounced the word *sabermetrics*, but Luhnow had quickly come to trust his intuition about an important quality in any young player that even James admitted he couldn't reliably evaluate: his character, known in scouting parlance as his makeup. When Luhnow and Cabell sat down with Correa and his parents at the Astros' spring training facility in Kissimmee, Florida, after a private workout that had confirmed all of Elias's observations about the shortstop's physical gifts, they couldn't help but notice how Correa had barely broken eye contact as he had answered each of their questions, a rarity for a 17-year-old.

"This kid's a leader," Cabell told Luhnow. Luhnow, speaking the Spanish he had learned as a boy, listened as Carlos Sr. and Sandybel told him about 24/7 and Hitler, and about the nightly drills, and about his consistent refusal to get caught up in his peers' partying. "Because he showed signs at such a young age to be as driven as he is to succeed, that's a strong indication that it's real and it's not something that he's doing for show," Luhnow said. Truth be told, Carlos Correa—a bilingual self-starter who had forced his way to the precipice of an unlikely career in pro baseball—reminded Luhnow of someone other than Derek Jeter or Alex Rodriguez.

If Luhnow was still running the draft for the Cardinals, the meeting would have been enough to boost Correa up his preference list, to make him an enticing option had the clubs ahead of him gone another way. That was no longer his task. Thanks to the Astros' miserable 2011, his first-ever draft pick as a major league general manager would be the first one of the first round—the one-one. "With the Cardinals, when we're picking eighteen or twenty-eight, there are so many different scenarios that you can't be sure of anything," Luhnow said. "At one-one you can be sure: If you like a guy, he's yours."

Added Luhnow: "All you have to do is call his name."

//////////

SOME YEARS, the identity of the one-one is so evident that the club holding the pick has only to perform cursory due diligence before selecting him. That was the case for the Washington Nationals, who, by virtue of their recurring awfulness, had the draft's top picks in both 2009 and 2010. In 2009, the country's best amateur was the San Diego State ace Stephen Strasburg. The Nationals took Strasburg. In 2010, the best amateur was the junior college slugger Bryce Harper, who, a year earlier at 16, had been billed on *Sports Illustrated*'s cover as BASEBALL'S CHOSEN ONE. The Nationals took Harper. Two years after that, behind Strasburg and Harper, Washington began a run of six straight winning seasons. Easy.

In 2012, there was no clear choice. "This is one of the most volatile, erratic, and weak drafts I can remember," a front office executive told *Baseball America* in May. "I've had some veteran guys tell me it's the worst ever."

That might have been true down where the Cardinals were picking, at No. 23, but at the top, Luhnow, Sig, and Elias were faced with a problem they'd never encountered in St. Louis: too many quality options, all of whom were confirmed by Sig's analysis and the Astros' scouts, as well as third-party sources like *Baseball America*, as locks to become major league stars in relatively short order. Three of them—Mark Appel, Kevin Gausman, and Mike Zunino—were college players, and after eight years of refinements, Sig's projection system for collegians had become far more accurate than it was when it spat out the name Jed Lowrie.

Appel and Gausman were both tall, strapping pitchers who struck out more than a batter an inning for big schools, Stanford and LSU, respectively. Zunino, of the University of Florida, was virtually flawless. While playing the game's most physically and mentally grueling position, catcher, he hit for power and walked almost as much as he whiffed, skills for which he won a rare trifecta of awards: the Golden Spikes, for the country's best amateur; the Dick Howser, for its best college player; and the Johnny Bench, for its best collegiate catcher. The only other player to win all three awards was Buster Posey, in 2008. Four years later, Posey was a stalwart for the San Francisco Giants and was on his way to winning the National League's Most Valuable Player Award.

Even more intriguing was a fourth option, one who appeared to be the closest thing to Mike Trout since Mike Trout. His name was Byron Buxton, and he was a six-foot-two, 180-pound high school center fielder from rural Georgia who could do it all: run, field, throw, hit for power, hit for contact. Buxton was the type of prospect that scouts called, always admiringly, a freak. He was considered the fastest amateur since Bo Jackson. He could throw a baseball 99 miles per hour and a football 82 yards. That he was a high schooler made him harder to project with certainty, though it also allowed him more time to grow. "The system works with high schoolers, but to a lesser degree," said Sig. "The information you're making sense of, there's less predictive ability." There was more of it for a high schooler from Georgia, where they played more games and against stiffer competition, than one from New Jersey.

The Astros' public relations staff liked to prepare bios of the club's conceivable top draft picks in advance, for immediate release upon their selection. As draft day—June 4, 2012—approached, they had several written, including for Appel, Buxton, Gausman, and Zunino. Those were the names that appeared at the top of *Baseball America*'s mock drafts, and the ones that were generating the most buzz inside the Astros' front office—many of whose members were holdovers from before Luhnow's arrival six months earlier. As Luhnow, Elias, and Sig huddled in the general manager's office as the clock ticked, those outside the room figured they were deciding between the two options for whom they had really been pounding the table: Appel, if they went with a collegian, and Buxton, if they went with a riskier high schooler. "Nobody had any darn clue of who we were taking," Luhnow said. Scouts all knew one another, from years spent in Courtyard by Marriott bars across the country. One injudicious text message could blow everything.

At the appointed hour, Luhnow emerged and, for the first time with the Astros, moved a magnet to the top of the draft board. It bore the name of a player who had only recently begun appearing in the lower fringes of the top ten on third-party mocks, never near No. 1. It was a stunner. The public relations staff rushed out to assemble a bio from scratch. And many incumbents in the Astros' front office knew their days in Houston were numbered.

///////////

Luhnow and his most trusted staffers had been waffling between Byron Buxton and Carlos Correa on the morning of the draft, and even as late as six p.m. central time, when they went on the clock. "They were both going to end up being great players, at the end of the day," said Elias, who officially became the Astros' scouting director a few months later. "If you took Cal Ripken instead of Ken Griffey Jr., it's really six of one and a half dozen of the other."

Carlos Correa with his brother and parents shortly after the Astros drafted him first overall in 2012.

"You never know if you're going to get another chance to pick first, and you want a player that can have the highest possible impact," said Luhnow. "For us, that was Correa. Buxton was right there, close to him. Tremendous tools. Young, exciting. But we really felt the short-stop component of it gave Carlos the edge."

Though Sig had to admit that Correa's performance metrics, mostly drawn from games against overmatched Puerto Rican high schoolers, were relatively unreliable, that only meant that his algorithms boosted the signals derived from the soft information the

Astros had gathered about Correa, which came from scouting him and meeting him. Glowing reports from good scouts like Elias and seasoned baseball men like Cabell had predictive value, too, and Sig's system concluded that Correa was the draft's top talent, no matter where he came from—especially because he was so young, still more than three months shy of his 18th birthday.

Every month mattered. It turned out that a high school senior who received a virtually identical evaluation as another who was, say, 10 months older—as Byron Buxton was compared to Correa—had a surprisingly elevated chance of future success. If the Astros didn't pick Correa because it felt risky, then they would have been standing on a 16 against a 7. And if they did that, what good were they? "It's one thing to get somebody with college-level statistics to create a model," Sig said. "It's another for the decision-makers to really use it. I don't mean use it as a tiebreaker, or to throw the analyst a bone late in the draft. I mean, really *use* it, from the first pick. That's what Jeff did."

"I don't think we have any special insights or special knowledge, or that we're any smarter than anyone else," said Elias. "I think we're operating with information and techniques that are more or less out there in the baseball community. More than half the teams use most of the information that we use." Buxton, Zunino, and Gausman were drafted with the three picks immediately following the Astros', and Appel went eighth—so low only because clubs knew his contractual demands would be significant. Continued Elias, "The thing that can be a competitive advantage for us is having the discipline and conviction in our information to stick with it even when it feels really wrong."

There was another reason why the Astros picked Correa: how much they were going to have to pay him, as far as his draft bonus. It was always a consideration, but never more so than starting in 2012. The league and the players' union had just agreed to a new collective bargaining agreement that included strict new rules about how much picks could be paid. Each club was assigned a pool of money to compensate its picks, based on the sum of recommended dollars for each pick in the draft's first 10 rounds. If you could reach an agreement to pay an early draftee less than the collectively bargained bonus his particular draft slot called for, you could spend more on players you picked later.

General managers like to talk about the difficulty of turning down the allure of "the first million," particularly for a player like Correa, a teenager who lived in a house made of cinder blocks and who, the industry believed, was otherwise unlikely to be taken before the seventh pick, which belonged to the San Diego Padres. The Padres had sent their vice president of professional scouting, a former big league catcher named A.J. Hinch, down to Puerto Rico to watch Correa for a full week in early May, and Hinch had liked what he saw. "As it turned out," Hinch said, "we had no chance at him." The recommended slot bonus for the one-one in 2012 was $7.2 million. If the Astros could get Correa to accept significantly less than that—a strong possibility for someone like him—then they could later draft a player who had indicated he would accept only an over-slot bonus.

They targeted two pitchers in particular. One was Lucas Giolito, a high school right-hander from Los Angeles who had been a one-one contender before he had sprained his elbow's ulnar collateral ligament, but who could always go to UCLA if he didn't like the financial terms he was offered. The second was a Tampa high schooler named Lance McCullers Jr., whose fastball was clocked at 97 miles per hour when he was 16. McCullers was relatively well-off—his father pitched in the majors for seven years—and he had made it known that he would be happy to honor his commitment to attend college at Florida.

The Astros offered Correa $4.8 million, $2.4 million less than the recommended slot bonus for the one-one. His mother, Sandybel, told him that he ought to go to college. He had scored a 1200 on his SATs, and had been offered a full ride to the University of Miami. Upon hearing his wife's advice, Carlos Sr. asked for a wheelchair. "Do you know how much construction I'd have to do to get $4.8 million?"

he reminded his son. "My work, your work, your son's work, and his son's work isn't going to add up to that."

Correa accepted the offer, which allowed the Astros to also sign McCullers—whom they picked 41st overall, after the Nationals took Giolito 16th—for $2.5 million, nearly double his recommended slot bonus. Luhnow thought he had emerged from his first draft in Houston with, potentially, both its best position player *and* one of its best pitchers, an outcome that would even outstrip what he had done with the Cardinals in 2009.

Correa never regretted his decision. The Cubs, now run by Theo Epstein, had told him they planned to take him sixth overall, one spot ahead of the Padres, but he had no promises higher than that. "That slot value was $3.2 million," he said. "When the Astros made the offer of 4.8? Which was 1.6 more, with the chance to make history as the first top pick out of Puerto Rico? There was nothing to lose, when I came from nothing."

////////////

CORREA'S GRADUATION FROM the Puerto Rico Baseball Academy was scheduled for a few days after he signed his contract, but well before he'd seen a dollar from it. He was not only the school's best player, but also its valedictorian. On paper he had secured not just his first million but nearly his first five, but he owned just one pair of shoes, and wore a borrowed suit to the draft. A family friend, the owner of a printing business who was one of the few wealthy residents of Santa Isabel, offered to take him shopping to buy him the first suit that he could call his own, to wear as he accepted his diploma. Correa couldn't stop looking at himself in the mirror of an Express in Puerto Rico, at the way the slim black garment with its silky dark blue lining clung to his body. *I'm a professional,* he told himself. *I've accomplished what I've always wanted.*

As he gazed into the dressing room mirror, Correa allowed himself to envision the years to come. How even though so many still said he would soon grow too big to stick at shortstop, he would follow a strict off-season diet to stay under 220 pounds—222, maximum—like a fighter perennially making weight. How he would give his autograph to most anyone who asked, with the same signature, quick and legible, that he had so often practiced in his school notebooks while he waited for his classmates to complete tasks he had already finished. And how neither he nor his father would ever have to work construction again, and could soon afford to buy anything they wanted, all the shoes and the clothes they had desired but could never have. "From now on," he said, "I will look nice."

His family knew there had never been a guarantee that such a future would be theirs. That all those nights ignoring their heckling neighbors would amount to anything. That Javier would receive the height and graceful athleticism of Sandybel's family, and not the stockiness of his father's. That his disciplined childhood would only build his character, not destroy it. "We think that Javier has always had an angel watching over him," Sandybel said. The Astros had been watching him, too, but he wasn't the only player who had captured their attention.

4

GROWTH MINDSET

In 2012, the year he had moved to Houston, Sig Mejdal did more than acquire a new job and a new home, if you could call his old fraternity brother's garage a home. He attended wedding number 89—his own. He had enjoyed every ceremony he had ever attended, but he had also analyzed what made some truly special and others less so. It's hard to find a band, as opposed to a DJ, that pleases everybody. The bridesmaids' dresses should not match the tablecloths. If you put a potted plant in a basketball hoop, guests will still know they are in a high school gym. For his own nuptials, he and his fiancée, Arati, a former journalist who had become a corporate social media manager and whom he had met at a conference, eloped to a rock off the coast of Stockholm. The officiant, provided by the Swedish government, pronounced the couple's names as Art and Sigrid, but Sig rated it very highly anyway. After that, Sig spent half his time in Houston and half working from North Carolina, where Arati and her 12-year-old son from her first marriage, Ross, lived.

Ross was very much like his new stepfather had been as a boy. He was bright, a straight-A student. He loved sports: tennis, but also baseball, especially after Sig came into his life. He was small and slight. He rarely hit the ball out of the infield, and he spent most of his Little League games in right field.

Unlike Sig, whose mother and father could barely grasp the difference between a ball and a strike, Ross had a parent who understood baseball pretty well. During the 26 weeks a year in which Sig worked remotely from Raleigh, he attended Ross's games. He always sat in the correct bleachers, but he spent most of the time grimacing at what he saw. The problem wasn't what the kids were doing. It was what their coaches were telling them to do.

Ever since there was such a thing as Little League, its coaches had preached the same hitting philosophy: choke up and swing away. Ross's did, too. "Like every coach in Little League, they're encouraging the kids to not strike out looking," Sig said. "The kids accommodate the coach by swinging at everything they can reach. It's a terrible habit. When you aren't Babe Ruth, it makes no sense."

For all his good qualities, Ross was not Babe Ruth. He knew that, but as the end of middle school approached, he set an ambitious goal for himself: to make his high school's baseball team. Here was something with which Sig could help.

He enlisted a friend of his from the Cardinals, a scout named Matt Blood, who also lived in Raleigh, to take turns with him pitching batting practice to Ross, and to imbue Ross with the plate discipline not of a Little Leaguer, but a major leaguer. It wasn't a matter of taking balls and swinging at strikes. It was a matter of identifying *which* strikes were worth a cut. Borderline pitches were no good. The Babe himself often couldn't do much with strikes that came in low and away but crossed over home plate's black border. But the strikes that arrived waist-high, especially over the plate's inside third? Those, Sig and Blood told Ross, were the good ones, the pitches that even a batter who was not particularly strong could drive over the shortstop's head.

In his Little League games, Ross did as he had been taught. He occasionally committed the cardinal sin of striking out looking. As he returned to the bench and his coach yelled at him, Ross caught Sig's eye and smiled. *He doesn't know what we know,* the look said. After tryouts at the beginning of the spring of his freshman year of high school, Ross anxiously scanned the junior varsity baseball team's roster. He found his name.

All those extra batting practice pitches led to one unfortunate result: Sig tore his rotator cuff. Even as he underwent surgery and then endured agonizing physical therapy, he felt Ross's new swing had been worth it. "He has a great growth mindset," Sig said, proudly.

//////////

GROWTH MINDSET: It was a phrase that would come to define baseball decisions with even higher stakes than Ross's. A superlative analytics department might get you halfway up the mountain. It was an intangible—the elusive but discoverable qualities of persistence and adaptability—that got you to the top.

While the Astros had badly deteriorated by the time Jeff Luhnow arrived, the organization still had some 300 baseball players under contract, the majority of whom had never played an inning in Houston. They filled rosters in Triple-A, at Oklahoma City; in Double-A, at Corpus Christi; in High-A ball, at Lancaster; in A-ball, at Lexington; in short-season A-Ball, in Tri-City; in rookie ball, at Greeneville and Kissimmee; and in the Dominican Summer League.

Luhnow got the job, in part, by promising Jim Crane he would rid his books of expensive players who wouldn't have lasted until the Astros were good again, and convert them into young future contributors. In reality, the highly compensated veterans Luhnow inherited accounted for only a fraction of the organization's players. Heading into the 2012 season, six were due to make more than a million dollars, and just two—slugger Carlos Lee and closer Brett Myers—were owed more than $8 million. What about everybody else?

Luhnow believed that the process he planned to install, which would synthesize hard data and human experience to draw the best out of both, would help him make good decisions as far as acquiring the right players to turn the organization around via the draft, trades, and free agency, and that their analytics-aided tactics and training methods would provide those players with the tools to succeed. At a certain point, the decisions were out of the front office's hands. They belonged to the players themselves: how hard to train, what to eat, how willing they were to use those tools to determine which pitches to swing at and which to throw.

That was where having a growth mindset was important. The Nerd Cave could provide a player at even the organization's lowest level with data that revealed exactly how he might improve his plate discipline or the mix of his pitches to find greater success, but that was just the start of it. It was up to the player to have the willingness to act upon that information in order to grow. That often meant changing the way he had always done things, particularly challenging because whatever these players had been doing had been good enough to allow them to get here, professional baseball.

One of Luhnow's and Sig's frustrations in St. Louis was that they had been siloed in the scouting department. They had so many ideas for better practices the Cardinals could implement, but the other departments were run by other executives, and some of them refused to speak to Luhnow, let alone listen to him. Now that Luhnow ran everything in Houston, he controlled the decisions about the important men who would translate the front office's new philosophies to the players, convince them to use them, and teach them how to do it: the coaches. He overhauled the organization's coaching ranks, filling them with people who not only understood the plan but were fully on board with it, even if it often violated orthodoxies in which they had previously believed.

Despite the Astros' decline, Luhnow knew that the organization, among the 300 players it already possessed, had to have at least a few young players who, due to their natural talent and their drive to improve, might prove a part of the future he envisioned. He planned to take a wrecking ball to the Astros, but there had to be some shiny copper piping worth salvaging. "Any GM is going to inherit a system with great players in there," Luhnow said. "It's a matter of which ones you're going to bet on."

Sig helped to guide those bets. He could run the same regressions on the Astros' own players as he always had on draft prospects, only now they were even more predictive of future success or failure. Some 140 games a year against Double-A pitching provided a much better data set than a few dozen against high school hurlers. He could also incorporate into his models the human observations, even the gut instincts, of coaches who knew the players far better than a scout might know a high schooler, whom he might have met a handful of times, if at all. Coaches spent every day working with the players in question and filed reports back to Houston after every game. The more Luhnow brought in coaches who were on board with his plan, the better the information they could pass along to Sig. Sig's models updated constantly. As the players incrementally grew—or didn't—so did their projections. Instead of indicating whether a player should be drafted, the Nerd Cave's algorithms suggested when he was ready to be promoted to a higher level of play, or to be cut.

Jim Crane made his own contribution to the process. Unlike many new owners, who might want a winner tomorrow, Crane understood that Luhnow's overhaul would take years, which permitted him time to avoid making rash decisions on very young players— trading them, for example, for immediate big league help—that might come back to haunt him. The owner's patience also allowed the Astros to benefit from the best friend of even the most disciplined gambler: luck.

///////////

THERE WAS ALWAYS ONE PLAYER in the Astros' system whom Luhnow was likely to keep around. The spring before their arrival in Houston, when they were still with the Cardinals, both Luhnow and Mike Elias had traveled to the University of Connecticut to scout a six-foot-three, 200-pound junior named George Springer. "He was a rare animal—a five-tool athlete in college," Elias said. "Guys with those kinds of physical tools? Who throw like that, run like that, have that kind of body? They usually get signed out of high school."

Guys like that were also rarely available when it was the Cardinals' turn to draft. With what would prove to be his last-ever first rounder in St. Louis, in June 2011, Luhnow used the 22nd pick on yet another undersized collegiate middle infielder, Kolten Wong of the University of Hawaii at Mānoa. To Luhnow's dismay, if not surprise, the Astros had removed Springer from his board 11 slots and nearly an hour earlier.

George Springer dives into first for UConn in 2011.

Springer always had the genes and the background to become a major league star. His grandfather, George Chelston Springer, emigrated from Panama at 17 in 1950 to pitch at the Teachers College of Connecticut. His father, George Jr., played in the Little League World Series, then walked on to the UConn football team before becoming a lawyer. ("I peaked at age twelve," George Jr. liked to joke. "Unfortunately, I didn't know that until age eighteen.") His mother, the Puerto Rico–born Laura, was a UConn gymnast who later coached the sport. George III and his two sisters grew up on floor mats. "The flips, the twists, I could do it all," he said.

In his first full season as a minor leaguer, in 2012, Springer displayed every bit of that explosive athleticism, batting .302 with 24 home runs and 32 stolen bases in 128 games. He also demonstrated a trait that gave Luhnow and Sig genuine doubt about whether Springer would ever play a role in their club's future, even though he would enter 2013 as *Baseball America*'s 37th-rated prospect: He played completely out of control.

That tendency sometimes revealed itself in the outfield, where he made as many blunders as wall-climbing catches, but more often at the plate. He swung from his heels no matter what. "I didn't have a plan," he said. "I always tried to hit a five-run homer instead of settling for the single down the middle."

He was so gifted that such an approach had worked at Avon Old Farms, the boys school to which he'd transferred as a high school sophomore, and later against Big East pitching. Springer played that way, all out, all the time, for a reason. At 15, he had been even smaller than Sig's stepson: five foot two and 100 pounds flat. "I wasn't the strongest, I wasn't the fastest," he said. "I was always trying to do things bigger." By the end of high school, he had grown a foot and doubled his body weight, but still maintained a little guy's mentality. "I just believed that I had to go out and give one hundred percent of who I am every single day," he said. "I think that led to trying to do things that I couldn't physically or mentally do. I'm a pretty high-energy guy as it is. You add in having fun, and competition, and you're looking at a recipe for *fast*."

Springer's recipe produced a lot of home runs during his first year in the minors, but more often led to an outcome that Sig's metrics had always flagged as significantly negatively predictive: strikeouts.

Springer strode to the plate 581 times in 2012 and retreated from it without having made fair contact after 156 of those at-bats. That computed to a strikeout rate of one per every 3.7 plate appearances, an obscene frequency. Only nine regular major league hitters exceeded it that year, and they were swinging and missing against the best pitchers in the world. Springer was doing it at Lancaster and Corpus Christi, against hurlers who, for the most part, wouldn't go much further.

It was hard to find a player who had struck out as often as Springer did at so low a level of play and gone on to become a major leaguer of any prominence. At the time, the majors' most strikeout-prone slugger was the White Sox behemoth Adam Dunn. Dunn owned four of the 13 highest seasonal strikeout totals in baseball history. It was impossible to imagine a genuine big leaguer whiffing more. And yet when Adam Dunn was in Single-A, he had on average swung through or looked at strike three during just one of 5.5 plate appearances—a rate that was nearly 50 percent *better* than Springer's.

If there was one reason for optimism to be gleaned from Springer's strikeouts, it was the nature of them. He actually had a developed sense of the plate, and drew a walk every two games, a lot for a young player. He didn't usually swing at bad pitches. He swung at good ones. He just swung so hard that he often missed them.

But Springer had more than just good genes, athleticism, and intelligence. While he hadn't had to overcome the economic deprivations of many of his teammates, he still had a strong growth mindset, the source of which revealed itself every time he tried to order at a restaurant or was called upon to speak in class: stuttering. It had started early, and by the time he was a junior at Avon Old Farms, it was debilitating. He woke up every day dreading the social interactions that lay ahead, but looking forward to his practices and games, where his performance spoke for him. "The baseball field was the only place where I felt like myself," he said.

For much of his youth, Springer felt lost when he wasn't on the diamond. "I just didn't think I would ever get past it," he said. "'This is who I am. This is how it's going to be.'" Years of speech therapy eventually helped Springer realize that this wasn't true. He used many strategies. He controlled his breathing. He spoke with his hands. He seamlessly substituted synonyms on which he knew he wouldn't stumble for words that gave him trouble.

Eventually, he felt little anxiety about talking in public, to the point where his inquisitors wouldn't have detected a hint of a stutter unless they were looking for it. He even became the national spokesperson for the Stuttering Association for the Young. So when his minor league coaches told him, based on directives they'd received from the top of the organization, that he had to swing softer, to hit the cutoff man, and, most of all, to slow down? That wasn't quite the same challenge as the one he overcame every time he ordered a meal. He knew how to adapt.

Springer debuted with the Astros in April 2014. By mid-May, he had four home runs. He'd also made six errors in right field and struck out at least once in 25 of his 32 games. He had two four-strikeout nights in a span of 10 days. Adam Dunn would record just one that entire season. The Astros' second year manager, Bo Porter, benched him for a few games. "He was overrunning balls, just seemed out of control," Porter explained. "In the batter's box, he was trying to hit the ball to Beaumont. I think a lot of that had to do with the excitement of arriving in the majors, and all the hoopla that was surrounding him."

The Astros new system was designed to guide Springer toward the changes he would need to make in order to thrive. And Springer reached for them. A calmer Springer hit two homers and drove in five runs on the evening of his return. Thereafter, while he still struck out a lot—once every three plate appearances as a rookie—he bent the curve the Astros had projected for him when he was in Single-A. His strikeouts decreased each year, to the point where Springer whiffed less in the majors than Adam Dunn had at Single-A. And while Dunn had one tool, Springer had five.

"I slowly figured out what kind of hitter I wanted to be, what kind of hitter I am, instead of getting in the box and blindly swinging," he said, without a hint of a stutter. "Slowing down, in all aspects, has helped me still play fast."

/////////////

MEANWHILE, LUHNOW HAD BEEN busy gutting the Astros' roster. Between December 2011 and September 2013, he made 25 trades, sending away 28 players, most of them major leaguers, and acquiring 41, almost all of them prospects. No one was safe, if he could be leveraged into a more promising return, not even Jed Lowrie. In February 2013, 14 months after Luhnow had made Lowrie the first player he'd acquired with the Astros, Luhnow traded him and a reliever to the A's for a package that included the pitcher Brad Peacock, the slugger Chris Carter, and the catcher Max Stassi.

"It is a purely statistical analysis," Lowrie told Evan Drellich, the *Houston Chronicle*'s beat writer, the next year, of the way Luhnow and the Astros operated. "I think you can't have that approach and expect to have good personal relations. That seems like a hard balance to strike, when you're judging someone strictly on numbers and nothing else, and I'm not talking about whether it's a good guy or a bad guy. But there are certain intangibles, and the perception is the numbers are trying to drive out the importance of those intangibles." Luhnow—and Sig, too—felt Lowrie was wrong, but, coming from him, it stung.

Luhnow's reputation for roster ruthlessness, for dispensing with most members of the organization he had inherited, reached even the Astros' youngest fans. One day, he received a handwritten letter:

dear Mr. Jeff Luhnow:

*hi my name is Will and I live in texes Please don't trade
gorge springer these are the reasons*

1. he is my favirte player
2. I get my hair cut like his
3. he is a team leader

Luhnow posted the letter to Twitter. "Sound logic don't you think?" he wrote.

///////////

DALLAS KEUCHEL WAS NEVER particularly small, when he was growing up in Oklahoma, and he was never particularly big. He loved to pitch, but he could never throw a baseball particularly fast. What he could always do, from the time he was eight, was throw it exactly where he meant to, every time. "Right away you could tell the kid could dot you between the eyes, if he wanted to," his father, Dennis, would tell *The Oklahoman* newspaper.

Dennis was a horticulturalist by trade, and he spent his entire working life outside. His passion, though, was for baseball, particularly for pitching. Each day, when he was done caring for other people's trees and plants, he came home and tended to something else: Dallas's left arm. They didn't just play backyard catch. They had target practice. Dennis would hold his glove directly over his heart. "Hit it," he would say. Dallas would. Dennis held his glove below his knees, inches above the grass. "Hit it." Dallas hit it. Dennis held it above his head. "Hit it." Dallas hit it. Every throw Dallas ever made, even when it looked like he was just fooling around and trying to get his arm loose, had a purpose, an intended location.

Dallas loved playing baseball video games, too, and if he'd finished his homework, he was permitted that diversion. Unlike many baseball dads, Dennis thought the games were useful, in that they allowed his son to develop a mastery of pitching strategy. Dallas's first game was a little handheld Atari, but over the years he graduated to Super Nintendo, then Sega Dreamcast, then PlayStation, then PlayStation 2. He enjoyed being John Smoltz, because Smoltz could blow his 98-mile-per-hour fastball by any of the tiny avatars he faced, then put them away with his nasty splitter. But Dallas learned more from playing as the pitchers who were more like him, those who couldn't throw hard but with whom he could still get Smoltz's results due to their pinpoint command: Greg Maddux, Jamie Moyer, Mark Buehrle, and, in particular, Tom Glavine.

In his real-life games, Dallas never had the kind of repertoire that stood out, especially not to scouts, even once he got to Tulsa's Bishop Kelley High. His fastball came in at 85 miles per hour, sometimes 87. "For a high school pitcher, his stuff was good, but I can remember facing a lot of guys who had better stuff than he did," said one of his opponents from Oklahoma. He received an invitation to just one all-star tournament and was never named all-state. When major league clubs held the 2006 draft, his name wasn't among the 1,502 they called. The worst part might have been that even though he started three state championship games for Tulsa Kelley, and won two of them, rival teams didn't even think enough of him to bother learning how to properly say his last name. "Kutchel," their announcers would say over the PA system. "Keekel." "Koykel."

That always motivated him. "It's *Kyke-el*," he muttered to himself, before, as often as not, shutting them out with stuff they were sure, next time, they were going to hit.

Keuchel pitched at the University of Arkansas for three years. He had a 5.88 ERA as a freshman, mostly out of the bullpen. By his junior season he was the Razorbacks' number one starter, their Friday night guy. Even so, major league clubs didn't tend to get worked up about a pitcher who couldn't hit 90. Scouts only flocked to his games if they were there to watch someone else. He struck out fewer than six batters per nine innings, and he allowed, on average, more than a hit each frame. Not great—though if you looked closer, most of those hits were weak tappers and bloopers. Even though he pitched in the highly competitive Southeastern Conference—the SEC—against hitters who wielded springy metal bats, just four of the 114 hits they produced against him as a senior were home runs. That was how, despite his otherwise unimpressive ratios, his ERA improved to 3.92. In June 2009, after major league clubs had picked 220 other amateurs—and 109 other pitchers, the first of them Stephen Strasburg—the Houston Astros took a seventh-round shot on the junkballer out of Arkansas.

In the minors, his results stayed the same as they had in college, even as he advanced through the system and faced increasingly talented opponents. He allowed more than a hit per inning, his strikeout rate hovered around six per nine, he didn't give up many homers, his ERA was around 4.00. He never came close to a top 100 prospects list, and the grades *Baseball Prospectus* gave him were consistent: a C in 2010, a C in 2011, a C in 2012. "He could be a fifth starter or a long reliever," wrote the authors of the industry's bible.

In 2012, when Keuchel was 24, the Astros got a new owner and a new front office, men who hadn't drafted him and had no attachment to him, and whose analytics didn't look favorably upon mediocre soft-tossers. Jeff Luhnow would have traded him, and thought little of it, but no other general manager wanted him. Luhnow knew his counterparts hadn't spent any time scouting the pitcher by the way they pronounced his name on the phone. "Kootchel?" they said, before quickly asking about someone else.

So the Astros kept him, and, since they so badly needed anyone who could pitch the major league innings they still had to play, they promoted him to Houston that June. His first three starts went surprisingly well. He allowed a single run in each of them, and in his second outing, against the Cleveland Indians, he even threw a complete game. Then the league caught on to him.

Since Keuchel's fastball came in at only 89, and besides that, he really only threw a changeup, he couldn't strike you out. All you had to do was sit back and foul off pitches until he gave you something you could drive. By season's end, he was 3–8 with a 5.27 ERA, and he had accomplished the almost impossible feat of walking more batters, 39, than he whiffed, 38. The Astros couldn't blame their rivals for declining to trade for him. They wouldn't have traded for a pitcher like that, either. Keuchel wouldn't have traded for himself. "I didn't feel like I belonged here," he said.

Over the winter, back home in Oklahoma with Dennis, Keuchel equipped himself with something he believed could change that feeling. He decided that if he was going to survive in the big leagues, to feel like he belonged, he had to be willing to adapt. Specifically, he needed a third pitch besides his sinking fastball and changeup, one that would help him keep batters off-balance and prevent them from digging in for long at-bats. "When you have three pitches, that puts doubt in hitters' minds," he said. He settled on a slider, a pitch he used to throw in high school but had abandoned in college and in the minors when his fastball and changeup proved good enough for him to get by.

When the Astros' players arrived at spring training in February 2013, they could be certain of only one thing: They were going to be bad. "There was no light at the end of the tunnel," Keuchel said. They'd lost 107 games the year before, and now the front office had traded away the few veterans, like Carlos Lee and Brett Myers, who had prevented them from losing even more. Many of the players, as they scanned a locker room that housed almost no one older than 26, saw a circus. Keuchel saw something else: an opportunity. "It was an open tryout for, like, fifty guys," he said.

One day during spring training, Luhnow and David Stearns called a team meeting for the club's pitchers, catchers, and infielders in the multipurpose room on the second floor of their stadium in Kissimmee. They laid out the way in which the club was now going to use analytics to guide their on-field tactics. Mike Fast, from the Nerd Cave, demonstrated how the club had accumulated and parsed years of data on every opposing hitter, which revealed how they performed against every type of pitch and where they tended to hit them. For one thing, this meant that the club's new manager, Bo Porter, would be calling for infield shifts against certain hitters, particularly lefties who liked to pull the ball, like David Ortiz and Adam Dunn. Even if the shortstop played on what was traditionally considered the wrong side of second base, he'd be in position to field the ball where the hitter more often hit it. Luhnow and Stearns promised it would, in the long haul, save pitchers runs.

Keuchel hated the idea. "I'm a stubborn SOB," he said. Most of his teammates hated it, too. During the half-hour meeting, some, like the 27-year-old starter Lucas Harrell, even told Luhnow and Stearns as much. But they had no leverage. None of them was John Smoltz or Tom Glavine. "Before we start bitching," Keuchel said to his teammates, "let's take a look."

Their early looks led to bitching, some of it from Keuchel. "The first time a ball goes to the regular shortstop position but there's nobody there, that's the only thing you can remember through the course of the game," he said. "The fourteen-hopper is the only thing that resonates in your mind."

But gradually, when he reviewed his outings, he realized that the shift was, on the whole, beneficial, especially for a pitcher like him who gave up few homers but a lot of ground balls. If the tactic could turn even one extra grounder a game from a hit into an out, that was a big deal. "More times than not, this shift thing is helping me," he said. He grew to love it.

He also grew to love the other part of Luhnow and Stearns's presentation in the multipurpose room, in which they revealed the newly developed analytical tools the Nerd Cave was going to give the pitchers to help them approach hitters, and vice versa. It could tell them, with video evidence, how hitters performed against each type of pitch thrown in each location at each point in the count. In other words, it could make even the game's best hitters predictable. It was cause and effect. While Porter and his coaches would incorporate the information into their planning and managing of games, at a certain point it was up to the pitchers to decide how much they wanted to use it. The Nerd Cave could always give them more, if they wanted it.

Keuchel had grown up trying to mystify video game hitters with Glavine's soft stuff. Now he had information that could help him decide how to do it with his own, including a slider that felt increasingly good as it left his hand.

Keuchel made the Opening Day roster. In many ways, 2013 would prove more disastrous for the Astros than he or any of their other players could have imagined during spring training, particularly the 15-game losing streak that closed it out, which included the demoralizing extra-innings loss to the Yankees on the season's final day and, worst of all, the Butt Slide. "At that point, I just really wanted to go home," Keuchel said. "There had never been another time I had been so relieved to get back to Oklahoma and just, like, hide. It was beyond embarrassing."

It also had a silver lining. Though Keuchel's ERA hadn't improved much from his rookie year, he had thrown his slider 20 percent of the time. That, combined with the analytical information he'd been provided on how to use it to attack hitters, led to improved underlying results. He struck out more than seven batters per nine, an 80 percent increase from the season before. He felt that he was now a pitcher with upside, with a path to further improvement.

The Dallas Keuchel who showed up for the next season, 2014, was different than the one the Astros or their opponents had previously seen. For one thing, the previously bare-cheeked pitcher had accepted a bet from two of his friends from Tulsa: to endure the entire year without shaving. He started the challenge at the end of spring training. Soon his beard extended to his collarbone, and he had to groom it as his father had shaped shrubbery. It didn't help him with women. "They either like the beard or they hate the beard, and that's brought to my attention within ten seconds of meeting them," he said. He remained a bachelor. But he found that the beard gave him an identity.

More significantly, over the winter, he had decided to fully embrace the analytical tools the Nerd Cave provided him. He barely knew anyone in the Nerd Cave. He might nod hello to Sig or Mike Fast in passing. But he appreciated their work. He realized their data could not only allow him to determine where each hitter typically hit the ball, but also predict how that hitter would perform against a left-handed pitcher who had a sinking two-seam fastball, a changeup, and a slider. A pitcher exactly like him.

He spent hours each day poring over video and scouting reports, to the point where he could himself position his infielders more precisely than even his managers or coaches could. If he planned to throw an inside slider to a left-handed batter, his ability to hit his target allowed him to predict exactly where he was going to deliver it, and he now knew exactly where the batter would probably hit it. Before the pitch, he could direct his second baseman to move two additional feet to his left.

Keuchel also learned that someone like him did best by pitching backward. Fireballers, like John Smoltz, could start hitters off with fastballs and then get them to swing through breaking balls. But most major league batters could hit first-pitch fastballs that came in at less than 90 miles per hour. The key, for someone like him, was often to start off-speed and then finish with a well-located fastball. By comparison, it would look to hitters as if it were coming in harder than it actually was.

§§§§§§§§§§§

ON MAY 13, 2014, Keuchel prepared to face a club that had consistently hammered him the season before: the Texas Rangers. In four starts against them in 2013, the Rangers' disciplined sluggers, led by Adrián Beltré, had either knocked Keuchel out of the game early by running up his pitch count, or teed off on him, or both. Over $25\frac{1}{3}$ innings, the Rangers strafed him for 15 earned runs on 25 hits and seven walks, and he hadn't beaten them once.

On that Tuesday night in May, the Rangers encountered a new Dallas Keuchel, not just a newly bearded one. They could still find his pitches with their bats, but only once did any of them make hard contact—a first-inning double to right by Beltré. The rest of their six hits were soft liners, bouncers, and bunts, all singles. Mostly they found that when they hit the ball, it went right to one of the Astros' fielders. Through the game's first eight innings, during which Keuchel hadn't thrown a single pitch that reached 90 miles per hour, he had lured the Rangers into three double-play grounders.

By the time there was one out in the top of the ninth, Keuchel had an 8–0 lead and a chance to induce one more double play, one that would end the game. There was a runner on first, and the batter was Prince Fielder, Texas's new left-handed cleanup hitter. At five foot eleven and 275 pounds, the 30-year-old Fielder was shaped like a cannonball, and had the destructive abilities of one. Over his last eight seasons, he had averaged 35 home runs a year for the Milwaukee Brewers and the Detroit Tigers. He had also built a track record of tendencies. Thanks to the Nerd Cave, Keuchel knew them.

Fielder, like many sluggers, crushed pitches that came in over either the middle or the inside part of the plate, which he could pull over the right-field fence. The season before, in Detroit, 23 of his 25 home runs were on pitches that arrived over the plate's inner two-thirds. But he also had trouble laying off balls that came in elsewhere. He had put 275 outside pitches in play in 2013, and only two of those had resulted in homers. Low and outside pitches gave him particular trouble: He had batted .172 against those, with no home runs at all.

It was, of course, no secret around baseball that Prince Fielder dominated the plate's interior two thirds. Most of the home runs he had hit in 2013 were off pitches that had been mistakes—those that had not gone where the pitcher had intended them to go. But Keuchel, with his ability to throw a baseball wherever he wanted, almost never made mistakes. He even intended his pitches that came in off the plate, and were called balls by the umpire, to end up there. In 2014, just more than 40 percent of his pitches were strikes, the seventh-lowest percentage in the league. That was by design. While such a low strike rate generally revealed a lack of command, in Keuchel's case it resulted from a formidable amount of it. He was confident enough in his control to throw lots of balls outside the strike zone on purpose, hoping to get hitters like Fielder to chase them and knowing that he could later throw strikes if he needed them.

He started Fielder off with a 79-mile-per-hour slider, down and away. Fielder held off. The next pitch was a sinking, 86-mile-per-hour fastball, also low and outside. Fielder declined to swing again. He was going to make a fight of it. Keuchel threw his third pitch, an 89-mile-per-hour fastball, out of the strike zone again, but this time it arrived high and outside, in an area in which Fielder also tended to struggle, batting just .250 in 2013. Fielder held off once more.

With a count of three balls and no strikes against him, Keuchel knew he had to find the strike zone with his next pitch. Even though he assumed Fielder would likely take the pitch, hoping to draw a walk and spark an unlikely rally, Keuchel wanted to assume as little risk as possible. His 89-mile-per-hour fastball was a strike, but over the plate's outer third. Fielder took it.

Now, even though it remained a hitter's count at three and one, Keuchel felt as if he had Fielder right where he wanted him. With his 108th pitch of the night, he threw another 89-mile-per-hour fastball within the strike zone. For the fifth straight time, he avoided the middle and inside portions of the plate. The pitch arrived over the plate's outer third, and low. Fielder did precisely what Keuchel anticipated he might. He rolled over it, tapping it weakly to the third baseman, Matt Dominguez, who had shifted to play on the far side of second base. Dominguez scooped it up, touched second, and threw to first, securing Keuchel's first-ever complete game shutout.

It was only the Astros' 13th win of the season, against 27 losses, but it showed progress. Wrote Evan Drellich in the *Chronicle,* "Even when this club is a contender someday—one assumes that will come before the Antarctic glacier fully melts—wins this thorough will be rare."

Even better than the result, for Keuchel, was the new feeling he had experienced that night. His three pitches, his control, and his hard-earned knowledge of each hitter's tendencies had clicked, all at once. He knew which pitches he had wanted to throw before each of the 31 batters he had faced, and he knew what was likely to happen when he threw them. Then, almost always, it happened. *This is a feeling I want to have each and every time out,* he told himself.

Dallas Keuchel smiles after another commanding performance.

Major league public address announcers continued to mispronounce his name. *Tonight's starter for the Houston Astros: Dallas Kookel,* they would say, as he shook his head while throwing his final warm-up pitches in the bullpen. Though Luhnow remained unopposed to the idea of trading Keuchel, he now wanted more in return, based on Keuchel's improved performance. "I thought he would be a useful back-end guy," Luhnow said, meaning a reliable number four or number five starter.

One of the problems with regression analysis was that it had trouble identifying outliers, such as a sui generis pitcher who could consistently outperform the sum of his measurable parts. Other clubs weren't clamoring for a pitcher who had an 89-mile-per-hour fastball, either. At the trade deadline, Luhnow dealt three players, headlined by Jarred Cosart, to the Marlins for a package of minor leaguers—the third baseman Colin Moran, the outfielder Jake Marisnick, and the pitcher Francis Martes—as well as a compensatory first-round draft pick. "That was going to be me in that trade," Keuchel said. He heard that the only reason he wasn't headed to Miami was that the Marlins preferred Cosart, another holdover from the previous regime, but one who was two and a half years younger than he was and threw a fastball that touched 99.

Keuchel didn't much care. Business was business, but what mattered to him was that he had finally cracked baseball's code. He felt as if he could now see the 0's and 1's that had dictated the actions of the opponents he had once tried to flummox with the digital avatar of Tom Glavine, but in real life. He finished 2014 with a 2.93 ERA, the American League's seventh best, over exactly 200 innings, the standard workload for a frontline starter. The season after that, he came off the trading block for good, and for the first time in his life he was no longer a regular victim of careless PA announcers. They all knew how to say the name of the winner of the American League's Cy Young Award.

///////////

IF IT TOOK JEFF LUHNOW years to realize that Dallas Keuchel was more than a back-end pitcher with good control, he saw right away that José Altuve was more than his height. When Altuve was young, his teammates in Venezuela called him *enano*—the midget. Professional teams deemed him something else: a nonprospect. In September 2006, he showed up at a local tryout for the Astros near his home city of Maracay, an industrial town of nearly a million residents near the Caribbean coast that had produced many of Venezuela's greatest players, including Bobby Abreu and Miguel Cabrera. He'd already auditioned for at least a half dozen clubs, including several of the league's savviest, such as the Giants and the Yankees. Each one had sent him home with the same message: Boys who stand five foot five and weigh 140 pounds at 16 do not become major leaguers. The Astros turned him away after the first day, too.

For a Venezuelan teenager, there was no prep school or college he might attend while waiting for a growth spurt that would never come. Altuve's father, Carlos—an engineering assistant at a chemical company—insisted he go back the next morning anyway. A special assistant for the Astros named Al Pedrique had by then gotten to Maracay. Altuve's speed impressed him: He was the fastest player on the field, running a 6.31 on his first 60-yard dash and a 6.29 on his second. Bo Jackson, the standard for baseball speed, ran a 6.18 when he was in college at Auburn. At the plate, Altuve got his bat on everything he could reach. That year, the Yankees signed another 16-year-old Venezuelan, the six-foot-three catcher Jesús Montero, for $1.6 million. Pedrique told Altuve he didn't have quite as much room in his budget. He could give Altuve a bonus of $15,000. Altuve didn't think twice.

Five years later, rosters generously listed Altuve at five foot six. In reality, he hadn't grown an inch. But he had hit .327 over five minor league seasons, and the Astros promoted him to the big leagues in the summer of 2011, a month after they drafted George Springer, who was eight months older. Despite the heightened competition, Altuve proved to be the same player he had always been: one who could steal bags,

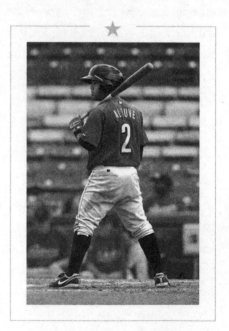

The five-foot-five José Altuve in 2010, his last full season in the minors.

play strong defense at second, and hit virtually any pitch thrown to him. As a rookie in 2011, he swatted at 55 percent of the pitches he saw, an aggressive rate that was exceeded by just six major league regulars, including a few of the game's top sluggers like Vladimir Guerrero, Josh Hamilton, Adam Jones, and Alfonso Soriano. But he made contact 88 percent of the time, a frequency none of those other free-swingers matched. Even the great Guerrero hit less than 82 percent of the pitches at which he hacked.

It is always difficult for an athlete to explain why he has a gift others don't—in Altuve's case, his hand-eye coordination—and Altuve struggled to do so. "I'm definitely not trying to *not* strike out," he said. "I just hit the ball." He imagined he might always remain the same type of player, one who slapped the ball around, rarely whiffed, and used his legs to stretch a lot of singles into doubles. That was who he was when Luhnow arrived at the end of 2011, and Luhnow and Sig knew that sort of player had value. "He has incredible bat control," Luhnow said. "He's able to foul off pitches and keep himself in the at-bat. He's got a really smooth, level, line-drive swing. And he's got a small strike zone, quite frankly."

In July 2013, when Altuve was in the middle of what promised to be a typical major league season for him—a batting average above .280, 30 doubles and 30 steals, single-digit home runs—Luhnow signed him to a long-term extension. It was modest money, by big league standards: a total of $12.5 million over the next four seasons and then another $12.5 million in options in 2018 and 2019, which could be exercised by the Astros. But it was a lot more than $15,000.

At minimum, Luhnow said, "We knew that we had at least an everyday second baseman on a second-division club," meaning a club that only harbored hopes of contending in the future. A player like that was worth about $3 million a year to any team, even a rebuilding one, no matter how tall he was. "You wouldn't bet on a five-foot-six player to make the big leagues," Luhnow said. "But once that five-foot-six player has demonstrated that he can perform on any level, and beaten out ninety-nine percent of the population, there's no reason to hold that against him ever again." The Astros' metrics suggested that Altuve might not be finished beating the odds.

Just because you can hit everything doesn't mean you should, unless you're Vladimir Guerrero. After Luhnow's arrival, the Astros' coaches began preaching a new philosophy to their diminutive second baseman, similar to the one Sig would later suggest to his stepson: Since you almost never strike out anyway, why not try limiting your swings to those pitches that you can turn on and drive, those on which you might really do damage?

For Altuve, like most hitters who were not the six-foot-three, 235-pound Guerrero, that meant pitches that came in not only over the plate, but over its inner two-thirds, especially belt-high. You could divide the strike zone into nine squares, ranging diagonally from up-and-in to middle-middle to down-and-away. That had helped Dallas Keuchel figure out how to approach Prince Fielder. As a rookie, Altuve swung at a larger percentage of strikes that were middle-away, 72 percent, than middle-in, 69 percent. And yet his slugging percentage on the middle-in pitches was twice as high as it was on the middle-away ones. What if he started hunting middle-in?

In 2012, Altuve became a much more selective hitter. He cut down his swing rate by more than 11 percent, and a player who a year earlier was among the league's freest swingers suddenly showed above-average discipline. His results didn't change much. His batting average improved modestly, from .276 to .290. But he had a new hitting philosophy, one that would stick. Two years after that, in 2014, he had a new body. An American diet of hamburgers and ice cream had ballooned Altuve's weight to 178 pounds, but he cut out junk food and came into spring training in 2014 at 160, muscled and lean. His singles turned into doubles—47 of them—to go with a league-best .341 batting average.

The next year, when he was 25, his doubles turned into home runs. He hit 15 in 2015, twice as many as he ever had before, while striking out less often than he had as a rookie. A player who had once been signed for $15,000, and whom the Astros paid $3 million, was now producing like one who was worth at least 10 times that. While the Astros might have contributed to that development as far as encouraging Altuve's selectivity at the plate, Luhnow knew they couldn't take credit for it. "What drives Altuve," Luhnow said, "is what's inside." Altuve couldn't grow physically, but no player had more eagerly consumed what the club was feeding him to grow anyway.

///////////

IN THE SPRING OF HIS SOPHOMORE YEAR, Sig's stepson, Ross, eagerly scanned his high school's baseball rosters once more. Then he checked them again. His name wasn't on any of them: not varsity, not JV. Though he had a major leaguer's plate discipline, he had been cut.

Although his baseball career had received an unlikely extension, it was now over. It was a disappointment, to be sure, but Sig helped Ross realize that people who focus on processes over outcomes, and who have a growth mindset, don't allow one setback to derail them. Ross had always enjoyed tennis. He might have liked it even more than baseball, before Sig came along. And tennis, in North Carolina, was a sport that was underplayed by high school boys, who gravitated to football and basketball and baseball. Ross's high school team had 12 starting spots—six at singles and six more in doubles—and not enough talented players to fill them all. The next spring, Ross tried out for the tennis team. He started every match, some in singles but most in doubles, and ended up with a winning record.

In Houston, the Astros' front office believed it had plucked the makings of a contender from the ashes that had been left by its predecessors. George Springer, Dallas Keuchel, José Altuve, and Carlos Correa, too: That was a core around which a winner could be built, and it remained thanks not only to the club's executives' decision-making and patience, but to the aptitude and character of the players themselves. It was easy to imagine a scenario in which Luhnow and Sig had screwed up—in which, for example, they traded away Keuchel before his belated development into an ace. They had certainly tried, and failed only because no other club possessed the wherewithal to recognize Keuchel's unusual alchemy. Such a near mistake showed the executives they, too, had room to grow. "He's arguably as good a pitcher as there is," said Sig. "We had him in our system, and we didn't realize that. If you think about that, remind yourself of that, it's impossible to be arrogant. We remembered that very well."

As they set about assembling the other 21 members of a future championship roster, they wouldn't always have the same luck that they had experienced with Keuchel. They would suffer poor outcomes after even probabilistically optimized processes, as Ross had. What happened then? There was no tennis team in the major leagues.

5

PEYTON MANNING
ON A SURFBOARD

To clubs picking first overall in the draft, there is one type of player riskier than a high school hitter. It's true that many high school hitters bust. Shawn Abner, Al Chambers, Steve Chilcott, Danny Goodwin: Nobody remembers those top picks except the men who came to regret drafting them. High school hitters can also turn into generational superstars. By Wins Above Replacement, the all-inclusive metric designed to capture a player's value over that of an average substitute, the best seven one-ones in the draft's history had all once belonged to the category: Alex Rodriguez, Chipper Jones, Ken Griffey Jr., Joe Mauer, Adrián González, Darryl Strawberry, and Harold Baines. As of June 2014, Carlos Correa, who was lighting up High-A ball, seemed likely to join them.

But high school pitchers? High school pitchers were terrifying for any club with a pick in the single digits. "It's the scariest, in terms of history," said Mike Elias. "There have been some wild successes, but the list of those picked high is littered with injuries and disappointments." So much could happen during the long window of time between the day you drafted a high school pitcher and his much-anticipated big league debut, years in which he would throw so much more than ever before and to hitters who were so much better than those he had ever faced. If a pitcher's arm was the most valuable and fragile asset in baseball, a pitcher's psyche was second.

In the 49 previous drafts, starting with its inception in 1965, clubs picked a high school hurler one-one just twice. In 1973, the Rangers chose a left-hander from Houston named David Clyde. Arm injuries ended Clyde's career when he was 26, after he had compiled a record of 18–33 with an ERA of 4.63. The Yankees tried again in 1991, when they selected a southpaw from North Carolina, Brien Taylor. Two years later, Taylor hurt his shoulder while trying to protect his brother during a bar fight. He went to see Dr. Frank Jobe, the orthopedic surgeon, who, in 1974, figured out he could reconstruct Dodgers pitcher Tommy John's left elbow by replacing its torn ulnar collateral ligament with a tendon from John's right forearm. Jobe saved not only John's career, but, as his procedure spread to operating rooms across the world, those of thousands of pitchers after him. He couldn't save Taylor's. He deemed Taylor's torn rotator cuff the worst he'd ever seen. Taylor became one of two one-ones, along with Steve Chilcott, never to play in the majors at all.

In 2014, after a season that had ended with their desultory 15-game losing streak, the Astros would become the first team in major league history to make the first pick in three consecutive drafts. If that was not the primary goal of Jeff Luhnow's long-term plan, it was certainly a useful by-product. "Fix it!" the Astros' few remaining fans always yelled as they filed past Luhnow's field box after yet another loss. Despite the pessimistic vitriol he received from around baseball for not just his annually atrocious teams but the apparently cold-eyed way in which he and his math nerds assembled them and directed their odd on-field tactics, Luhnow didn't intend to lose forever. He remained confident his first two one-ones would help. In 2013, the year after he picked Correa, he'd taken a player who had seemed even safer: Mark Appel, who had failed to reach an agreement with the Pirates the year before, returned to Stanford, and reentered the draft. Though Appel suffered through tendinitis in his right thumb and an appendectomy, and had an ERA of 11.93 through his first $14\frac{1}{3}$ innings in Single-A in 2014, he was still *Baseball America*'s 31st-rated prospect and appeared a good bet to turn things around.

Luhnow imagined that the Astros' string of one-ones would likely end at three, meaning that going forward, they would no longer have their pick of the best player in the country. Compounding matters was that most of the Astros' rivals had improved their own drafting by incorporating the type of analytics that had once given Luhnow and Sig such an advantage in St. Louis. If their opponents by and large hadn't mastered how gut instinct played into the equation, the importance of collegiate park factors and strength of schedule were no longer a secret. Usually, the Astros could now count on the other players they had considered candidates for the first pick to be chosen in short order, often in a predictable row, by the teams drafting behind them. As soon as the next year, a drop in draft position would likely mean the Astros would no longer have a hope of ending up with the player they most coveted.

At the beginning of 2014, the Astros began selling a new T-shirt in the gift shops of Minute Maid Park, one that succinctly defined the primary thing their fans could genuinely root for, though it remained far more abstract than a winning team. PROCESS, the T-shirt read, in bold capital letters. The diehards bought them. This last one-one might represent the Astros' final chance to maximize their process through the draft, and to provide the finishing piece on the teams that Luhnow envisioned would move pallets full of championship apparel in the relatively near future. They had to nail it.

////////////

As 40 MEMBERS OF the Astros' front office staff assembled in a conference room on the second floor of the club's offices in Houston's old Union Station, they felt the familiar weightiness of the task ahead. As in St. Louis, Luhnow had his staff sit at tables arranged in a large U-shape. The men included Luhnow, Sig, Elias, David Stearns, Kevin Goldstein, all the scouts, and certain special assistants like Craig Biggio, who the next year would enter the Hall of Fame as an Astro.

It was 10 a.m. on June 4, the day before the draft's first two rounds would be conducted, and the men were there to provide their expert opinions on the six players who were still in the running for the one-one. Two of them were high school pitchers. "All right," said Elias, who, officially in his second year as scouting director, ran the meeting. "Six players. We can only take one. Everybody really hit it out of the park in terms of giving us everything we need in terms of material evaluation. The area guys who know these guys best and have covered them for years, we're listening closely to you on this. This is your opportunity to air it out."

The Astros' front office meets to discuss their third straight No. 1 overall draft pick.

For the next 100 minutes, the room discussed each of the prospects one by one. The discussions were structured. As Elias introduced each player's name, video clips depicting him were projected on a screen at the front of the room, on a loop. It was so dark that it was sometimes hard to make out the face of the person who was speaking. What mattered was the information, and getting everyone who had provided that information on the same page. First, the area scout who had been responsible for the player, and who knew him best, would introduce him with a quick report. Then anyone else who had seen him—Elias, the national cross-checker David Post, special assistants like Biggio—would chime in. Then Luhnow, who had also traveled to see each of the six in person, would ask questions. Then analyses of the player's swing or pitching mechanics, to which coaches within the organization contributed, would be read aloud. Finally, Sig's team would weigh in with its statistical projections.

It eventually became clear that while the Astros obviously liked each of the players very much, two of them were unlikely to end up as the one-one. The first was Aaron Nola, a right-hander from LSU who was the first-ever back-to-back winner of the SEC Pitcher of the Year Award. Everyone agreed that Nola was the most polished pitcher in the draft. "At times, it's a boring game to watch," a scout said of Nola's starts. That was a compliment. "It's strike after strike after strike." As soon as the following summer, Nola might become a club's number three starter, and remain as such for the next 15 years. That was a valuable commodity. But with the first pick, the Astros wanted an ace.

The other highly regarded player the Astros discussed, but whose name they were unlikely to call the next evening, was Nick Gordon, a high school shortstop from Orlando who was the son of former major league closer Tom Gordon and the half brother of the Dodgers' speedy second baseman, Dee Gordon. Like Nola, the scouts viewed Gordon as distinctly above average across the board, with no obvious flaw. The area scout graded him a 60 for power, a 60 runner, a 60 thrower. "A big leaguer all the way," he said. Said Elias, "You start dreaming about the hit tool a little bit," but you couldn't quite dream about it until it became equivalent to that of Alex Rodriguez or Carlos Correa.

That left four genuine options: Carlos Rodon, a left-hander from North Carolina State; Alex Jackson, a slugger from Rancho Bernardo High in Southern California; and Brady Aiken and Tyler Kolek. The last two were the high school pitchers.

A year earlier, the six-foot-three, 235-pound Rodon had been considered almost as sure a thing to go one-one as Stephen Strasburg had been in 2009. A slightly down junior season had raised some doubts, but you wouldn't have known it based on the report delivered by Tim Bittner, the area scout who had covered him. "He's been the dude since he stepped on campus," Bittner said. "The big thing for this guy is he has a pitch you don't see normally. It's a seventy-grade slider, at eighty-eight to ninety-one miles an hour. It's a weapon. It's a weapon now, it's a weapon on all levels." Sig's team revealed that one of the players to whom its metrics suggested Rodon was comparable was Chris Sale, the White Sox' ace and an annual Cy Young candidate.

Rodon shared something else with Sale, and with most number one starters: an authentic desire not just to get every hitter out, but to dominate him. "They'll come try to take him out, he'll refuse, and the head coach will retreat with his tail between his legs," a scout said approvingly. Elias concurred. "This dude has a fire-breathing, in-your-face, competitive drive," he said. "That's what you prize in what you're getting here. He's going to bleed out there to win Game Seven—and he's probably going to win it, too."

You could sense the scouts' views of Jackson before the discussion of him had even begun. "Mmmm," they grunted each time he unleashed his violently powerful swing on the video screen. "Mmmm." Jackson hit 47 home runs in high school, five short of Mike Moustakas's California state record. "Physically, he looks like Magglio Ordonez," the area scout said, comparing him to the White Sox' and Tigers' six-time All-Star. "A three or four hitter. Potentially hits thirty homers, with a .300 average. I must've seen him hit a home run in ten straight games. The big thing with this kid is the huge raw power."

"What about his swing?" Luhnow asked.

"Graded eighty out of eighty," came the reply.

Area scout Brad Budzinski was similarly unequivocal about Brady Aiken, a six-foot-three, 210-pound lefty from San Diego's Cathedral Catholic High who had committed to UCLA and who threw a mid-90s fastball to go with an unusually developed curveball and changeup. "I love everything about this kid," Budzinski said. "To me, we're getting possibly the next Andy Pettitte. Makeup-wise, I feel like it's Peyton Manning on a surfboard. A lot of people say they want to be a Hall of Famer, but I believe for this kid it's a realistic goal, to be one of the best pitchers of all time."

Budzinski had followed Aiken since the pitcher was 15, and had gotten to know him and his family. His sister, Budzinski noted, was a six-foot-one college volleyball player, suggesting that Aiken might have even more room to grow. He painted a portrait of someone who had been assiduously groomed to become a big leaguer. "They've controlled his innings since he was a kid," Budzinski said. "Limited his travel ball, limited his summer innings. In his first three seasons on varsity, average of 72.5 pitches per start. This year, low eighties, from what I can gather. They've done a really, really nice job controlling his usage. Charismatic kid, good-looking, successful, confident. I think this kid handles the pressure of being one-one. The kind of guy you can use as a poster boy for the franchise. We take him first, I sleep real good at night, not worried about this kid going off the deep end."

"What kind of work does he do between starts?" Luhnow asked.

"He's a five a.m. guy," Budzinski said. Aiken woke up at that hour every day to work out.

"If the stuff stayed the same right now," said David Post, "it's more than enough to pitch and have success in the big leagues."

Though Sig's department only lightly incorporated high school stats into its algorithms, it recited Aiken's anyway: "K's per nine of almost seventeen."

"Did he say seventeen?" one of the scouts whispered.

"I don't think UCLA is harboring any hopes of getting him next fall, one way or another," Elias said.

Kolek was also attractive, in different ways. He stood six foot five and weighed 260 pounds, and his fastball touched 102 miles per hour. "This is the kind of guy that's at the front of the rotation and overpowers hitters for a long, long time," said Ralph Bratton, the veteran scout with the white walrus mustache. "He's gone wire to wire, mid-nineties, upper nineties, he's maintained that velocity week in and week out. It's what gives him the ceiling. It's power all the way."

"The stuff is as good as we've ever seen from a high school kid," Elias said. "I think we can all agree this is as seriously as we've considered taking a high school righty, and with good reason."

Kolek had other things going for him. He attended Shepherd High, less than an hour northeast of Minute Maid Park, and the allure of drafting a local boy—and one who reminded everyone of Roger Clemens—was considerable. "They've got a cool setup out there on their ranch," Elias reported. "They've got a pond to fish in. They've got tractors that they drive around, chasing animals."

The Yale graduate's novice description of hunting drew laughs from the many outdoorsmen in the room, and one in particular. "Now, where are you from, Mike?" boomed a deep Texan voice. It belonged to the 67-year-old Nolan Ryan, who had pitched for the Astros for nine of his 27 big league seasons, was the father of the Astros' president, Reid Ryan, and served as an executive advisor to the club.

"Nolan, how hard did you throw at his age?" a scout asked the all-time strikeout king, who had watched Kolek pitch for Shepherd.

"There weren't radar guns in those days," Ryan said. "But I can tell you, Nolan Ryan wasn't even close to what this kid is as a senior in high school. This kid commands the ball. It wouldn't surprise me if this kid came pretty quick."

The meeting drew to a close at 11:40 a.m. It had been the type of wholly collaborative session Luhnow had always envisioned during those contentious June days in St. Louis, one in which each scout had focused only on delivering information that would benefit the entire organization, as opposed to trying to prove the superiority of his way of evaluating over the analysts'. There had been no grumbling. Each man knew his skills were valued and would factor into the ultimate decision. "All right, it's a good group," Luhnow said to his 39-man brain trust. "Flip a coin now, or later?"

"If we take one of the high school pitchers, we have to be really convinced that this guy is the guy, and that's not real easy to settle on," Elias said that afternoon. "Especially when you've got other good options, like a top college pitcher and a high school hitter. We're still debating it." The Astros' decision engine had one more day to determine what it was going to do.

////////////

As SIX P.M. CENTRAL TIME approached on the evening of Thursday, June 5, the Astros' scouts and analysts milled around the club's draft room on the fifth floor of the former train station. The room had metal walls, covered with rectangular name-bearing magnets clustered according to their projected rounds. The staffers were waiting, like the rest of the baseball world, to see which of the magnets the team's leadership would place atop the board. Whereas the day before they had been dressed in khakis and polo shirts, they now wore suits and ties. If there was any need to remind them of the caliber of player they hoped to draft, there was the dinner they had just been served: Nolan Ryan Beef Brisket and Nolan Ryan Jalapeño Sausages.

Though the front office was now entirely composed of people Luhnow had either affirmatively retained or brought aboard himself—another reason for the harmony of the previous morning's meeting—he still had not tipped his hand to them, to make sure that their analyses were always unencumbered by what they thought he wanted to hear and to prevent even innocent leaks. "Even if we had made up our minds six months ago, I don't think anybody in that room would have had any idea," Luhnow said. Only his innermost circle did.

Finally, at 6:05, Elias emerged from Luhnow's office, where he had been ensconced with the general manager as well as Stearns and Sig. Elias nonchalantly slapped the magnet bearing their pick's name at the top of the draft board. Minutes later, Commissioner Bud Selig announced the pick from the MLB Network studios in Secaucus, New Jersey. On the fuzzy big-screen TV mounted at the front of the room the Astros' staff watched as the player, whose reaction the network's cameras was covering live from his home, buried his face in his hands.

"Oh no!" a scout called out. "I don't want him to cry!"

Astros scouting director Mike Elias just after slapping
Brady Aiken's name atop the draft board.

There would prove to be no tears from Brady Aiken, the California high school lefty whose name was printed on Elias's magnet. Soon, Brad Budzinski, the young scout who had followed Aiken since the pitcher was 15, accepted congratulations—"That's your guy,

Budz!"—and handshakes. "A lot of seasoned scouts have never even had a first rounder, let alone a one-one," a dazed Budzinski said.

Luhnow tried to call Aiken on his cell phone, but Budzinski had given him the wrong number. "How well do you really know this guy?" Elias teased the scout. Then Luhnow appeared to connect. "Hey, Brady, it's Jeff Luhnow with the Astros," he said, as everyone listened in. Luhnow paused dramatically. "Give me a call back when you get this." Laughter reverberated off the room's metal walls.

Brady Aiken (left) and Jeff Luhnow (right) are all smiles after the Astros picked the high school pitcher first overall.

In the end, the decision to select Aiken over Kolek, Rodon, and Jackson—who would be picked second, third, and sixth, respectively—was not a last-minute one. "We decided the morning of the draft," Elias said. "I think we all woke up with the same notion of what we wanted to do."

By then, Sig and the Nerd Cave had coded every bit of information the Astros could have possibly gathered about each prospect into their algorithms. In truth, while a new bit of actionable intelligence might have emerged from the previous day's one-one meeting—which was designed, in part, to get all the organization's front office staffers excited about whatever player it ended up selecting—the Astros' top decision-makers already had the vast majority of data points they might conceivably use. Much of the data about Aiken had come from the three years of hard work Budzinski had put into him.

Budzinski played junior college baseball in Wisconsin back in the early 2000s, and always knew he wanted to become a scout. After college, he ran a small virtual tour business and then got into real estate, but his desire to work in baseball was so great that he drove around the Midwest to scout players for free—bird-dogging, it was called—even though the region typically didn't produce top prospects. The Astros hired him in 2008, and Luhnow kept him on because he proved himself the type of scout who bought into Luhnow's system, and understood his role within it.

While the Astros could help a scout like Budzinski improve by telling him, based on the Nerd Cave's regressions, if his grades revealed a tendency to consistently overrate or underrate a certain type of player, and even specific qualities in players, they mostly wanted him to trust his judgment. "No one's ever asked me to do things any different than I did before, speak any different than I did before," he said. "It's the analysts' job to do the analytics, and it's our job to scout. If we start trying to cross over into their area, you're double counting. I think you get the best results when you stay in your lane."

Sig's job was to merge the lanes. Aiken had received the draft's best grades from not only Budzinski, but from at least three-quarters of the Astros' executives who had seen him play, a group that included Luhnow, Elias, Stearns, Goldstein, and Enos Cabell. Once Sig's system had done its work—stripping those grades of biases, and incorporating other predictive information like his age and mechanics—he remained the draft's number one talent, even though he was a high school pitcher in a strong class.

"They were kind of knotted up in every analysis, but Aiken was consistently at or tied for the top spot pretty much every way we looked at it," Elias said. "The mere fact that we were willing to take a high school pitcher one-one for the third time in history, even though the first two didn't pan out, showed us how strongly we agreed. And we feel good enough about our farm system, that there's enough coming through, that we don't want to look back in ten years and say, 'Oh, jeez, we passed on the best high school lefty ever just to get something a little quicker.'"

Years of scouting reports, funneled into and regressed in Sig's algorithms, all suggested that Aiken was the draft's best player. So did the less quantifiable facts that he was a five a.m. guy, and Peyton Manning on a surfboard, which meant that both the injuries and pressures that often overwhelmed high school pitchers might not reach him. Picking someone else, simply because he was not a high school pitcher? That would've been standing on a 16.

In the draft room, there were more immediate matters at hand. The big league club was at the moment playing against Albert Pujols and the Los Angeles Angels. Pujols had left St. Louis, as a free agent, the same winter that Luhnow, Sig, and Elias did. "We're losing one to nothing," Biggio announced, holding his smartphone aloft.

"Already?" said Luhnow. It was just the top of the first. "How'd that happen?"

"Albert hit a sac fly."

It wasn't long before the Astros started scoring themselves. Three RBIs came off the bat of George Springer, and the Astros were on their way to their ninth win in their last 12 games.

"Oh good, more points!" Sig said drolly, glancing up at a TV.

"They're not points, Sig," said Kevin Goldstein.

Everyone chatted and joked. Though they still had 40 picks ahead of them over the following two days, they'd made the big one, and virtually everyone either agreed with it or understood it, the type of organizational consensus for which Luhnow had always longed. Now all they had to do was get Brady Aiken to Houston, give him a medical exam, sign him, and introduce him to the hometown fans. That was just a matter of course. Almost always.

///////////

AIKEN ARRIVED IN HOUSTON with his parents, Jim and Linda, and his older sister—Halle, the six-foot-one outside hitter for San Diego State—on June 23. It was almost three weeks after he had nearly wept when the Astros drafted him and a comfortable four before the league's signing deadline. "I'm really excited to take this next step in my life," Aiken said.

The step promised to be lucrative. Aiken's agent, Casey Close, had clout. He represented superstars like Derek Jeter and Clayton Kershaw and was married to Gretchen Carlson, the 1989 Miss America turned Fox News host. Close had negotiated a $6.5 million signing bonus for Aiken, which was $1.4 million less than the recommended slot bonus for the one-one but still a fortune for a 17-year-old pitcher.

With their savings, the Astros planned to sign another California high school pitcher who was represented by Close, Jacob Nix, who had, like his friend Aiken, traveled to Houston with his family. Like Lance McCullers two years earlier, Nix had made it known that he would go to college—at UCLA—unless he received a significantly over-slot bonus. The Astros confidently drafted him in the fifth round and tentatively agreed to pay him $1.5 million, more than four times the sum the Cardinals had given the pick directly before him, Florida Atlantic pitcher Austin Gomber. The Astros would only have room in their bonus pool to sign Nix after they locked in Aiken, but that appeared a formality. The last one-one to fail to agree to terms with the club that drafted him was the pitcher Tim Belcher, back in 1983.

Astros fans expected to meet their future ace as soon as the next day, when he would ceremonially pull his new jersey over his shirt and tie at his introductory press conference before heading to Kissimmee to begin his journey back to Houston. Boxes of replica jerseys bearing his name had already arrived at a souvenir shop in Minute Maid Park.

The next day, however, nothing happened. Nothing happened the day after that, either. Then Brady Aiken and Jacob Nix flew home to California.

The problem was Aiken's left elbow, the one he used to pitch. Though he was in formidable shape from all those early mornings in the gym, and had never been injured or even overworked, the medical exam the Astros' doctors had given him upon what ought to have been an auspicious arrival in Houston hadn't turned up clean. Unlike in the NBA and NFL, baseball held no pre-draft combine at which prospects could submit to physicals, and they were not otherwise compelled to do so. That meant that organizations drafted using information that was necessarily incomplete. Luhnow and Elias selected Aiken based upon everything they could see and analyze, but it was only afterward, via an MRI, that they got a look at what they couldn't. It looked, in their estimation, like the reddest of flags.

Medical privacy laws prevented anyone from disclosing anything about Aiken's exam, and the club consistently declined to publicly do that. Eventually, Evan Drellich, of the *Chronicle*, got to the bottom of it. The issue was the state of Aiken's ulnar collateral ligament, the half-inch-thick band that connects the arm's humerus with the ulna. It was the part of a human's anatomy that is most stressed by throwing overhead and that, when it tears, must be repaired by Tommy John surgery if he or she is ever to throw the same way again.

Of course, an MRI of every pitcher, no matter how much his pitch counts have been limited, would reveal an abnormal UCL. If a club demanded perfect ligaments, it would never draft any pitchers at all. But Aiken's UCL wasn't only worn; it was, reportedly, congenitally small. "He may have some of it, but not much," a source told Drellich, adding that Aiken's anatomy would make a strong prognosis after a future Tommy John surgery less likely.

Luhnow lowered his offer to Aiken to $3.1 million. To his frustration, Luhnow couldn't explain what his doctors had seen in Aiken's exam that had led him to react that way, out of respect for Aiken's medical privacy, so publicly it appeared as if the notoriously cheap Astros were lowballing their one-one. Immediately, needles that were longer and sharper than ever before prodded at Luhnow's skin, calloused as it was from years of criticism. The needles came from all angles: from fans who were sick of rooting for the worst team in baseball; from the media; from agents; from the players' union.

Luhnow felt he hadn't operated any differently from the way the majority of the league's general managers would have, had their doctors detected a land mine on an MRI. Just the year before, the Marlins selected the pitcher Matt Krook 35th overall. Krook failed his physical after he'd agreed to terms, wasn't signed, then tore his UCL after pitching 45 innings for the University of Oregon.

But the Astros weren't any team, and Luhnow wasn't any general manager. It was one thing to appear not to be trying to win, another to be parsimonious, and another still to view talented humans like numbered cattle, but it was something else to be messing with the futures of not one but two teenagers, Aiken and Nix, during what were supposed to be the best days of their lives and when they hadn't done a single thing wrong.

"We are extremely disappointed that Major League Baseball is allowing the Astros to conduct business in this manner with a complete disregard for the rules governing the draft and the twenty-nine other clubs who have followed those same rules," the normally media averse Casey Close told Fox Sports. "Brady has been seen by some of the most experienced and respected orthopedic arm specialists in the country, and all of those doctors have acknowledged that he's not injured and that he's ready to start his professional career."

"It is disappointing on any number of levels to think what has happened in that situation," said Tony Clark, the head of the union, which was considering filing grievances. "The manipulation that we think happened in this case is going to lead us to have some conversations."

The headline of the post the sports blog *Deadspin* published about the matter was less circumspect. THE ASTROS ARE TRYING TO DICK DRAFT PICKS OUT OF THEIR MONEY, it read.

Although Jim Crane maintained an all-green policy, he wasn't impervious to bad publicity, which, as an experienced businessman, he knew had a monetary and operational value of its own. On

July 18, the last day for major league teams to sign their picks, the owner directed Luhnow to submit three offers, each better than the last, to Aiken's camp in a final effort to bring both him and Nix on board. The third came with five minutes to spare before the five p.m. eastern deadline. It was for $5 million, more than Carlos Correa had received two years earlier and more than any member of the 2014 draft other than Kolek and Rodon commanded.

Aiken and Close did not respond to any of the offers. They had made up their minds. Due purely to the Astros' malfeasance, as the public believed, Aiken would become the first top pick in 31 years not to sign, no matter the allure of the first million. Peyton Manning would return to his surfboard for at least one more year.

The Astros' red flag immediately turned into another black eye, perhaps their most throbbing yet. Their failure to sign Aiken not only also cost them Nix—because the evaporation of Aiken's entire slot budget meant they were no longer allotted the portion they had intended to pay Aiken's friend—but also another high school pitcher they had drafted in the 21st round and intended to pay more than his slot recommended, Mac Marshall of Georgia. Perhaps, some wondered, the Astros weren't run just cynically, but ineptly. "I do feel genuine empathy for the players involved," Luhnow said. "It was bad luck all around. I understand that, from a fan's perspective, we got nothing."

That wasn't just the fans' perspective. Concluded the ESPN national baseball writer Buster Olney, "The perception of them is shattered, and they will have to pay for its reconstruction, one way or another."

From Luhnow's vantage point, that wasn't necessarily the case. In fact, the value he appeared to have lost by not signing Aiken—as well as Nix and Marshall—could be recouped, and even exceeded, in one specific way. No decision, even one as considered as drafting Brady Aiken, was final until every possible angle had been exhausted, and the Astros had one left. "All the outcomes won't present themselves for years to come," Luhnow said. Black eyes fade. By July

2014, the Astros had already identified someone who might press a cold sirloin to theirs.

/////////////

THE KEY NUMBER IN the Astros' negotiations with Brady Aiken was the sum to which Luhnow knocked down his original bonus offer: $3.1 million. Major League Baseball's rule book included the following provision:

> *If a drafted player fails a Club-administered physical examination, and the Club does not subsequently offer the player a bonus at least equal to 40 percent of the player's Signing Bonus Value, the player will become a free agent if no agreement is reached by the signing deadline. In such cases, the Club would not receive any compensation for the unsigned player.*

The Astros knew each and every rule. The assigned slot value for that year's one-one was $7,922,100. And 40 percent of $7,922,100? It is $3.1 million—or $3,168,840, to be precise. The Astros made sure that if Aiken declined their lowball offer, a strong possibility, they would be in line to receive compensation because of it. The compensation would be valuable: the No. 2 overall pick in the next year's draft, on top of the other relatively high selection their record would earn them. It was even possible that the No. 2 pick could turn into a player who was better than Aiken, Kolek, Rodon, or Jackson would ever be.

The decision really came down to whether Luhnow felt that a presumably healthy No. 2 in June 2015 would be worth losing Brady Aiken, whom he had loved only weeks before but who had since taken on a different risk profile, as well as Nix and perhaps Marshall. Despite his late attempt to sign Aiken and deflect the venom spewed at his club, it was clear which side of the decision Luhnow preferred.

Baseball's scouting cycles do not run year to year. Clubs begin the work of evaluating prospects long before the season in which they become draft-eligible. They have often been following college players for half a decade or more, since they were in high school. So when Brady Aiken and Casey Close failed to respond to Luhnow's messages on July 18, 2014, and the five p.m. deadline passed, the Astros' scouting department did not need to switch gears to identify the player it might take eleven months later with its unexpected No. 2 pick, the one who would allow them to recapture, and even potentially exceed, Aiken's lost value. They already had a strong idea of who it was going to be.

He was a shortstop at LSU, where, in his first two seasons, he established exactly the type of statistical profile Sig's metrics had always prized: a high on-base percentage, better than .400; an excellent OPS, over .900; a disdain for striking out, which he did just about once every three games. The Astros also had an unusual advantage in their efforts to collect soft information about him, too. The father of one of their scouts, J.D. Alleva, was LSU's athletic director, Joe Alleva. They learned that the player was a strong student, which suggested a growth mindset, and the right kind of confident: not performatively cocky, a quality that could evaporate during snowballing slumps, but genuinely so, a quality that didn't. He was unflappable. He didn't give a shit about anything but playing.

The knock against him within the industry was a familiar one to the Astros' decision-makers, Luhnow and Sig and Elias: his size. LSU's roster listed him at a flat six feet, which, as always, meant that he wasn't. After their experiences with Jed Lowrie and José Altuve, the Astros knew that while a small stature was not ideal in a general sense, it wasn't disqualifying, only a data point. The player's size had never before proved an impediment to him, as it hadn't for Lowrie and Altuve, and it likely never would.

In October 2014, *Baseball America* released its first list of Top 100 prospects for the following June's draft. It ranked the LSU shortstop 13th, 11 spots behind an again draftable Brady Aiken.

IN ORDER TO RETAIN the draft eligibility that would have been delayed for three full years had he enrolled at a four-year college, Aiken went to IMG Academy in Florida to train. In March 2015, he made his first competitive outing since his final one for Cathedral Catholic the spring before, during which Brad Budzinski clocked his fastball at 97 miles per hour. After just his 13th pitch for IMG, Aiken experienced a burning sensation in his left elbow. "Something felt a little wrong," he said.

A lot was wrong. His ulnar collateral ligament had sheared in half. He had to undergo Tommy John surgery.

"It's going to be frustrating, and not just from a baseball perspective," he wrote shortly afterward for *The Players' Tribune,* the website owned by Casey Close's greatest client, Derek Jeter. "When it's 90 degrees at home in Cardiff and the waves are perfect and I can't surf, that'll be tough, too." He had no regrets about his decision to reject the Astros. "The money wasn't the only factor to consider. I wanted to play somewhere I felt comfortable, with a support system I felt would lay the groundwork for a successful and long career. Making sure I had that in place was worth the frustration of not being able to get on with my career sooner."

Luhnow had no misgivings about his own decision, especially now. Despite his elbow, Aiken was picked by the Cleveland Indians, 17th overall, in the 2015 draft and was paid a bonus of $2.5 million, precisely half of Luhnow's final offer to him the year before. Over his first two seasons in the Indians' minor league system—through 2017, the year in which Budzinski had once projected he might make his major league debut—Aiken went 7–18, with a 5.05 ERA, and walked nearly as many batters as he struck out. He had yet to advance above Single-A.

Over the next three years, none of the other five amateurs the Astros had discussed in their one-one meeting the morning before the 2014 draft had shown signs of becoming the type of franchise-changing talent for which any club picking first would have hoped. Carlos Rodon and Aaron Nola, the college pitchers, went third and seventh to the White Sox and the Phillies, respectively. Both reached the majors in 2015, had ERAs just under 4.00, and struck out around one batter an inning. They were steady third starters.

Meanwhile, not one of the high schoolers had come close to the big leagues. Nick Gordon, picked fifth by the Twins, was in Double-A, an annual Top 60 prospect who did everything well enough to imagine that he'd arrive in Minnesota soon, but nothing spectacularly. The Seattle Mariners selected Alex Jackson sixth, but the swing at which the Astros' scouts had once appreciatively grunted proved too long to consistently catch up with professional pitching. Just two years later, the Mariners traded him to the Braves, in whose lower minors he struck out more than four times as much as he walked. And Tyler Kolek, the other high school pitcher, the one whose fastball had impressed even Nolan Ryan? The Marlins took him second overall, but he blew out his elbow early in 2016. Over the next two seasons he pitched just $3^2/_3$ innings, those in rookie ball.

Fifteen slots before the Indians took Brady Aiken in 2015, the Astros went on the clock to make the pick they wouldn't have owned had they signed Aiken the summer before, at No. 2 overall. The prospect who appeared at the top of all the external mock drafts was a different college shortstop, Vanderbilt's Dansby Swanson. Everyone in the Astros' draft room prayed that the Diamondbacks, who held the first pick, would do what they were supposed to and pick Swanson. They did. The Astros then quickly selected the shortstop from LSU.

Alex Bregman might have been small, but he was as clear-cut a top pick as any member of their front office had ever experienced. He was first, above Swanson, on everyone's list: Sig's, the scouts', Elias's, Luhnow's. He agreed to a deal for a $5.9 million bonus, $1.5 million under slot, on June 24, and passed his physical. The next afternoon, he was introduced at a press conference in Minute Maid Park in which he buttoned an Astros jersey over his white shirt and light blue tie and then sat down between Elias and Luhnow. "Everything we knew about him as a player and a person checked every box for us," Elias told the media. "We're just very comfortable with and excited about his talent."

"I'm just very excited to get to work," Bregman said. The day after that, he reported to Quad Cities to officially begin his journey back to Houston.

6

SUMMER OF SETBACKS

As the 2014 season wore on, the analytically grounded ratio-nalists in the Astros' front office began to wonder if at least one su-pernatural phenomenon was real: the *SI* Jinx, which had long held that an appearance on the magazine's cover portended disaster. The Astros, as bad as they were, didn't appear to have any farther to fall. The weeks after George Springer appeared in mailboxes across the country, not long after the club drafted Brady Aiken, proved other-wise. "Everything that could have gone wrong that summer seemed to go wrong," Jeff Luhnow said.

Failing to sign Brady Aiken, and fielding the resulting schaden-freude and sometimes R-rated opprobrium from across baseball be-cause of it, was just the start. The Astros had promoted Springer in mid-April, and he slugged 10 home runs—"Springer dingers," as Houston's finally invigorated fans called them—in May alone. In July, though, he strained his quad, and spent the last two and a half months of his rookie season on the disabled list. A promising

Single-A season for Carlos Correa also ended early when he broke his leg sliding into third base.

Mark Appel's struggles in the minors deepened. While Appel was three years older than Correa, the 2013 first overall pick had also only advanced as far as Single-A, where someone who not long before was the most polished collegiate pitcher anyone had ever seen had become, by his own reckoning, "maybe the worst pitcher in professional baseball." After one particularly awful start, a July outing in which he allowed seven runs in less than two innings, Appel returned to the clubhouse, screamed, and fired 80 baseballs, one after another, through the particle board that served as the room's wall. Meanwhile, Kris Bryant, a collegiate slugger on whom the Astros had passed to pick Appel, was on his way to slugging 43 home runs in Double- and Triple-A, and was a certain bet to debut as the Cubs' third baseman early the next season. (Appel would retire from baseball three years later, after having been traded to the Phillies, as the third one-one after Steve Chilcott and Brien Taylor never to play in the majors.)

Then one of the Astros' minor league stadiums was nearly swallowed by the rain-engorged Mississippi River, and another caught fire. There was no combination of data and human intuition that could have predicted any of that.

One day in late June, Luhnow, Sig, and the entire Astros organization got a real surprise. *Deadspin*, the sports blog, published a post titled LEAKED: 10 MONTHS OF THE HOUSTON ASTROS' INTERNAL TRADE TALKS. The post linked to documents ripped from Ground Control, the club's proprietary internal database and the clearinghouse for its collective brainpower, that included dozens of notes the Astros' executives had made about negotiations they'd had with other clubs between June 2013 and March 2014. One revealed that Luhnow had engaged in discussions with the Marlins' general manager, Dan Jennings, about the potential of acquiring one of the game's leading sluggers, Giancarlo Stanton, and included information about which of his own players he was willing to sacrifice, specifically the pitcher Jarred Cosart and the outfielder Delino DeShields Jr:

JL talked to DJ and said we had interest in Stanton. DJ
said he doesn't think he'll trade Stanton and the only deal he
could think of from us that would work would be Springer
and Correa. JL said that would not work. JL posited a deal
around Cosart and Deshields.

The Astros had not only been hacked. They had been targeted by someone with an ax to grind—someone who wanted to publicly embarrass them. "It was like coming home and seeing your house has been broken into," Luhnow said. As the FBI began an investigation, Luhnow had to apologize to each of the league's other 29 general managers, as well as to his own players whose names had been discussed. Then the story became more sordid.

The next summer, *The New York Times* would report that the FBI had discovered that the hack had originated from a house in Jupiter, Florida—one used by executives from Luhnow's and Sig's old club, the Cardinals, during spring training. Luhnow's organization had been violated by someone he likely knew very well. Then the perpetrator was identified. It was Chris Correa, the former analyst who had once helped to scrape Division II and III data from the internet, leading Luhnow to draft Matt Adams in 2009, and who by 2015 had become the Cardinals' scouting director.

The feds determined that Sig had turned in his Cardinals laptop, along with its password, to Correa when he followed Luhnow to Houston in December 2011. Sig used a similar password for his new Astros webmail account, and Correa had figured it out, giving him unfettered access to Sig's email—and then to Ground Control, which Correa had gone on to access at least 60 times on 35 different days between March 2013 and June 2014. Those accounted for the intrusions the authorities had been able to document. He had likely done it far more often than that.

Correa asserted that he had been attempting to determine whether Luhnow and Sig had stolen proprietary data from the Cardinals when they left for Houston. That didn't make much sense. The value of such data would have been ephemeral anyway, and Jim Crane had hired Luhnow and Sig not for the contents of old spreadsheets, but of their minds—the residual intellectual property, as it was known, that had created the Cardinals' own database, called Red Bird Dog, to begin with. And it didn't explain why Correa had accessed Ground Control so many times, including on the days of the 2013 draft, when he had viewed the Astros' scouting reports, analytical rankings, and draft board, and presumably incorporated that information into his and the Cardinals' own decisions about players.

The timing of the leak to *Deadspin* was especially suspicious. It had arrived, by anonymous email, on June 28, 2014, two days after *SI*'s cover story predicting that Luhnow and Sig would lead the Astros to a World Series in 2017 appeared online.

The feds concluded that the cover and story had made Correa, left behind in St. Louis, jealous of his former colleagues. Feloniously jealous. As an unsealed court document put it, "Mejdal was one of Correa's rivals. They previously worked side by side in the Cardinals' analytics department, and in separate discussions with the FBI, reported having heated disputes with each other. In January 2012, when Mejdal left to join the Astros, they both assumed similar positions as heads of their respective analytics departments for teams that until 2013 played against each other in the same NL Central division. And now, this rival was now being praised even though his team had not yet begun to win."

The 35-year-old Correa eventually pleaded guilty to five counts of unauthorized access to a protected computer. "You broke into their house to find out if they were stealing your stuff?" US District Judge Lynn Hughes asked Correa.

"Stupid, I know," Correa responded.

"That didn't strike you as peculiar?"

"It was stupid."

Correa later said, "I broke the law. I violated my values, and it was wrong. I behaved shamefully. This episode represents the worst thing

I have done in my life, by far, and I am overwhelmed with remorse and regret."

Chris Correa in January 2016, after pleading guilty
to five counts of unauthorized access of a protected computer.

Despite Correa's contrition, in July 2016 Hughes sentenced him to 46 months in a federal prison in Maryland, which he began serving the next month, and ordered him to pay $279,000 in restitution. The following January, Major League Baseball commissioner Rob Manfred levied his penalty on the Cardinals for an act of corporate espionage that was unprecedented in the sport. He fined one of the league's most distinguished organizations $2 million, and commanded it to hand over its top two draft picks in 2017 to the Astros.

Even had Correa been a lone wolf—as the proceedings, at least, concluded he was—it was impossible to measure the advantages the Cardinals had gained from his 15 months of access to the Astros' internal database, as well as the damages the Astros had sustained from one of their bitter rivals knowing every one of their moves before they made them. "It's difficult to assess the effect," Luhnow said when the Cardinals' involvement first came to light, "but we have continued to execute our plan, and we are making progress."

While the Astros implemented stricter data security measures, there was little else they could do. They had always expected to encounter setbacks along the way, even if the cluster they experienced in 2014 was uniquely shocking. But those setbacks—the injuries, the flood, the fire, even the hack—had not been self-inflicted, and none of them had revealed a fundamental flaw in the decision-making engine that guided their plan. Even Appel's mysterious struggles had been entirely unpredictable. They always expected some bad luck, and now they had gotten it.

That year, however, brought another unfortunate event, one for which the Astros were solely responsible. It was a decision they thought had been as carefully considered as all their others, backed by both artificial and human intelligence. And it was a decision that immediately revealed itself to be a mistake for which they had no one to blame but themselves.

///////////

DURING J.D. MARTINEZ'S FIRST FEW TRIPS between his team's hotel in Venezuela and their ballpark early in the winter of 2013, he didn't understand why the bus driver always took a different route and always drove at a terrifying speed, barely braking at red lights. Then one of his teammates on the Leones del Caracas explained it to him. It was for the same reason that their team bus was always accompanied by men on motorcycles who were strapped with semiautomatic rifles—so they wouldn't be hijacked.

Martinez was 26, and had already spent parts of three seasons in the Astros' outfield. He was accustomed to life in the big leagues, with its smooth transportation and reliable hot water. But he wasn't playing in the Venezuelan Professional Baseball League, which had operated between October and January since the 1940s, for its luxuries. He was trying to save his career.

Martinez had always believed he was doing everything right. Though he was just a 20th-round pick out of Fort Lauderdale's Nova

Southeastern University in 2009, he'd blasted his way through the minors and reached Houston just two years later. In 2012, Jeff Luhnow's first season as GM, Martinez led the 107-loss Astros in RBIs, even if that required only 55 of them. After his first three years and 252 games with the Astros, though, he was batting just .251, with 24 home runs. Clubs increasingly looked to on-base-plus-slugging percentage as a way to measure the combination of a player's patience and his power. Martinez's OPS was .687, lower than that of the slap-hitting version of José Altuve. Each season, his production had declined.

J.D. Martinez strikes out once again as a member of the Astros.

One day in July 2013, Martinez took a pregame batting practice session in the cage beneath the Rangers' ballpark in Arlington, Texas. He noticed that the Astros' hitting coach, John Mallee, was quiet. "How'd it look?" Martinez asked Mallee when he was finished.

"Looked good," Mallee said unconvincingly.

"Dude," Martinez said. "What do you want?"

Mallee beckoned Martinez to sit down next to him. "J.D., you're not even a career .700 OPS hitter," he said. "You don't steal bags. You're not a Gold Glover. You *have* to hit. Your numbers are OK. You can have a career. You can bounce between the big leagues and the minors. You can make enough money to live off of, at least until you become too expensive to keep around. But that's it. Unless you change something."

Martinez was taken aback. "You're asking me to change my swing, to change my way of making money?" he said. "Are you coming with me when they send me to Triple-A after I go oh for twenty, because I'm trying to figure out a new way to hit the ball? No. You're going to stay right here—and I'm going to be screwed."

Still, Mallee's message stuck with him. A few weeks later, Martinez sprained his left wrist while sliding into a bag in Toronto. He began spending most of his time in the Astros' trainer's room, which had a TV that was always tuned to ESPN. The channel kept showing highlights of the Brewers' slugger Ryan Braun, though not for a positive reason: He had been suspended for the remainder of the season for using performance-enhancing drugs. As Martinez watched clips of Braun, a five-time All Star with an OPS that was more than 35 percent higher than his own, hitting home run after home run, he realized something: *My swing doesn't look anything like his.*

He looked at clips of the game's other leading power hitters, like Miguel Cabrera and Albert Pujols, and saw that their swings were similar to Braun's, which meant that they didn't look like his, either. Then he began focusing on one of his own teammates, the catcher Jason Castro, who had just made the All-Star Game and was on his way to tripling his career high in home runs. *Holy crap*, Martinez thought. *Castro's got the same fucking swing they do.*

While Martinez chopped down at the ball, the sluggers he studied swung with a smooth uppercut. The head of his bat finished low. Theirs finished high. He asked Castro how he had learned to swing like that. "You've got to see my guys in California," Castro said.

Martinez returned from the disabled list in September. Over his final eight games, he hit .174. The day after the season ended, he had his first appointment with Castro's guys in California: Craig Wallenbrock, who was in his late 60s, and his 27-year-old assistant, Robert Van Scoyoc. Neither Wallenbrock nor Van Scoyoc had ever played past college, but they ran a batting cage out of a warehouse in an industrial park in Santa Clarita where they had steadily earned a reputation as gurus of a modern approach to hitting. "I want to finish my swing the way Jason Castro does," Martinez told them. On his first day, he noticed an inscription on one of the many bats that hung from a rack on the batting cage's wall. "Thanks for everything," it read. "I wouldn't be where I'm at today without your help." Below that was Ryan Braun's signature.

Like his friends José Altuve and Dallas Keuchel, with whom he'd advanced through the Astros' minors in near lockstep, Martinez always had a growth mindset, one instilled by his parents. He had grown up in South Florida with five older sisters, all of them from his parents' previous marriages. His mother, Mayra, was a nurse, and before another overnight shift at the hospital she would often drop J.D. off at the Domino's franchise where his father, Julio, worked. J.D. spent most of his grade school years popping slices of pepperoni into his mouth while Julio flipped pizzas. Julio eventually started his own roofing company, which he grew until he had 35 employees. So when Wallenbrock and Van Scoyoc told Martinez that his swing was the worst they'd ever seen from a major league player, he viewed it not as an insult but an opportunity. He had made the big leagues, and stayed there, with a garbage swing, one that he now could hardly bring himself to watch on video. *How the fuck did I ever get this far with that swing?* he asked himself. And how good might he get if he learned to swing properly?

The problem wasn't just the way he finished his swing. That was bad, but it resulted from everything he did that led to it. He started with his hands low and, as a pitch arrived, raised them into hitting position. Braun and Castro kept their hands quiet. He tended to lurch forward at the ball. Braun and Castro stayed balanced. In batting practice, his goal was to drive the ball to the net at the back of the cage. Braun and Castro targeted the cage's roof, aiming for an elevated launch angle that would be more likely to produce extra base hits. Martinez spent five hours a day for two weeks in Wallenbrock and Van Scoyoc's warehouse, revamping his swing and then consuming video that revealed his rapid improvement. "It was like I was hitting in a room that was dark, and somebody turned the lights on," he said. He went to Venezuela, a winter option that was usually unappealing to an established big league player, to confirm that his improvements were real.

Officials with the Leones had one piece of advice for players staying in the team's hotel. "You're safe here," they said. "But don't ever, ever, *ever* go outside." Caracas was soon to pass San Pedro Sula, Honduras, as the most violent city in the world. Martinez had no intention of sightseeing. "All I did was watch video and pray the Wi-Fi was working so I could watch more video," he said.

Once he made it to the ballpark, by whatever route the aggressive driver had chosen, he encountered an environment unlike any in which he had previously played. For rivalry games, the first row of the outfield bleachers was occupied by police with riot shields. The Leones' Estadio Universitario held fewer than 21,000 fans. They sounded like 100,000. They chanted, *"Ponche! Ponche!"*—"Strikeout! Strikeout!"—whenever a batter had two strikes against him, even if he happened to play on the team for which they were otherwise rooting. *I'm not* ponche-*ing*, Martinez said to himself. *No way.*

In his first game with his new swing, Martinez hit two home runs. He would hit six during his month in Venezuela, batting .312 with an OPS, .957, that was superior to Ryan Braun's, albeit against worse competition. Better than the results was the way he now felt when he hit the ball. "The first time, it was like, What just happened?" he said. "It felt like I was cheating. Like the ball was stuck to my barrel and I could do whatever I wanted with it."

When he arrived in Kissimmee for spring training, he sat down with Luhnow and Bo Porter, who was entering his second season as the club's manager. "I'm not the guy I was before," he told them. "I went down to Venezuela, and I discovered this new thing. Anything you want me to do, I'll do it. Just give me the same at-bats as anyone else. Let me show you what I learned."

He thought they agreed. They didn't. Sig's algorithms indicated that the probability that an outfielder who was already 26, and who couldn't run or field particularly well, would get better was vanishingly small. And Porter, eager to move ahead with younger outfielders who might turn into winners, had little interest in giving Martinez the opportunity to demonstrate the effects of the changes he said he'd made. The future, Porter believed, was not just in George Springer, but in Robbie Grossman, L.J. Hoes, and Marc Krauss. He gave each of those players at least 40 at-bats during spring training. Martinez got just 18, half of them one-off pinch-hit appearances that prevented him from continuing the rhythm he had begun in Venezuela. "That's not an opportunity," Martinez said. "That's an opportunity to fail."

In his 18 at-bats, Martinez had three hits. Near the end of spring training, Luhnow called him into his office. The Astros were releasing him. "I was in shock," Martinez said. "Dude, I just got cut from the worst team in baseball." Then he got mad.

"What happened?" he asked Luhnow. "I've always been cool. I've never thrown anyone under the bus. I've never been a dick. I've always been very respectful. What did I do? What went wrong? When we sat down and I asked for an opportunity to show what I'd learned, you said I'd get one. I only got eighteen at-bats."

By the time Luhnow finished explaining that they hadn't envisioned him making the team, and they wanted to give him the opportunity to go somewhere that he might, Martinez's thoughts had already turned to the future. As he packed up his belongings in the clubhouse, his old friends José Altuve, Dallas Keuchel, and George Springer came by his locker to shake his hand, one by one. "I'm sorry, bro," they said. "Keep your head up."

"You guys are going to see me," Martinez said. "Don't worry about it. I'll be good. I promise you."

The Tigers signed Martinez two days later. He made the hour

drive from Kissimmee to their spring camp, in Lakeland. A few days after that, he was back in Kissimmee to play for the Tigers' minor league side against the Astros' equivalent. Luhnow watched from the stands, as did several of Martinez's old teammates. Martinez went three for four, with a home run and five RBIs. After his homer, he tossed his bat as far as he could. The next day, the Tigers' minor leaguers played the Astros' again, this time in Lakeland. Martinez hit three home runs, which could have been four if his last shot hadn't hit the top of the wall. After the third blast, the Astros' shortstop, a prospect named Carlos Correa, playfully threw his glove at Martinez as he trotted past him. "Get out of here, bro," Correa said. "Who *are* you?"

Luhnow had some idea. Martinez was the new hitter he'd promised he'd become, and who hadn't had an opportunity to show it. *What did we just do?* thought Luhnow.

It quickly became clear that they had released, for nothing in return, the very thing that their entire process was designed to find: a cheap superstar, and one whose contract they would have controlled for the next four seasons. After hitting 10 home runs in 17 games with the Tigers' Triple-A affiliate in Toledo, Martinez debuted with Detroit in late April. In mid-June, he was named the American League Player of the Week for a seven-game stretch in which he batted .444, with four homers and 11 RBIs. Shortly thereafter, he returned to Houston for the first time as a visiting player. When he was finished with batting practice, he found a familiar face waiting for him on the top step of the dugout. "I just want to tell you a few things," Luhnow said. "I want to tell you congrats. I want to tell you that I wish you the best, and that I'm really happy for you. And I want to tell you that you were right. But take it easy on us."

"Thanks," Martinez said. "I truly appreciate that. And I won't." Over the next four years, which he began with the Tigers and finished with the Diamondbacks., Martinez batted an even .300 and averaged 32 home runs. Robbie Grossman, L.J. Hoes, and Marc Krauss combined to hit a total of 38, and none of them remained in Houston after 2015. Martinez's on-base-plus-slugging percentage of

.936 was not only 56 points higher than that of the Astros' leader, the new version of Altuve, over that time period—it was nearly 100 points better than Ryan Braun's.

Martinez acknowledged that every athlete who has ever been cut from a team feels aggrieved. What hurt most was how the Astros had done it. "They had all this data, all these nerds and geeks, and I think they forgot that at the end of the day, everybody is still human," he said. "And a human can adapt, and a human can adjust."

In the years to follow, J.D. Martinez would serve as a reminder of a few things—an inescapable one, as the Astros' executives rarely flipped on their TVs without seeing him hit another home run. One, as Sig said, was "the feeling that we are smart is our enemy. That's what we strive to avoid. *SportsCenter* reminds us of that every couple of days."

Another reminder was not to overreact to even humiliating setbacks, but to use them to evolve. When a player was adamant that he had made a change over the off-season, the Astros committed to gathering enough information to determine whether it was a meaningful one. "Nine out of ten times, when people tell you they've gotten better in winter ball, it turns out it's not true," Luhnow said. "Sometimes it's actually real. I am so happy for J.D. I give him a big hug every time I see him. I think about what could have been. And I also feel disappointed that he didn't get more playing time to show us the new him."

/////////////

DESPITE THE SERIES OF BLOWS they sustained in 2014, the year brought at least one welcome surprise: The Astros were much better. There had been so much losing, over so many mortifying seasons, that few people noticed when there began to be a bit less of it. The accumulated results of their decisions since the end of 2011 finally seemed to have some promise. Their minor league system, considered the game's most barren only a few years earlier, was now loaded and ranked among the league's best, buoyed by many of the young players into whom Luhnow had converted the mature assets he'd inherited. Luhnow had planned for it to take three to four years to reseed the Astros' farm, but it happened in just two. The system was led by Correa, who even with a broken leg remained the sport's fourth most promising prospect, according to *Baseball America*.

Behind all those Springer dingers, the major league club had gone 15–14 in May, its first winning month since September 2010. Altuve broke out to hit .341 to win the league's batting title. Keuchel pitched to a 2.93 ERA over an even 200 innings. By September, Collin McHugh was throwing his straight fastball less than ever, with only around a quarter of his pitches. He finished the season 11–9 with a 2.73 ERA, sixth best in the American League among pitchers who worked more than 150 innings.

Still, they could have done without *Sports Illustrated*'s cover, for reasons that were not metaphysical. The cover, with its attention-grabbing prediction, was as much a surprise to the Astros' front office as it had been to other readers, including Chris Correa and Alan Shipnuck. "You have a big, gaudy, major magazine cover prognosticating that you're on the way to win a World Series," said David Stearns. "Obviously, that was the goal, and everyone was working towards that. But the cover put a definitive time frame on it. I think it put a result out there that everyone could peg on the Astros, rather than a process, which was what we were focused on." Jim Crane issued a directive to his employees: We're done talking about how we're going to win, until we win.

They weren't doing it regularly yet. The 2014 Astros still lost a lot of games, but 92 instead of 111. Despite the nicknames fans still wore on their chests—bootlegged LASTROS and DISASTROS T-shirts still outsold the authorized ones that read PROCESS—they didn't even finish last, but second to last, three games ahead of the Rangers.

Even so, September brought another upheaval, this one planned. Luhnow fired Bo Porter. Luhnow had always respected Porter, which was why he had given him his first big league managing job to begin with. The 42-year-old Porter was a good baseball man, and a winner. He had been an All–Big Ten safety at Iowa and had then played 10 years of professional baseball, spending parts of three seasons in the majors before working his way up the coaching ranks. But the job of manager, as Luhnow envisioned it, had become very different from what it once was, and even from the one Porter had learned coaching in minor league dugouts. A skipper was in some senses the pivotal member of the organization, both the conduit and filter between its executives and players. He not only had to embrace the Astros' process and convince their players to buy into it, but to provide feedback to the front office if elements of that process required rethinking.

He also couldn't fail to provide someone like J.D. Martinez enough at-bats for the organization to make an informed decision about him.

Luhnow sought to replace Porter with someone with a résumé that was both specific and rare. He had to have extensive major league playing experience so he could understand the players' side of things. He had to have worked on several levels of an organization so he knew how they all interacted. He had to have an extensive knowledge of, and respect for, the power of analytics. And he had to know what it meant to be data-driven, as the Astros conceived it.

Luhnow asked each of the 10 candidates he interviewed for the job the same question: "Are you OK with me sending down the lineup every day?" Many said they would be. That was the wrong answer. While the front office would provide the manager with a workshop full of tools to aid his decisions about optimal lineups and pitching matchups and tactics, the ultimate calls couldn't be made by a computer. "My preference is to make sure people are armed with these resources, but then let them do their jobs," Luhnow said. Only a manager could each day possess information that could undercut statistical trends, like whose legs were sore, who had a cold, who had slept poorly the night before, who had lost confidence in his slider. Only a manager could have the universe of knowledge that could lead him to violate the probabilities and follow his gut to make a crucial move, although he might be required to explain his rationale to his bosses later. And only a manager who the players knew had that power could truly command authority within a clubhouse, and inspire them to play their best for him each night.

Luhnow found his man by the end of September: 40-year-old A.J. Hinch. Hinch had spent parts of seven seasons in the big leagues, as a catcher for the A's, Royals, Tigers, and Phillies. He had become a manager, at 34, for the Diamondbacks, after having already served as their vice president of player development. Catchers tended to make good managers because they spent their playing careers involved in all aspects of their teams, including game-planning with pitchers and massaging their psyches. Hinch worked as the Padres' vice president of professional scouting after that, the role in which he had spent a week in Puerto Rico positively evaluating a young Carlos Correa. Luhnow even felt that Hinch's undergraduate degree, from Stanford, would help. It was in psychology.

"This is about the players, this is about the front office, this is about the coaching staff all playing their part in this big puzzle that is getting more wins than your opponent," Hinch said at his introductory press conference in Houston. For three years, the Astros had mostly discovered novel methods of losing. Now, under Hinch, they were ready to find new ways to win.

Hinch would have more to work with than Porter had. Jim Crane committed to acquiring free agents again, as he had always promised he would, and by Opening Day of 2015, the Astros' payroll exceeded $72 million, nearly three times what it had been two Aprils earlier. Their highest-paid position player would be an undersized 31-year-old infielder whom Luhnow signed away from the A's on a three-year, $23 million contract. It was Jed Lowrie.

IN SEARCH OF
CARLOS BELTRÁN

FOR FOUR MONTHS IN 2004, HOUSTON'S KILLER B'S OF JEFF BAGWELL, Lance Berkman, and Craig Biggio had another member: Carlos Beltrán. Beltrán had spent the first six years of his career in the baseball purgatory then located in Kansas City, where despite the Royals' continuing irrelevance he established himself as one of the league's best all-around players. He could bat from both sides of the plate, and almost every year he threatened to slug 30 homers, to hit .300, to steal 30 bases, to play a spectacular center field. By 2004, the Royals knew there was one thing that the 27-year-old Beltrán, who was to become a free agent that winter, couldn't do: reverse their fortunes all by himself. Kansas City had just one winning season with Beltrán in the lineup, and in 2004 they were worse than ever, careering toward 100 losses. So they traded Beltrán to the Astros in June. During the 90 games that remained in the regular season, he hit more home runs than Bagwell, Berkman, or Biggio, 23 of them. He drove in more runs, 53. He swiped more than three times as many bases, 28. Then, in his first-ever playoffs, he outdid himself.

A 22-year-old Carlos Beltrán in 2000, flanked by Royals teammates Johnny Damon (left) and Jermaine Dye (right).

Over the course of 12 games that October, batting second in the lineup between Biggio and Bagwell, Beltrán hit .435 with eight home runs, 14 RBIs, and six steals. In the decisive Game 5 of the Astros' National League Division Series against the Braves, he slugged two homers off Atlanta starter Jaret Wright and drove in five runs. Then he homered in each of the Astros' first four games in their National League Championship Series against the Cardinals. No one had ever before hit home runs in five straight playoff games. "Every player has two weeks in the year where you feel like you don't care who is on the mound, you don't care if you've got two strikes, you don't care if you have guys in scoring position," Beltrán said. "You're just seeing the ball, hitting it, and getting incredible results. Those were my two weeks."

Biggio, Houston's leadoff hitter, had a different way of describing Beltrán's performance: "He was Superman."

The Astros lost the seventh and final game of the NLCS in

St. Louis. Their pitchers couldn't get Albert Pujols out, and even Beltrán couldn't help them with that. A few months later Beltrán became the 10th player in baseball history to receive a nine-figure contract. The $119 million deal given to him by the Astros' more lovable fraternal twin, the New York Mets, promised to keep him off the market for seven years, until the kryptonite that was age had likely begun sapping his skills. Even so, a young Cardinals executive never forgot Beltrán's preternatural fortnight.

Jeff Luhnow was then in his first season as St. Louis's vice president of baseball development, and he watched Beltrán's heroics from the stands in both Busch Stadium and Minute Maid Park. Twelve winters later, as the 2017 season approached, Luhnow was armed with many more data points to guide his decision-making than those contained in his own memory. In fact, he and Sig Mejdal could exploit the type of hard information that they had only dreamed of acquiring when they started in St. Louis.

In 2015, Major League Baseball installed a system called Statcast in each of its 30 ballparks. Statcast, powered by a technology called TrackMan, used a combination of high-definition cameras and Doppler radar to accurately measure a range of player movements that was far broader than its predecessor, PITCHf/x, which had once turned the Astros on to Collin McHugh's underutilized breaking ball. They now knew not only the spin rate of each pitcher's pitches, but also the exit velocity and launch angle of each ball a hitter contacted, the precise speed and acceleration with which he ran on the base paths and in the field, even the efficiency of the angle by which a fielder chased a batted ball in an attempt to get his glove on it.

By the end of the 2016 season, Carlos Beltrán still performed well by most of Statcast's metrics, remarkably so considering that he was about to turn 40 and become the league's second-oldest position player, after the 42-year-old Ichiro Suzuki. Though he was no longer a base stealer, he still ran well, with a top sprint speed of 26.6 feet per second. More than a third of the league's regulars, some of whom were nearly two decades younger than he was, were slower. And while he played his final game in center field in 2012, he remained no worse than exactly average in right. Statcast determined that the standard outfielder would have caught 81 percent of the balls hit in his direction, based on the vectors with which they were struck. Beltrán came up with 81 percent of them.

Every source of data confirmed that he could still hit. During the previous season, Statcast revealed the continuing quickness of his bat. Balls rocketed from his barrel at an average speed of 90.1 miles per hour, a velocity that ranked him in the top 20 percent of everyday players. If Beltrán no longer smacked the ball as hard as someone like Aaron Judge, the towering Yankees rookie whose average exit velocity exceeded 95, it was still enough to slug 29 homers during a season he split between the Yankees and Rangers.

So Beltrán intrigued Luhnow not only because of what he had done a dozen years earlier, but what he could continue to do, which was potentially hit home runs in a lineup that lacked a dependable designated hitter. But Luhnow also felt that Beltrán could imbue a club with something else, a variable that neither Statcast nor any of Sig's other metrics could begin to track.

///////////

In 2015, the Astros became a contender sooner than anyone expected, threatening to jump not only *Sports Illustrated*'s timeline for their turnaround but also their own front office's. It happened in large measure thanks to a very young player who provided expediting contributions that Sig's models hadn't predicted would come so soon.

Carlos Correa's broken leg in 2014 only slightly delayed his climb through the minors. Luhnow and Mike Elias visited him in the hospital after his surgery. They were solemn, at first. Correa wasn't. "Chipper as ever, smiling, asking questions about the other players on the team," Elias said. "You knew if there was anyone that was going to apply himself in that situation, it was going to be him." He made his major league debut for the Astros less than a year later, on

June 8, 2015, beating Byron Buxton, whom the Minnesota Twins had snapped up with the No. 2 pick in 2012 and given a $6 million bonus, by six days.

When the Astros called up Correa from Triple-A, they were 34–24 and in first place in the American League West. On the eve of his promotion, considering that Correa was about to become the majors' youngest everyday player and at a taxing defensive position, one of the Astros' executives predicted that over the remaining 104 games in the season, he would bat .250 with eight home runs and 10 steals, and provide an unlikely contender with a modest if energetic boost. Correa hit his eighth homer in his 34th game and stole his tenth base in his 57th, and locked up the Rookie of the Year Award early.

As Elias had always hoped, Correa quickly showed that he could be a spectacular big league shortstop, despite his six-foot-four height. On July 25, in a tie game against the Royals with two outs and a runner on third in the bottom of the ninth, the fleet-footed Kansas City outfielder Alex Ríos hit a bouncing grounder toward the hole between short and third that seemed a certain game-winner. Correa darted to his right and backhanded the ball. In one motion, with his momentum carrying him onto the left-field grass, he leapt in the air and threw a rope to first, beating Ríos by half a step. Viewers weren't alone in being reminded of another great shortstop, one who had retired the year before after 20 seasons in New York and whose signature play Correa had mimicked thousands of times on the practice field in Santa Isabel. "When I made that play, obviously Jeter came to my mind," he said.

Luhnow didn't need to consult Sig to see where Correa's overall performance had fallen in the range of the expected outcomes his algorithm had modeled. It was in the 99th percentile.

Not long after Correa arrived in Houston, he moved into a two-bedroom apartment, with an open floor plan and immaculate modern furniture, on the penthouse level of a high-rise. It was exactly the type of dwelling that anyone would imagine a 20-year-old who had already become baseball's best shortstop would call home. Perhaps the only feature it shared with his family's house in Santa Isabel was its exposed concrete—a necessity there, a design feature here. If not for a few personal touches, like a trophy on a sideboard that read JUNE 2015 ROOKIE OF THE MONTH, it might have been a suite in a hotel that caters to guests who can list their favorite DJs. Correa's walk-in closet contained every model of Yeezy, the Kanye West–designed sneaker that sold for thousands on eBay, in size 13. "I *love* going shopping," he said. He owned 15 different fedoras.

When Correa first toured the apartment, the real estate agent pointed out that it had a view of Minute Maid Park from each of its floor-to-ceiling windows, and then added, strangely, that if Correa saw that the park was engulfed in flames, he would know not to go in that day. The agent's sales technique was almost perfectly misguided, though Correa rented the place anyway. "I wake up every single day, look over there, and am like, Let's get to work," he said.

Correa's schedule was always the same when the Astros were at home. He arose at 11. He watched something on the enormous TV that dominated his living room—*The Walking Dead*, *The Blacklist*, *Sons of Anarchy*, *Prison Break*, anything starring Kevin Hart—and drove his white BMW to the ballpark, where he spent the next 10 to 12 hours. He was asleep by two a.m. He still declined to indulge in any sort of nightlife—"No girlfriends, just baseball," he said—and he did not understand why virtually every day at least one person pointed out to him that he could not yet legally buy a beer. "Never drank a beer before," he said. "I've had wine and champagne, but never a beer. I don't think that will happen. I don't know why people look forward to that."

From many 20-year-olds, a statement like that might come off as judgmental, if not insincere, but from Correa it simply seemed straightforward. That was the quality Luhnow and Enos Cabell sensed in him, one Bill James admitted he couldn't detect or measure. Prodigies like Correa were often prima donnas, undermining the clubs they are supposed to help due to their behavior and their older teammates' resentment of it, but that was not a risk with him. He was mature, but not an automaton. During his first big league spring training, in 2014, his teammates prepared a special locker for him: a laundry basket, with an overturned bucket for a seat. He used it, happily. Early the next season, when Correa was still in Triple-A, José Altuve wrote Correa's name on a piece of athletic tape and affixed the faux nameplate over the empty locker next to his. "I wanted him here," said Altuve. "I was saving his locker."

Lance McCullers also reached the majors that year. His call came three weeks before Correa's, and he pitched to a 3.22 ERA and on average struck out more than one batter in each of his $125\frac{2}{3}$ innings. "McCullers has got to be in that 95th to 99th percentile as well," Luhnow said. Behind McCullers, at shortstop, Correa played with Altuve to his left and another player who wasn't much taller than Altuve to his right: Jed Lowrie, who shifted from short to third base to make room for his new teammate. "The talent is so easy to see," said Lowrie, who watched from close range as Correa torqued his body to pull off jump throws like Jeter and hit home runs like A-Rod. That might have been true now, but just two and a half years earlier, only the Astros were equipped to identify it for what it was.

Carlos Correa leads the Astros to the playoffs as a rookie in 2015.

Correa and the Astros finished the 2015 regular season with a record of 86–76, a 35-win improvement in the span of just two years. They won their first playoff game in a decade, as Dallas Keuchel conjured six shutout innings to lead them to a 3–0 Wild Card–round victory over the Yankees. That event occasioned Correa's first taste of beer, amid the celebration in the visitors' clubhouse at Yankee Stadium. His review, in full: "It tastes bad."

In the next round, the Astros blew a two-games-to-one lead in the best-of-five American League Division Series to an opponent that was not only finally good, but cohesive and relentless in a way that was hard to explain. The opponent was the Royals, Carlos Beltrán's old team, who were on their way to winning their first World Series in three decades. A month later, with the Astros' shortstop position now filled for the next six years at minimum, Luhnow traded Jed Lowrie to the A's again.

The next season, the Astros regressed. They started 2016 cold, and by May 22 they were 17–28 and already 10 games behind in the AL West. It was too much ground to make up. They ended up winning two fewer games than in 2015, going 84–78, and missed a Wild Card spot.

Maybe, after the outlier that was 2015, they had simply returned to the normalized improvement curve Luhnow and Sig had once imagined. But perhaps, Luhnow speculated, their clubhouse was missing something crucial in both seasons. They had turned the club around by ridding its roster of expensive veterans and focusing on acquiring and developing the right young players. But that meant they had almost no veterans. None of their key performers was yet 30 years old. Several, like Correa and McCullers, weren't close to 25. "We had some veterans in there, but they weren't necessarily the types of guys that create followership," Luhnow said. Luhnow reflected on the 2015 ALDS and the intangible dynamic the experienced Royals had, one that his precocious Astros lacked.

Perhaps the club was missing a player who could not only hit home runs but who had experienced virtually everything a player could in professional baseball, one who knew what it was like to be very young and very old, to make the league's minimum salary and more than almost anyone, to make All-Star games, to win awards, to win playoff series and lose them, to play like Superman and to be too injured to play at all for months at a time during a few seasons. A player who had faced 1,498 different pitchers in his career and shared a dugout with nearly 700 different teammates.

Perhaps it was missing Carlos Beltrán.

//////////

THE ANALYTICS COMMUNITY'S VIEW of the impact of a team's chemistry on its bottom line performance had evolved in the 25 years since Bill James had sprayed his acid, as he had put it, at Sparky Anderson for continuing to play Enos Cabell almost every day. In 2002, Theo Epstein's Red Sox hired James as an advisor, and baseball's consummate outsider received his first regular access to the inner workings of a club—something that he had once not been sure was ideal for a cold-eyed analyst who sought to avoid cognitive biases at all costs. By 2010, he'd had eight years of exposure to the rigors of the players' workplace, filled with highly competitive people who spent most of their waking hours together for as many as eight months a year, with few days off. "Whether you sell insurance or you're a school teacher, obviously the people you work with can make you more productive or less productive," James told *The Seattle Times*. "Baseball would be quite a remarkable activity if it was the one place in the world where your co-workers didn't have any impact on how productive you were."

James had less patience than ever for the argument that while chemistry might exist, it was so difficult for anyone to measure that it was best to ignore it. "If you divide the world into shit that you know and shit that you don't know, and you study the stuff that you know, then you're not going to learn very much," he said.

Luhnow and Sig had spent their careers in baseball trying to devise ways to turn the shit they didn't know into shit they did. By the winter before the 2017 season, the value of team chemistry remained in the first bucket. Most hard-core analysts, the type who attend wonky if increasingly star-studded events such as the annual MIT Sloan Sports Analytics Conference, no longer scoffed at the concept as simply a result, and not an independent cause, of winning or losing. It was no longer enough to witheringly conclude that good teams always had good chemistry, and bad teams had bad chemistry, but that bad teams were never bad despite good chemistry. But it remained difficult to prove, let alone to assign a weight to its impact.

At 2017's Sloan Conference, held in March, three analysts tried. A professor from Indiana University's Kelley School of Business and two economists from the Federal Reserve Bank of Chicago presented a paper called "In Search of David Ross," which found that the concept of chemistry as something that could cause a club to consistently outperform the individual contributions of its players was real. There was a reason why the voluble, relentlessly positive Ross, a backup catcher, had appeared on two different World Series champion teams, the Red Sox and the Cubs, in the span of four years. It was not his .229 career batting average.

The equation-heavy, 43-page study calculated a 20 percent variation in team wins from what might be expected if victories were simply a result of the sum of a club's players' performances, and further asserted that 44 percent of that difference could be accounted for by chemistry, which the study's authors called the David Ross Effect. "Players such as David Ross are true 'diamonds-in-the-rough' according to our analysis, with their full impact on team performance likely to fly under the radar according to traditional performance metrics," the authors wrote.

The paper was not definitive, more a valuable entry into an area of study that remained in its infancy. It focused its analysis on interactions between players on the diamond, not those in the dugout or the clubhouse, which could potentially be even more important. The industry remained a long way from developing a metric to measure the positive impact of someone like David Ross on a club's results—a

Chemistry Wins Above Replacement, or ChemWAR, perhaps. One of Jeff Luhnow's strengths was that despite the data-driven approach that had led to the Astros' turnaround, he realized that only a fool would ignore the potential value of the shit he didn't know—the shit for which his data couldn't account.

"Just because you can't quantify it doesn't mean it doesn't exist," he said.

For Sig, the idea of paying a lot of money for something he agreed was real but couldn't value, funds that could otherwise be spent on qualities that he definitely could assess, made him a bit squeamish, if he was being honest. What *was* chemistry, anyway? Was it how players got along, how they shared information to attain a common goal, how they rooted for one another? Was having experienced players always beneficial, or might there be such a thing as too much experience held by players who pushed outmoded ideas on their younger teammates? Might it be better if players didn't get along perfectly, to drive healthy internecine competition? And while it certainly seemed like good chemistry mattered, and provided a team like the 2015 Royals with an edge, was that an availability heuristic? Not only did Sig have zero predictive information related to chemistry, but he didn't even know what he might try to predict. How could you try to reach a goal if you couldn't define its parameters?

But Luhnow made the decisions.

If Luhnow sought simply a short-term deal for a player who could reliably hit 25 homers from the Astros' open DH slot, the free agent market presented several options. There was 32-year-old Mitch Moreland and 34-year-old Brandon Moss, each of whom might have signed for around $6 million. For a few million more, Luhnow could have had 31-year-old Michael Saunders or 36-year-old Mike Napoli. Months before the 2017 Sloan Conference, with all those possibilities still available, Luhnow had already winnowed his list of candidates for the Astros' open DH slot to two free agents. One was Matt Holliday, who had hit 295 homers in his career and whose leadership and willingness to mentor younger players Luhnow had witnessed firsthand during the three seasons they overlapped in St. Louis. Holliday was to turn 38 in January. The second candidate was even older.

On December 5, 2016, the Astros signed Carlos Beltrán. Luhnow gave him a one-year deal worth $16 million, committing to compensate him more in 2017 than anyone else on an Opening Day payroll that had nearly quintupled in just four years, to $124 million, thanks to other measured forays into the free agent market for veterans like the outfielder Josh Reddick and the pitcher Charlie Morton. Beltrán, in turn, would receive more than just $16 million. He would, he believed, get a real chance—perhaps his last one—to experience one of the only things he hadn't during his 19 years in the majors, and his three and a half decades playing baseball: a World Series victory.

//////////

THE ROYALS PICKED BELTRÁN in the second round of the 1995 draft, not long after he turned 18. He found that his pursuit of improvement was often as lonely as it had been on the empty field in Manatí, Puerto Rico, where he had spent his boyhood tossing balls to himself and dreaming of becoming Roberto Clemente. He asked veteran players for tips any chance he could. Sometimes they even gave them to him. One who did was a fellow Puerto Rican switch-hitter named Luis Alicea, who joined the Royals in 2001, when he was 35 and Beltrán was 24. Two seasons earlier, Beltrán had been the American League Rookie of the Year, batting .293, with 22 home runs, 108 RBIs, and 27 steals, but he slumped the next year, hitting .247, with seven homers in 98 games and losing the center-field job. Alicea didn't have Beltrán's gifts, but he knew how to maximize those he did possess. That was how someone who stood five foot nine and never hit more than six homers in a season lasted 13 years in the majors.

It was one thing to try to keep a single swing in working order, Alicea told Beltrán. Switch-hitters like them had to keep track of two—one from the right, one from the left. They had to work more than twice as hard as everyone else. On-field batting practice sessions before games were not enough. "Meet me in the cage," Alicea said. There, the two players hit a total of 320 balls—80 from the right and 80 from the left for each of them. "This is something we're going to do every day," Alicea told Beltrán. "Get to the ballpark early."

"OK," Beltrán said. "We'll do it." Beltrán played 152 games in center field that season. He hit .306, with 24 homers and 101 RBIs.

Beltrán became obsessed with his swing, with maintaining and perfecting two sets of mechanics, and he began spending long hours in the Royals' video room watching his at-bats for any sign of a flaw, any inefficiency. Soon, his eyes drifted to the pitchers. He began to realize that after watching them enough times, he was able to pick up on any tendency they might have that he could exploit. He became particularly adept at discerning if they tipped their pitches, meaning if they did anything different before they threw one type of pitch as opposed to another, or before they targeted one part of the plate as opposed to another.

He'd reveal his findings to his skeptical older teammates. "Guys, you see what he's doing?" he'd tell them. "No, no, I don't want to know," they usually replied. "It's too quick to do anything about it anyway." It wasn't too quick for Beltrán.

One day, Beltrán was studying video of a pitcher whom the Royals faced often, as he also played in the American League Central: Bartolo Colón of the Cleveland Indians. It was long before Colón began his endless baseball second life as a lovable, portly junkballer nicknamed Big Sexy. Back then, he was an annual Cy Young contender whose fastball reached 100 miles per hour. Beltrán thought he saw something interesting. He rewound the screeching VHS tape and pressed play. There it was again. He rewound. Yes, there it was again.

Pitchers were creatures of habit, and Beltrán saw that Colón had developed a bad one. When he was about to throw a breaking ball, he hurried through his pitching motion. When he planned to throw his blazing fastball, however, he took his time, as if to be sure that he gathered every ounce of might he could possibly put into it. Even

100-mile-per-hour heat was hittable if you knew it was coming. Beltrán knew, every time.

Beltrán made 15 plate appearances against Colón in 2001. He reached base on more than half of them, and he hit three homers and two doubles, for a batting average of .462 and an on-base-plus-slugging percentage of 1.841. Almost every pitcher, he thought, had a tell. And if a pitcher had a tell, he could find it and, thanks to the work he put into his swing, take advantage of it.

Beltrán made a promise to himself. When he was a veteran, no young teammate would have to seek him out to mine him for his knowledge about how to prepare, and no young teammate would be left to his own devices to figure out how to attack pitchers. He would always make himself available, if someone wanted his help. *The weight of my living,* he thought, *will be to use my time to try to do things for the people that are coming after me.* He also thought that he'd be doing something for himself: fostering a team that had a better chance of winning.

/////////////

BELTRÁN KNEW HOW INTIMIDATING it could be for younger players to approach older ones, even those with whom they shared a clubhouse for eight months a year. In July 2007, at the All-Star Game, he found himself in the same locker room as the veteran whose record of eight home runs in a single postseason he had tied three years earlier and whose brain he had always wanted to pick most. While Beltrán was by then well-established, an All-Star for the fourth time, 42-year-old Barry Bonds, of the San Francisco Giants, was about to make his 14th All-Star appearance. Bonds was weeks away from passing Hank Aaron to become the all-time home run king, but he had earned a reputation for something besides his hitting genius and his alleged use of steroids: his orneriness. The game was to be played in Bonds's home stadium, AT&T Park, and in the home clubhouse Bonds had an entire corner to himself, which contained both a reclining massage chair and a hulking slugger. Beltrán steeled himself and asked the glowering Bonds when he might have time to discuss the art of hitting. Bonds's face brightened. He pointed toward the batting cage. "OK, Carlos," he said. "Let's go."

In the cage, Bonds showed Beltrán how he liked to set the pitching machine to top speed, more than 90 miles per hour, and then gradually move closer and closer to it, training himself to react to pitches that arrived quicker than any human could throw them from a mound. Even more useful, to Beltrán, was the way he described his mentality. "Sometimes you're in an oh-for-ten slump, and you might start to doubt your ability," Bonds said. "But you have to understand that every time you walk to the plate, the person who is in trouble isn't you. It's the pitcher."

A decade later, when Beltrán arrived for his first spring training with the Astros in February 2017, he knew that he appeared to his young teammates as Bonds once had to him. He was at least seven years older than almost all of them, earned 30 times more than some of them, and was by then a nine-time All-Star who had hit 421 home runs. During his first days with the Astros, he approached each one of them not just the other outfielders, and not just the budding stars like Altuve and Correa and Springer, but everyone, pitchers included. "My friend, I am here to help you," he said. "Even if it looks like I'm busy, you won't bother me. If you sit down next to me and ask me a question, I would be more than happy to give you the time that you need."

By 2017, the Astros' young players had a world of tools at their disposal that Beltrán hadn't had when he sat alone rewinding tapes of the future Big Sexy. The club's video room hummed with computers loaded with clips that could reveal pitchers' tendencies to the percentile. A given night's starter might throw a first-pitch fastball 75 percent of the time, and 85 percent of those first-pitch fastballs came in on the inner half of the plate.

It was useful information, particularly as pitchers, on average, threw much harder than they had when Beltrán was young. Hitters who walked to the plate without a plan of attack, who intended to simply react to what the pitchers threw them, no longer had a chance. But the analytical information didn't capture the other side of hitting, the one that Bonds had stressed.

"Analytics people, they understand the statistics, the matchups, the percentages, and analytics are now a big part of the game of baseball," Beltrán said. "But they don't understand what the player is thinking. What is causing his launch angle to be what it is? What is going through the player's mind that is causing him to hesitate, instead of being aggressive?" Further, what beyond the data could give a player the confidence to believe that every time he stepped to the plate, it was the pitcher who was in trouble, not him? And what could someone like Beltrán detect in a pitcher's habits that could equip a teammate to understand not just what the probabilities suggested the pitcher would likely throw, but to know for certain?

Beltrán's impact was impossible for the Nerd Cave to quantify, but Carlos Correa attempted to attach a number to it: seven. Of the 24 home runs he hit in 2017, by the end of the regular season Correa attributed precisely seven to Beltrán's influence, to Beltrán's showing him how to use video to break down opposing pitchers to a depth Correa had never before imagined, to his identifying their tells. "Maybe they're doing something with their glove that allows you to figure out if it's a fastball or a curveball," Correa said. "The biggest thing I've learned from him is to look at the bigger picture. It's not only about playing defense and catching the ball and throwing the ball and hitting it. It's way more than that. He showed me how to prepare the right way every single day to be successful out there." Proper preparation, it turned out, meant more than watching a Kevin Hart flick, picking the right fedora and the right pair of Yeezys, and heading to the ballpark.

During games, between the at-bats Beltrán regularly received as the Astros' designated hitter, he spent much of his time in the clubhouse consuming video of not just the opposing pitcher, and not just of his own swings, but of his teammates' plate appearances as well. If they had developed a bad habit, he saw it and let them know, with visual evidence. If George Springer started swinging too hard again, Beltrán told him. "I could be pulling off the ball, I could not be following through," said Springer, who, like Correa, would set a career high in homers, 34, under Beltrán's tutelage. Couldn't a hitting coach, earning a sliver of Beltrán's salary, do the same thing? "You always just think a coach doesn't know what he's talking about, as a player," Springer said. "He's a player."

Beltrán aided the Astros' pitchers as well. In 2016, the season after Dallas Keuchel broke out to win both the Cy Young Award and Houston's Wild Card game, his performance had disintegrated along with his team's. His ERA jumped by more than two runs, from 2.48 to 4.55. His walk rate spiked, and his strikeout rate dropped. The first time Beltrán met Keuchel, in spring training, he gently suggested one reason why.

"Sometimes you held your hand above your glove last year before a pitch," Beltrán told Keuchel. "If the ball showed, it was a fastball. If it didn't, it was an off-speed pitch."

"I appreciate you telling me that," Keuchel said. Keuchel threw seven shutout innings against the Mariners on Opening Day. By the end of July, his ERA remained below 2.00.

Had Beltrán, in reality, accounted for just a fraction of the 40 percent boost in production that Correa attributed to him—not just for the young shortstop, but for all the Astros he mentored, even the pitchers—then he would have been worth far more than the $16 million the club paid him. After 19 years in the big leagues, Beltrán knew that he might help Houston win in other ways, too.

//////////

ONE NIGHT IN 2009, an academic named Kate Bezrukova found herself watching a Yomiuri Giants baseball game in the Tokyo Dome, alongside a colleague named Chester Spell. Bezrukova was an assistant professor in the psychology department of Santa Clara University, and she and Spell were in Japan to attend an annual conference hosted by the International Association for Conflict Management. Bezrukova, who stands five foot ten, had always loved both watching and participating in sports, and she was excited to see how the Japanese played baseball. To her surprise, not all the players were Japanese. Most were, but others were Korean, American, Venezuelan, and even Australian. And yet they still combined to form a successful team. That year the Giants would go on to win their record 21st Japan Series.

Born in Siberia and raised in Crimea, Bezrukova—whose given first name is Yekaterina—had all sorts of friends as a child: Russian, Ukrainian, Tartar, Jewish. After she earned her doctorate in social and organizational psychology from Moscow State University in 1999, she moved to the United States to continue her studies as a postdoctoral researcher at Wharton, where she worked alongside academics from China and New Zealand and all over the globe. Her intellectual interests began to align perfectly with her personal experience. Why, she wondered, did some diverse groups get along well while others clashed? Why did some international teams of academics collaborate productively while others didn't?

In the Tokyo Dome, Bezrukova and Spell realized they had happened upon the ideal type of organization to study how demographic differences, called fault lines, could affect performance. In a lab, it was difficult to measure performance, and even to define its parameters, but baseball teams provided not only demographically diverse groups to analyze but externally valid results, most of all wins. "This is a brilliant situation for us," Bezrukova told Spell. "Let's get our students on the project." Bezrukova and Spell directed their research assistants to perform fault line analysis on the demographics of all 30 major league teams between the 2004 and 2008 seasons.

Those rosters revealed several different potential fault lines that could divide a team into rigid factions, called in-groups and out-groups, and hinder its performance. They could run between position groups: not just pitchers and hitters, but starters and relievers, and everyday players and reserves. They might be based on status, pitting older and better-compensated subgroups against younger, underpaid blocs. And they could result from nationality, which could divide a clubhouse along fault lines of culture and particularly language. Such divisions could shift a team's focus from its ultimate goal—winning—to what the researchers called task-irrelevant cues, like competition and distrust between isolated subgroups, as well as restricted communication of information and advice.

Bezrukova and Spell estimated that a major league team's fault lines could account for three extra wins, or three extra losses, in a given season. A six-win swing could mean the difference between a club that won a World Series and one that didn't even make the playoffs. Intriguingly, the teams that performed best in Bezrukova and Spell's fault line analysis were not those who were the most demographically similar—mostly young, low-wage Hispanics, say, or older, highly compensated Americans. They were instead those that had players who could cross-cut between a mix of subgroups, who could facilitate a complementarity, as opposed to a rivalry, based on their differences. Perhaps they had a player who was older and American, but made relatively little money because he was a reserve catcher, like David Ross. Or perhaps they had someone who was older and highly paid, but also Hispanic, and was particularly motivated to, in academic parlance, deactivate his club's fault lines.

///////////

ALTHOUGH BELTRÁN'S FORMAL EDUCATION lasted only through Manatí's Fernando Callejo High School, he soon became an unwitting expert in the effects of fault lines. When the Royals drafted him in 1995, he spoke not a word of English. His postgame interviews could have been among those that caused a young Carlos Correa to cringe at their awkwardness, had Correa been old enough then to even watch baseball.

Beltrán became known for standing at the back of the line during outfield drills. The problem wasn't that he couldn't do what his coaches asked. He could stay behind the ball and use his body's momentum to power his throws to the infield better than anyone. The problem was that he couldn't understand the specifics of the coaches' instructions. He copied his teammates' motions, devoting most of the energy he ought to have directed toward improving to simply trying to figure out what he was supposed to be doing. Though he bonded with the organization's other Spanish-speaking minor leaguers, like the Dominican infielder Carlos Febles, he spent most of his time feeling stressed and isolated. In 52 games in rookie ball in 1995, Beltrán didn't hit a single home run.

Beltrán knew that most of his teammates thought he was odd, a loner, and probably unintelligent, by the way they steered clear of him. One day, he was approached by a fellow outfielder named Ricky Pitts. *"Hola, mi hermano,"* Pitts said to him. *"Cómo estás?"* Besides their position and height—six foot one—Pitts had little in common with Beltrán. As a 34th-round pick in 1994, he was not a top prospect, and he came from Seattle. But he had a natural inclination to connect with his teammates, whoever they were. While Pitts figured his career in baseball was likely to be short, he wanted to emerge from it with skills that would help him in the future, such as a mastery of Spanish.

The teenagers made a promise to each other. Wherever the years to come were to take them—to Lansing, and Spokane, and Wilmington—they would help one another learn each other's language, a few words a day. "Say it however it comes out," Pitts told Beltrán. "If you say something crazy, I won't laugh at you."

By 1998, Beltrán had reached Kansas City, while Pitts was forever stuck in Single-A. If Beltrán could by then follow only half of what his first big league manager, Tony Muser, said in his pregame addresses, he could at least haltingly communicate with teammates other than Febles, like Johnny Damon and Mike Sweeney. During games, he often found himself distracted by his fear of what would happen in the clubhouse afterward, how he would stumblingly try to answer the questions reporters asked him. But he was on his way to full fluency, to the point where he no longer felt isolated and would soon muster the courage to introduce himself in English to a famously grumpy slugger and talk hitting with him. Ricky Pitts had given him the key.

Sixteen years later, Spanish-speaking players comprised a quarter of the league, but many of them still had to rely on the kindness of teammates like Pitts. When Beltrán joined the Yankees in 2014, the club had three Japanese players, the pitchers Hiroki Kuroda and Masahiro Tanaka as well as Ichiro. Each had his own personal translator, provided by the team. And yet the Yankees' spring training roster had five times as many Latin players, three-quarters of whom could speak no English. After team meetings they would all rush over to Beltrán to find out what Joe Girardi, the Yankees' manager, had said. Beltrán, then 37, began lobbying the league and the players' union to require each club to hire a full-time Spanish translator. Two years later, thanks largely to his efforts, they did.

Still, when you walked into any big league locker room during any given club's downtime, you almost always found two groups hanging out, separate from each other: the English speakers and the Spanish speakers. There might as well have been a jagged fracture running down the middle of the clubhouse's low-pile carpet. Beltrán thought there had to be a better way.

///////////

IN HOUSTON, BELTRÁN WANTED TO create not only an environment in which useful information could freely flow between players, but also the type of inclusive, unified culture that he had longed for when he was young. Basically, he wanted the clubhouse to be fun. He focused much of his effort on mending the natural division between its American and Latin inhabitants. The Astros' Opening Day roster included 17 Americans and seven Latinos. While many of the club's native Spanish speakers, including Altuve, Correa, and the utility-man Marwin González, had become bilingual at younger ages than Beltrán had, in previous seasons they tended to stick together and speak in their natural tongue, while the Americans did the same. When an American player asked him a question, though, Beltrán intentionally often answered in Spanish before repeating his reply in English. He wanted to normalize both languages.

He quickly realized he had a 23-year-old ally.

Alex Bregman, the LSU shortstop whom the Astros selected with the 2015 compensatory pick they received due to their failure to sign Brady Aiken the year before, sailed through the minors even faster than the Astros had hoped. His rise from Quad Cities to Houston took just 13 months, even though it had included the learning of a new position, third base, as shortstop belonged to Correa. Minor league pitching proved no match for someone with his skills and fearlessness. Neither did a language barrier. Altuve and Correa had to laugh as Bregman incessantly chattered at them in what he professed was nearly perfect Spanish, a subject in which he swore he'd received straight A's in high school in New Mexico. It wasn't close to perfect, but they appreciated the effort and admired the way he never had any qualms about giving amusingly butchered postgame interviews to Spanish-language TV stations. "I'm speaking Spanish fifty percent of the day," Bregman said. "I want to be able to connect with guys from all different backgrounds. I think that's what leaders do."

Beltrán noticed that Bregman spent a great deal of his time communicating, or trying to, with one teammate in particular. Though he was 32, Yuli Gurriel had lived in the United States for less than a year. He defected from Cuba in 2016, a shock to that nation, as he was not only one of the baseball-mad island's greatest players but belonged to one of its leading baseball families. The Astros signed him to a five-year, $47.5 million contract, which contributed to their skyrocketing payroll. Gurriel arrived knowing virtually nothing about his new country's culture or customs, and spoke no English at all. He was exactly the type of player who could become isolated and resentful in an American clubhouse. Bregman refused to let that happen to his first baseman. The two yammered at each other in Spanglish all day long.

Bregman, Beltrán realized, was Gurriel's Ricky Pitts. Beltrán could have taken the lead in helping Gurriel himself, but he knew it was better for the club's dynamic for someone like Bregman—younger, a fellow infielder, American—to do it. "Keep it up," Beltrán told Bregman. "Imagine how you make Yuli feel, to know he has a friend who is trying to comprehend him."

"When Beltrán came over, that merged the clubhouse, really," said Bregman. "This year, we're all just way closer."

Beltrán instituted other bonding strategies. He never understood why even the very good teams he had been on tended to treat regular-season wins as a matter of course. Most of the time, after cursory handshakes and fist bumps, players would shower, dress, and go their separate ways mere minutes after they'd recorded the final out. It was, he thought, a missed opportunity.

During spring training, he had enlisted the president of the World Boxing Organization, a friend, to commission two championship belts for him. After Keuchel pitched the Astros to a 3–0 win over the Mariners on Opening Day, Beltrán explained to his new teammates what they were going to do with those belts. After each victory, before anyone hit the showers, every member of the team would sit at his locker for the awarding of the belts, one to the hitter of the game and one to the pitcher of the game. Beltrán would distribute them that night, but thereafter the belt-holders from the previous victory would decide who got them. Each new awardee had to give credit to the other players who had performed well that game before beginning his own acceptance speech. Failure to participate would result in a $500 fine from the club's kangaroo court, over which, of course, Beltrán presided.

The first night, a couple of players had watched the proceedings from the entrance to the shower room, with towels already around their waists. That was 500 bucks. "Baseball players, when you mess with their money, they listen," Beltrán said. Nobody was fined after that. Soon the players acquired a new clubhouse sound system, to blast music during the ceremonies, and whirling party lights. When reporters entered the clubhouse, as they were permitted to do after the ceremonies had concluded, they sometimes had trouble making out the faces of the players they were trying to interview. That was because of the fog machine.

One day in mid-July, Beltrán arrived at Minute Maid Park to find a curious message scrawled on the clubhouse's whiteboard. FUNERAL FOR CARLOS BELTRÁN'S GLOVE—3:30, it read. Though Beltrán still did fine in the outfield, and Statcast indicated that he got to precisely the percentage of balls he should have, it had been two months since he had played anything but designated hitter. He walked onto the field at the appointed time to find the rest of the Astros solemnly kneeling in a semicircle in the outfield around a box that contained the leather implement that had once won him three straight Gold Glove Awards. Brian McCann, the Astros' catcher, stood in a priest's billowing robes next to three faux tombstones, ready to deliver the eulogy.

Brian McCann presides over the burial of Carlos Beltrán's glove.

Beltrán couldn't stop laughing. He whipped out his phone to record the ceremony. It was funny, but also something more. It was one thing for him to try to build what he believed to be a winning culture by sharing the knowledge he had accumulated, demolishing demographic walls, and buying a few boxing belts. But for his teammates to collectively concoct a way to tease him like this, someone who was far older and richer and more accomplished than any of them were? *That* was chemistry. Everything he had tried to do was working. No one would ever have dared to hold a funeral for the glove of Barry Bonds.

//////////

DURING THE SUMMER OF 2017, Beltrán experienced something he never had before, not in Manatí, not even when he had felt so stressed and lonely in the Royals' minor leagues. Jessica—his wife of 17 years—and their children, two daughters and a toddler son, had moved into his place in Houston after the girls finished their year at a private school in Manhattan. The previously quiet rented house vibrated with energy and laughter. Then 2:15 p.m. approached, time for Beltrán to head to the ballpark. For the first time in his life, he didn't want to go.

He didn't even tell Jessica at first, and nobody with the Astros sensed that anything had changed. He prepared just as hard as always, and probably harder. "You don't walk into the clubhouse and see him there checking his phone," Luhnow said. "He's on the video, he's into the game, he's watching. That's something the other players would look at. This is a Hall of Famer. He's towards the end of his career. And he's still working to get better every day?"

He oversaw the club's belt ceremonies as enthusiastically as ever. There were many more of them than anyone could have anticipated. By the end of July, the Astros had a dozen more wins than any other club in the American League—69 of them, against just 36 losses. They were a juggernaut, leading the majors in runs scored, on pace to accomplish the virtually unthinkable offensive feat of hitting more homers than any other team in baseball while recording the fewest strikeouts. Nobody knew precisely how much credit Beltrán deserved for that, but everyone was certain it was a lot. Secretly, Beltrán's reluctance to head into work became a daily phenomenon. He finally admitted it to Jessica. "I think this year is it for me," he said.

Carlos Beltrán, at 40, during his return to Houston.

His body felt good. In the cage, the club's hitting coach, Dave Hudgens, could diagnose no mechanical issue. "Man, your swing, your bat speed, it's there," Hudgens told him. And Beltrán usually knew exactly how an opposing pitcher would try to attack him. But although the Astros had few regrets about giving him that $16 million because of all the intangible and often unclassifiable ways he helped the club, the individual results he produced on the field did not match his salary. His exit velocity dropped by nearly 2.5 miles per hour from the season before, to 87.5, below average. By July's end, with more than half the season over, his on-base-plus-slugging percentage had declined by 145 points from 2016, to .705, and he had hit just 12 home runs. It appeared as if Carlos Beltrán had finally gotten old.

Beltrán knew the issue was deeper than that. Analysts could detect and parse launch angles and velocities, but they couldn't know what inside a player contributed to those numbers. Beltrán did.

In August, as Jessica and the kids prepared to go back to New York for school, Beltrán's slump deepened. That month, he batted .210 with two home runs in 26 games. The Astros, who had spent most of the season looking like the World Series favorite, declined with him, going 11–17 in August. Suddenly, they were the DISASTROS again.

Some of it had to do with injuries, which piled up as the summer wore on. Correa tore a ligament in his left thumb while taking a swing in July, putting him on the bench until September. Soon, the Astros' disabled list required scrolling. It included nearly a third of their roster: Springer; McCullers; both their catchers, McCann and Evan Gattis; and three relievers, Michael Feliz, Will Harris, and Tony Sipp. After a July in which they scored more than seven runs a game, in August they averaged just four. No one slid face-first into a rival's posterior, but it was a genuine malaise.

As the month neared its end, a once promising season—the one for which Jeff Luhnow, Sig Mejdal, Mike Elias, and Jim Crane had spent six years assiduously building—was falling apart. Even Beltrán's steadying influence seemed unlikely to save it. Luhnow believed that a clubhouse with good chemistry could persevere through periods of failure better than one without, and Kate Bezrukova and Chester Spell's research independently confirmed that concept: Deactivated fault lines could prevent poor results from snowballing. Even so, as August approached Luhnow knew he had to do something even more drastic, for someone with his worldview, than paying for a quality he couldn't quantify.

8

TWO SECONDS
TO SPARE

THE HOUSTON OF 2017 WAS NO HINTERLAND JERKWATER. IT HAD BE-
come the roaring, international metropolis of which Roy Hofheinz
has always dreamed. In 1960, when the Judge was busy conceiving
the Astrodome, Houston's population had been one million and relatively homogenous: 74 percent white, 20 percent African American,
and six percent Latino. Now it had more than doubled in size, to
2.3 million, and it was the most diverse city in the United States:
38 percent white, 36 percent Latino, 17 percent African American,
and nine percent Asian. Its citizens spoke some 145 different languages, and more kept arriving. By 2030, Houston was expected to
pass Chicago to become the country's third-largest city. Hofheinz
would have loved it. More customers. More green.

Hofheinz himself might have coined Houston's new marketing
slogan: "The City with No Limits." The motto mostly referred to
its friendliness to free enterprise, one the Judge had helped foster.

"The ideological thrust in Houston in the twentieth century has been anti-government, anti-regulation, anti-planning, anti-taxes, anti-anything that seemed to represent, in fact or fantasy, an expansion of the public sector or a limitation on the economic prerogatives and activities of the city's business community," wrote a University of Houston professor in 1989.

That philosophy persisted, and even broadened. Oil, shipping, and aerospace were joined by information technology, biotech, and finance as thriving industries. Were Houston an independent nation, its economy would have been the world's 24th richest. The 2017 Fortune 500 included 18 Houston-based companies, fed by its continually booming population. They were headquartered in soaring office towers that regularly reshaped the downtown skyline. Houston had 37 skyscrapers taller than 150 meters, or 492 feet, the 29th most of any city in the world, tied with Abu Dhabi, Moscow, and Mumbai. Two more were under construction.

Houston grew not just up, but out. There were no geographical barriers to stop its sprawl, just flat coastal plain, and, unusually for a major city, no zoning laws to hinder it. The city covered 350 square miles in 1960, but by 2017 it had annexed enough adjacent communities to expand to 655 square miles, enough land to fit all of Baltimore, Chicago, Detroit, and Philadelphia within it. You could get in your car at Houston's southwestern border, point it northeast, set your cruise control to 60, and remain in Houston an hour later.

All that unfettered expansion, driven by the city's entrepreneurial spirit, had required the concreting over of wetlands, such as those on which the Judge had once built the Astrodome. Most of Houston sits on a clay-heavy soil called black gumbo, which experts consider one of the least absorbent soil types. When it rained, especially heavily, the water had nowhere to go. Neither did the people, the majority of whom, as in even the richest of cities, spent the sunniest of days trying to get by.

On August 26, 2017—a Saturday—it began raining, and it didn't stop.

Dallas Keuchel was thinking about getting in bed early. It was 10:30 p.m. central time on August 31, 2017, near the end of a week that had been taxing for him and the Astros but devastating for many others in Houston. Hours earlier, Keuchel and his teammates had peered down from the portals of the Astros' plane upon the outskirts of a city whose landscape they barely recognized. Where there had once been neighborhoods, there were now wreckage-strewn lakes dotted with rescue boats. Exhausted, and finally home, Keuchel sat down to unwind as he usually did late at night, with a video game controller in his hand. Then his phone started to vibrate.

Keuchel looked at the screen. *Shit, I'd better answer this,* he thought. *It's the Big Dog.*

Exactly a month earlier, on July 31, Keuchel had been furious with the Big Dog—that was Jim Crane—as well as Jeff Luhnow and everyone else in the Astros' front office. As the non-waiver trade deadline approached, Keuchel watched as his club's rivals loaded up with new aces to bolster their rosters for playoff runs, even though it meant coughing up top prospects to acquire them. The Dodgers traded for Yu Darvish. The Cubs added José Quintana. The Yankees got Sonny Gray. The Astros, meanwhile, had secured only Francisco Liriano, a bullpen arm who might be able to get some left-handed hitters out here and there.

"Disappointment is a little bit of an understatement," Keuchel, the top starter on a first-place team, told reporters. He did so for two reasons. One was that he was being honest. It was how he felt. He and his teammates, particularly José Altuve and George Springer, hadn't endured what they'd endured—the Butt Slide, the losing streaks—only to have management come up one piece short of building a champion. The second was that although the trade deadline had passed, he knew Luhnow had one more way to add that final piece, and he wanted the general manager to feel the players' longing for it.

As August progressed, Luhnow felt it. He figured his scuffling offense would rebound once Correa, Gattis, McCann, and Springer got healthy, but his pitching rotation had fallen apart, too, and even the return of McCullers—who was nursing a sore back—wouldn't be enough to rejuvenate it. In August, his starting staff pitched to an ERA of 4.83, a spike of nearly a run per game from the season's first four months. Only Collin McHugh registered an ERA of less than 4.20. Keuchel, working his way back from neck discomfort, allowed 20 earned runs in 35^2/$_3$ innings, for an ERA of 5.05. Mike Fiers, the number five starter, was even worse, yielding 27 in 32^2/$_3$, for an ERA of 7.44. If the Astros had any hope of playing deep into the playoffs, the rotation needed the boost Luhnow hadn't given it.

The month of August, though, offers a reprieve to general managers who miss the trade deadline at the end of July. Players can still change hands, with limitations, through August 31 and remain eligible for postseason play, making that one of the most important dates on the baseball calendar. Players could be traded in August as long as they had first been placed on revocable waivers, which meant that they and their contracts could be claimed by any of the league's other 29 teams, essentially in reverse order of their win-loss records.

Putting a player on revocable waivers carries little risk for the club that employs him. If he is claimed by a rival, the club has three options: It can pull him back, and keep him for at least the rest of the season. It can work out a trade for him with the team that claimed him. The third option explains why many highly compensated players pass through waivers entirely, which means they are free to be traded to anyone until the arrival of September: The club that owns him can decide to simply let him go and put the claiming club on the hook for his exorbitant salary, a significant financial risk. But at the stroke of midnight eastern time, all those options evaporated. Playoff-bound clubs had no choice but to move forward with who they already had.

Even before Luhnow had emerged from the July trade deadline with only Francisco Liriano, he and the Astros had earned a reputation among baseball's other general managers. "They don't give up anything in deals," one griped.

That wasn't exactly true. While Luhnow had spent his first three summers in Houston as a deadline seller, methodically trading away all his club's veteran assets for prospects, he reversed course when the Astros proved a surprising contender in 2015. That July, he worked out a deal for Cole Hamels, only to see it fall apart when the Phillies' ace invoked a clause in his contract that allowed him to block trades to nine teams, including the recently toxic Astros. Hamels ended up with the Rangers. Luhnow still acquired three major league players—starter Scott Kazmir from the A's, and Fiers and center fielder Carlos Gómez from the Brewers—in exchange for a total of six minor leaguers.

Those trades hadn't worked out. Despite their new talent, the Astros still washed out of the playoffs that year against the Royals, and all they had to show for it was a half dozen fewer minor leaguers, four of them Top 100 prospects. Now, in 2017, they were contending again, yet this time Luhnow had added only Liriano. He could easily rationalize why. As July's non-waivers trade deadline approached, he'd had conversations with every general manager who might have a pitcher to sell. He had even struck a deal for Zach Britton, the Baltimore Orioles' All-Star closer, only to see the Orioles pull the plug at the last moment. It was a letdown, but Luhnow knew that a subsequent trade made out of emotion, even desperation, would have likely been a bad one. From a valuation perspective, most deadline deals were ill-advised.

His goal had always been to build not just a one-time winner, but a sustainable one. Talented prospects, who could continually replenish his roster at sub-market wages, were key to that effort. Sig's algorithms almost always advised against deadline trades, which required the sacrificing of years of cheap production for, sometimes, a couple of months of starts from an expensive and aging pitcher.

"The reality is that any economic modeling which includes projections is not going to like a deadline deal, where you're trading what could be an enormous amount of future value for a decent amount of present value," Luhnow said. "The question all general managers have to grapple with is, how much of a deficit can you take on one deal? No, the math does not support these types of deals. It's a matter of using your best judgment."

Luhnow's judgment had changed in the month since the non-waiver trade deadline, due to a few developments for which no algorithm could account. His inaction in July demoralized not only Keuchel but the entire clubhouse, which surely combined with the injuries the club sustained, like Carlos Correa's damaged thumb, to lead to its August swoon. By the month's end, the Astros remained a lock to win the American League West and reach the playoffs. They were 80–53, with an 11.5-game lead in the division. But they no longer seemed likely to advance far in an October that had once held so much promise. "Things were pretty bleak," Luhnow said.

They were bleaker in the Astros' hometown, which needed any cause for optimism that it could get. Even the all-green Jim Crane was willing to pay for that boost. Hurricane Harvey, with its 130-mile-per-hour winds and five feet of rain, had by then slowly swept through Houston, routing more than 30,000 people from their homes and causing what would prove to be $150 billion in damage. While all the Astros' players and employees had been miraculously spared Harvey's wrath, as had Minute Maid Park, Crane told Luhnow that it was the club's duty to do something big, to provide some measure of hope for the now battered city in which he had made his fortune.

By 10:30 p.m. central on August 31, half an hour before the waivers trade deadline, Luhnow had come close. He had agreed to trade for a player who had not only passed through waivers unclaimed, due to his enormous salary, but who would represent the season's most significant acquisition, bigger than José Quintana or Sonny Gray, bigger than even Yu Darvish: Justin Verlander, the longtime ace of the Detroit Tigers. Darvish, Gray, and Quintana were all frontline starters. Verlander was a future Hall of Famer.

That was the first piece of information the Big Dog passed along when he called Keuchel. The second was that Verlander's contract included a full no-trade clause, meaning that he could not be officially dealt unless he agreed to it. Would Keuchel phone Verlander and convince him of the charms of both the Astros and of Houston?

"Hell yeah, I will," Keuchel said, before remembering whom he was talking to. "Sir."

////////////

SIX DAYS EARLIER, on August 25, Luhnow had left Houston with his wife, Gina, and their three-year-old son, Henry, to accompany his club on what was supposed to be a quick three-game road trip to play the Los Angeles Angels in Anaheim. Luhnow always brought his family on trips to California. Gina grew up on the West Coast and her parents still lived there. As forecasters were predicting Harvey to make landfall in Texas as soon as that evening and churn a course toward Houston, Luhnow had taken several precautions before he left. He moved his family's furniture to the second story of their house near Rice University, and positioned a few webcams so he could remotely monitor his property for potential flooding. Luhnow and his family stayed with Gina's parents, in west Los Angeles, but he intended to return to Houston to hunker down with his front office in order to focus on the final days before the August 31 trade deadline. He knew it might prove the most significant of his six years as the Astros' general manager.

Luhnow first talked with Al Avila, the general manager of the Tigers, about Justin Verlander in July, but they hadn't come close to a trade. As the Astros scuffled in August, the 34-year-old Verlander had shaken off a rocky first four months and recaptured his old dominance. Over 42 innings he went 4–1, with a 2.36 ERA and 50 strikeouts. Those numbers came over a small sample size of starts, but might have been almost commensurate with his contract, which called for him to earn $28 million in 2018 and $28 million more in 2019, making him one of the eight highest-paid players in the sport.

Justin Verlander in 2011, when he won both
the American League Cy Young and MVP Awards.

As August progressed, Luhnow and Avila exchanged dozens of permutations of potential deals. In Luhnow's mind, the odds of his acquiring Verlander fluctuated from as high as 70 percent to as low as five percent. By the month's last week, he felt his chances were good as long as he was able to make it back to Houston for final consultations with his assistants, scouts, analysts, and medical staff. As it did for so many Houstonians, in ways far more tragic, Harvey's direct hit dashed his plans.

While his webcams revealed his property had escaped damage, Luhnow couldn't get to Houston. The airports were closed. So, as his club flew across the country to play a series against the Rangers that had been hastily relocated to the Tampa Bay Rays' home ballpark in St. Petersburg, Luhnow stayed behind in California to attempt to negotiate with Avila from one of the only spots in his in-laws' house that received cell service: their dining room table.

As Henry and two of his young cousins ran screaming circles around him, Luhnow, in shorts and a T-shirt, tried to clarify to the household what he was up to. "It took me a while to explain to my in-laws that there are kind of *two* trading deadlines," he said. He did his best to keep in touch with Avila. By the morning of August 31, he determined the probability of reaching an agreement to be at a low ebb. Verlander's contract was simply too expensive, and the prospects the Tigers kept asking him for had too much value. Despite the Astros' recent play, and Crane's encouragement, he felt as if it would likely turn out to be in the club's best long-term interests to move forward without Verlander. So he felt comfortable scheduling other activities for later in the day, even though the deadline would be approaching. He agreed to attend and speak at his 11-year-old nephew's baseball practice, and then planned to go on a dinner date with Gina.

Gina was Luhnow's second wife. He had gotten divorced from his first in 2009, when their two children, Elizabeth and Jeffrey, were in grade school. It was the same year he had assembled one of history's best draft classes as the Cardinals' scouting director, but he knew his single-minded focus on finding players like Shelby Miller, Joe Kelly, Matt Carpenter, Trevor Rosenthal, and Matt Adams had come at a personal cost. "Baseball is tough on marriages, there's no question about it," he said. "The roles I had in St. Louis were intense travel roles. I would imagine the divorce rate in baseball among players and scouts is higher than in the general population." His older children frequently attended Astros games with him and he maintained a cordial relationship with their mother, who eventually moved from St. Louis to Houston. But he wanted his relationship with Gina, whom he married in February 2012—two months after he became the Astros' general manager—to be different. He would bring her and Henry along on road trips as often as he could, and he would honor commitments he made to them, even if they happened to coincide with the busiest days on baseball's calendar.

At 5:30 p.m. Pacific, three and a half hours before the deadline, Luhnow arrived at his nephew's San Fernando Valley ball field, the same one on which the 1976 movie *The Bad News Bears* had been filmed. As he approached the diamond, his cell phone rang. It was Avila.

The potential for a Verlander trade was not only back on, but higher than it had been over the preceding two months. The Tigers, after dealing slugger Justin Upton to the Angels for two minor leaguers earlier in the day, were now fully committed to a rebuild. That meant they were motivated to convert Verlander into prospects, too.

Still, Luhnow had a promise to keep. As his mind raced, he addressed 15 rapt middle schoolers and their coaches about the importance of practice, and of maintaining a growth mindset. "Carlos Beltrán, he's forty years old and the most accomplished player on the team," he told them. "But he watches video every day to figure out how to make his swing better." When practice concluded, he raced back to his in-laws' house.

He got there at 7:45 p.m., 75 minutes before the deadline, to find a living room full of producers. He had forgotten that Gina's parents, who were in the movie business, were hosting a dinner party that night. After a hurried explanation—*two deadlines!*—he rushed upstairs to take what he intended to be the fastest shower of his life, to clean up for his and Gina's date.

With the water running, his phone, which unexpectedly had found a signal, rang again. The Tigers would agree to pay $8 million per year of the salary Verlander was still owed, leaving Crane on the hook for $20 million per annum. That was a lot, but Crane could stomach it. Additionally, the deal no longer had to center upon one of the Astros' very best prospects, the pitchers Forrest Whitley and Francis Martes and the outfielder Kyle Tucker. Avila still insisted on a trio of minor leaguers with whom Sig's metrics indicated Luhnow should not part. They were outfielder Daz Cameron, the son of former major leaguer Mike Cameron; catcher Jake Rogers; and, crucially, starter Franklin Pérez, whom Astros international scouting director Oz Ocampo had signed for a $1 million bonus in 2014 after having camped out in Venezuela for a week. Luhnow had previously refused to discuss the six-foot-three, 197-pound pitcher's name in any other deal.

Those were Avila's final terms, and he had a negotiating advantage over Luhnow: Avila had no deadline. "We genuinely, absolutely love Justin Verlander, and there was a part of us that wanted him to stay here and finish his career," Avila said.

The Havana-born Avila, who was 59, had been a baseball executive for a quarter century, starting as the Florida Marlins' assistant director of Latin American operations in 1992. He was the Tigers' assistant general manager when the club drafted Verlander in 2004, and watched as he and slugger Miguel Cabrera—whom he had helped the Marlins sign out of Venezuela when Cabrera was a teenager—led Detroit to four playoff appearances. Those included World Series defeats in 2006, to Luhnow and Sig's Cardinals, and in 2012 to the San Francisco Giants. The Tigers' success under Avila's predecessor and longtime boss, Dave Dombrowski, had led them to lag behind the data revolution. When Avila took over from the fired Dombrowski in August 2015, a dozen years after the publication of *Moneyball*, the Tigers' analytics department still consisted of exactly one employee. Avila committed to bolstering their analytics operation, hiring, among others, a former Apple executive. By 2017, the club's first internal database, called Caesar, had only just come online, and their farm system reflected that. While five of *Baseball America*'s preseason Top 100 prospects were Astros—including Franklin Pérez, at number 54—just one was a Tiger.

Avila knew his rebuilding effort, which was likely to take several years, required prospects, but he could always trade Verlander for them later. He figured Luhnow needed Verlander now. "Those are the three guys," Avila told Luhnow, referring to Pérez, Cameron, and Rogers. As the bathroom's mirror steamed over, Luhnow agreed to let them go. For the first time since the executives had begun negotiating in July, they had the parameters of a deal in place. There was just one problem.

"Have you talked to Justin?" Luhnow asked Avila.

Luhnow had heard that Verlander only wanted to go to the Cubs, Dodgers, or Yankees, and perhaps not anywhere. His no-trade clause meant the deal's viability came down to his decision.

After his shower, Luhnow went back downstairs to reclaim his critical spot at the dining table, which was now set for Gina's parents' dinner party. He had to ensure that everything from the Astros' side, every form and medical approval, was in place in the event that Verlander said yes. Avila called at 8:35 p.m. with 25 minutes remaining on the deadline clock. "Justin has not approved the deal," he said. "It's not clear which direction that's going to go."

Over the next 20 minutes, the dinner guests began filling their plates with food from the kitchen buffet and settling in around Luhnow. "We've got four minutes left!" he shouted into his phone to his staff, drawing quizzical glances from the diners. "We've got to do this now!"

By nine p.m.—midnight eastern time, the deadline—Luhnow still didn't know if Verlander had agreed to become an Astro. He did the only sensible thing. He went on his date with Gina. As he sat down with her at a nearby restaurant, his hands were still shaking. He ordered a Tito's vodka and soda, with lime. Then he thought better of it, and made it a double.

//////////

JUSTIN VERLANDER also went on a date on the night of August 31. Just before 11:30 p.m. eastern, as Luhnow was entrenched at his in-laws' dining table in Los Angeles, Verlander and his fiancée, Kate Upton, were walking back from a late dinner to the apartment they shared in a suburb northwest of Detroit. Verlander had first met Upton, the part-time actress and full-time supermodel, when they appeared together in a commercial for the video game *MLB 2K12*. He was 28 and she was 19, but they hit it off. Six years later, as they strolled home from the res-

Justin Verlander and his fiancée, Kate Upton.

taurant, they chatted about how they hoped the day of their wedding, which was to be held in Italy in early November, would prove as temperate as this one. To Verlander there was nothing so beautiful, aside from Upton, as a Michigan summer. He would know. It was his 13th.

Verlander grew up in the small town of Goochland, Virginia. He could always throw hard. One day, when he was in 10th grade, he was short the 50 cents he needed to buy a chocolate milk. His best friend, Daniel Hicks, had two quarters. He sized up Verlander's right arm, which could already propel a baseball at 90 miles per hour. Hicks handed the coins over on one condition. He drew up a contract on a napkin: "I, Justin Verlander, promise to give Daniel Hicks 0.1 percent of my signing bonus if I sign a pro baseball contract." Verlander signed it. By 2004, Verlander had grown to six foot five and could throw faster than 100, and the Tigers picked him second overall out of Old Dominion. They gave him a signing bonus of $3.12 million. "Was a chocolate milk worth three thousand dollars?" Verlander asked. "I want to say yes. I was parched." He made his big league debut just a year later, his first taste of a summer in Detroit. In 2006, he joined the Tigers' rotation for good, and ran away with the American League Rookie of the Year Award. Hicks never cashed the check Verlander dutifully wrote out to him.

Over his first five seasons with the Tigers, Verlander proved a prototypical power pitcher, one who could regularly exceed 200 innings, strike out around 200 batters, and finish with an earned run average in the mid-threes. He became a favorite of Tigers owner Mike Ilitch, the aging founder of Little Caesars, who was known around his hometown as Mr. I. In 2010, just before Verlander turned 27, the 80-year-old Ilitch signed his young ace to a five-year contract extension worth $80 million. By the next season, it appeared as if Mr. I had gotten a discount that was better than those he gave his pizza customers.

Verlander's average fastball velocity dropped in 2011, to 95.6 miles per hour, but that was by design. He was so in command of his arsenal, which also included a changeup, curveball, and slider, and so certain of how each opponent would try to hit it that he no longer had to throw his hardest from the first pitch. His fastball rarely topped 92 in the early innings, as he saved his 102-mile-per-hour heat for when he would need it later on.

A list of the results of Verlander's starts that season looked like the product of someone's attempts to type a web address using a keyboard with sticky keys. *WWWWWWW*, read his game log from May 29 to June 30. *WWWWWWWWWW*, it read from July 21 to September 7. The W's stood for wins. He finished 24–5, with a 2.40 ERA and 250 strikeouts in 251 innings. He not only won his first American League Cy Young Award. He also became the first pitcher in 19 years to be elected a league's Most Valuable Player.

"It's hard for me to put a finger on what I know," he said that year. "But it's there. Time. Experience of pitching at this level for a while now. You log it all away, and it opens up a new game to you, almost. You remember a lot of things, and recognize a lot of things." That was how a 28-year-old ace sounded when he had reached his prime, when his competitive intellect had grown to match his physical gifts.

In 2013, Mr. I tore up Verlander's old contract and gave him another, for seven years and $180 million, the most lucrative a pitcher had ever received. It also included the no-trade clause, a relatively rare provision in that it affords players control over something that most employees in other industries take for granted: the city in which they work. Only five dozen or so of the game's top players owned such a clause; the rest could have their lives and families displaced at a moment's notice, without any say in the matter. Neither Mr. I nor Verlander believed Verlander would ever play anywhere but Detroit.

That deal soon appeared less of a bargain than the first. In 2014, Verlander's ERA spiked to 4.54, his strikeout rate plummeted to 6.9 per nine innings, and he didn't throw a single pitch that touched 99 miles per hour. While he understood opposing hitters better than ever, it appeared as if his inevitable physical decline had begun, that his 31-year-old arm had become worn down after the strain of 1,772 major league innings. Though he was too proud to admit it, that wasn't the problem. A few months before the season, he'd had surgery to repair two sports hernias and to reattach an adductor muscle. He was still recovering. "I still threw two hundred innings, and every single one of them hurt," he said. "I'm not going to tell anybody that I'm dying out there."

He returned to form in 2015, and in 2016 he finished a close second in Cy Young balloting to the Red Sox' Rick Porcello, even though he topped Porcello in ERA, Wins Above Replacement, innings, and strikeout rate, and had more first-place votes, too. Many thought he'd been robbed, chief among them the person who had become the most emotionally invested in his career. Tweeted Kate Upton, "Hey @MLB I thought I was the only one allowed to fuck @JustinVerlander?!"

After an inconsistent start to 2017, by late summer Verlander had again rebounded to show that, even at 34, he was far from done. On August 30, he'd allowed one run over six innings against the Colorado Rockies to bring his ERA down to 3.82, and he was the constant in a season of change in Detroit. Mr. I had died in February, at 87, Cabrera's production had severely diminished from his own MVP standards, and the Tigers were on pace for their worst record of Verlander's 13 seasons. Even after Avila traded Justin Upton earlier in the day, suggesting the team was about to launch into a rebuilding effort, Verlander figured he might stick around to see it through, for at least two more years, in the city that he and his fiancée had adopted as their home. He had his no-trade clause, and as the couple walked home from dinner, they figured there was no way he would have cause to invoke it, at least not in 2017.

While he had mentioned to Avila the Yankees, Dodgers, and Cubs as destinations he'd consider, that was primarily because he figured those were the teams that could afford his contract. He hadn't much thought about whether he would ultimately be willing to go anywhere at all. He always imagined he'd be afforded at least a day to make a decision, and just a few hours earlier, Avila had texted to say he had nothing in the works. What could possibly happen with just a half hour to go before the deadline?

Then Verlander's phone rang. It was Avila. They had a deal in place with Houston. Verlander had until midnight to choose whether he would accept it—but it would ideally be a few minutes earlier than that, or else they wouldn't have time to submit the paperwork to the commissioner's office. "All of a sudden," Verlander said, "I have to decide whether to uproot my life, our life, in a thirty-minute window."

Verlander and Kate Upton jogged the rest of the way home. He had so many people to call: his agent, his family. His phone rang again: an Oklahoma number. It was Keuchel, whom he had only previously met in passing. "There's one thing you're missing," Keuchel told him. "That's a World Series ring. You're not going to regret your decision to come here, if you do."

"I'd really like to chat more, but I don't have much time," Verlander said. But Keuchel's message, about how he wouldn't have any regrets? That resonated.

At 11:45, Verlander and Upton came to a new realization. They were deciding whether to move to a city that had just been slammed by a hurricane. "Holy crap, we don't know what the situation is down there," Verlander said. "I don't even think we can fly in there right now. Will we even be able to find anywhere to live?"

Verlander was now pacing back and forth through his living room with his eyes closed, as Upton sat on the couch. Although she was only 25, she had already spent more than six years beneath the international spotlight. She first appeared in the *Sports Illustrated* Swimsuit Issue at 18, and she was savvy about the best way to make career decisions. "Trust your instincts," Upton said.

"Trust your instincts, trust your instincts," Verlander repeated. "But what the hell are they telling me?" Then he stopped and looked at his fiancée. His heart was attached to Detroit, but his gut told him something else. He wanted to win. "Screw it," he said. "We're going to Houston."

"Hell yeah," Upton shouted.

He called Avila with his decision, and also a concern. With midnight just minutes away, how was he going to sign the document that would officially waive his no-trade clause? Avila had that covered. As he often did on the night of important deadlines, the general manager had invited his front office to his house to enjoy his wife's cooking: seafood with rice, and beef filets. When his talks with Houston intensified, and it appeared that Luhnow was finally willing to give up Franklin Pérez, Avila had dispatched two of his executives to drive the three miles to Verlander's apartment building and wait outside with the necessary form, just in case. They were sitting out there right now.

Verlander and Upton raced out their door in their pajamas. They pressed the button to the elevator, but then they thought better of it. The elevator was slow, and what if it stalled? They sprinted down four flights of stairs and let the two men into their building. Verlander signed his name. The men took an iPhone photo of the document and emailed it to the league office in New York. They thought they'd pressed send a few seconds before midnight, but had the file been slow to upload? They couldn't be sure.

/////////

OUT IN LOS ANGELES, Jeff Luhnow was trying to enjoy his dinner with Gina, which meant not looking at his phone. Finally, at 9:14 p.m. Pacific, 14 minutes past the deadline, it buzzed. It was the commissioner's office. This was it.

"The deal's been approved," the executive said. "But, Jeff? Don't ever put me through that again. We received final verification from Verlander at 11:59 and 58 seconds."

Luhnow took a long pull from his Tito's and soda. With two seconds to spare, he'd gotten his man. But what did that mean? By sacrificing 18 controllable future years of cheap young talent for two years of an expensive veteran, had he saved the Astros' season and given his city a modest reason to hope again? Or had he done what he had long ago vowed to never do: hit a 20 against a 10, aiming, however improbably, for a 21?

None of his players harbored similar doubts. Carlos Correa was in a motel room in Frisco, Texas, that reeked of urine. That's the type of lodging you get in Double-A, where the shortstop was in the final stages of rehabbing his thumb. He finally had a girlfriend: Daniella Rodriguez, whom he had met when she threw out the first pitch at an Astros game in August 2016, in her role as Miss Texas USA. Despite her crown, Rodriguez didn't mind sitting with Correa as he played *FIFA* soccer on PlayStation 4, and she didn't even mind the room's aroma. "She's stayed in worse places," Correa said.

Correa looked at his phone and gleefully threw his PS4 controller across the room, shattering it against the wall. There would be no more *FIFA* that night, but he didn't care. When he finally rejoined the Astros a few days later, he would have a new teammate. Forget his club's record in August, forget his thumb, forget even the hurricane for the moment. "It's on, baby," he said. "It's on."

///////////

TWO OTHER FACTORS CONVINCED LUHNOW to ultimately override Sig's algorithms to acquire Justin Verlander. One was that the Astros' front office suspected its economic models, as sophisticated as they had become, weren't properly assessing Verlander's value. Just before he had signed the document that waived his no-trade clause, Verlander and his agents had squeezed Luhnow into eliminating an option in his contract that would have vested had he finished in the top five of the Cy Young balloting in 2019, and would have locked him in at a $22 million salary for 2020. That would have represented a pay cut for him after a year in which he would by definition have remained among the game's best pitchers, and would also have delayed his entry into the free agent market by a year. But even though the Tigers agreed to pick up $16 million of his salary over the two years that remained, the Astros were still on the hook for $40 million, a sum their metrics indicated would likely prove to be an overpay even for a pitcher like him, especially when factoring in the future value of the prospects they had relinquished.

In the league's current economic climate, however, you couldn't simply buy a pitcher like Verlander for anything close to two years and $40 million on the open market. It was a unique opportunity in a pitching exchange whose specific dynamics Sig knew his probabilistic models weren't accurately capturing. Two winters earlier, a pair of similarly elite, if slightly younger, starters—David Price and Zack Greinke—had earned contracts worth more than $200 million apiece, from the Red Sox and the Diamondbacks, respectively, at average annual values of more than $30 million. Although Verlander was already 35, were he a free agent, he would have likely commanded at least a four-year deal that stretched into nine figures. The opportunity to pay him a sub-market wage for two years had to come with a great deal of unquantifiable surplus value.

The other factor was that the Astros believed Verlander had recently become a superior pitcher to the one he was earlier in the 2017 season, for reasons that extended past his improved results and to his fundamentals. Despite his success, and the generations of financial comfort Mr. I had given him, Verlander had always liked to experiment. Between every start, he sought new ways to stay a step ahead of both opposing hitters who were committed to catching up to him and his advancing age. After the rough first three months of 2017, Verlander knew he had a genuine problem to solve. His slider had long been a dominating pitch for him, a bewildering counterpoint to a fastball that still approached 100 miles per hour. All of a sudden, though, hitters began teeing off on it. Whereas the season before, when he had nearly won the Cy Young, opponents batted just .169 against the pitch, in June 2017 they hit .438 against it. And if they knew they could hit his slider, they could sit back and wait for his fastball. They started hitting those, too.

Verlander wasn't certain why it was happening. His slider felt the same way when it left his hand, but it traveled to the plate faster. It came in at more than 90 miles per hour, on average, meaning it represented less of a change of speeds from his fastball. It also arrived flatter, with less break. He suspected that Major League Baseball had introduced different baseballs, wound tighter and with lower seams, which led to reduced drag and higher velocities. The commissioner's office consistently denied it, but it was the same culprit that many analysts fingered to explain the skyrocketing league-wide home run rate. Verlander knew the baseballs were unlikely to change again. That meant that he had to.

He began tinkering. He gripped his slider farther back in his hand, and slightly adjusted the position of his wrist, to impart more downward movement on it. On June 21, he struck out 11 Seattle Mariners in just 5²/₃ innings. "I was giddy about it," he said. "I came home and told Kate right away: 'I found it.'"

By what would prove to be his last start with the Tigers, those six innings in which he yielded one run against the Rockies, the average velocity of his slider had dropped to just over 86 miles per hour, and he had gained three extra inches of vertical break. Opponents were swinging over his slider again. They hit just .196 against it in August. Major league bats, after all, were by rule allowed to be no more than 2.61 inches thick.

When Verlander arrived in Houston, the members of the Nerd Cave—especially Mike Fast—had been assiduously analyzing each of his starts, via video and Statcast, for months. They were dying to ask him one question, though they didn't want to come on too strong. "By the way," they asked, "did you change your grip, or something?"

Verlander was stunned. From afar, the Astros had followed his tinkering every step of the way. While he had solved the problem on his own, the Nerd Cave would soon reveal to him a world of data, to help guide future refinements, that he'd never had with the Tigers. As much as he missed Detroit, and Michigan summers, he knew right then that his instincts hadn't led him astray.

Luhnow hoped that *his* hadn't, either. He had watched as his competitors had added new aces and declined to deliver a counterpunch that his data suggested would be unwise. His models remained inconclusive about Verlander, but those couldn't fully account for the specific exigencies of the Astros' circumstances, including their terrible, morale-sapping August and, least of all, a hurricane. In the end, he had relied on what would always be the ultimate tiebreaker: his gut.

///////////

As Harvey pummeled Houston, the Astros kept playing, though their minds were elsewhere. José Altuve, for instance, had brought his wife, Nina, along with him on what was supposed to be a quick trip to California, but had left their 10-month-old daughter back in Houston with his parents. While they safely endured the storm, the uncertainty that remained in its aftermath was unbearable for Altuve, and all the Astros, especially during their bizarre three-game set against the Rangers in Florida.

Hurricane Harvey dumped 50 inches of rain on Houston in late August 2017.

Almost no one showed up for their relocated games in the dusty, echoing Tropicana Field in St. Petersburg. The Astros might as well not have been there for the series, either. They lost its first game 12–2. They lost its second game 8–1. While they somehow won the finale, in front of a crowd of 3,385 mostly geriatric curiosity seekers, they couldn't wait to fly the 1,000 miles back to Houston. "We haven't been playing our best in this series, and now we get on a plane and get home," said A.J. Hinch. "It's the best news of the day." The city had changed in their absence. The Astros were changed, too, and not only in composition.

On September 1, an off day, the Astros fanned out over Houston, contributing to relief efforts. Keuchel served food to police officers. Lance McCullers, an animal lover, volunteered at an animal shelter. Altuve, who had already pledged $30,000 to the city's recovery and secured a donation of $25,000 worth of sneakers from one of his sponsors, led a contingent of 16 Astros players and staff members to the George R. Brown Convention Center, which stood two blocks from Minute Maid Park and housed more than 9,000 evacuees. For nearly two hours they posed for pictures, signed autographs, played with children, and distributed supplies. "I feel like I owe Houston something, after all they have done for me," Altuve said.

On September 2, wearing patches over their hearts that read H STRONG, for Houston Strong, they whipped the Mets in both ends of a doubleheader. It was six and a half hours of emotional baseball, each game attended by more than 30,000 fans who had made their way to the ballpark, at least 5,000 of whom had come on tickets donated by the Astros to the mayor's office. Thousands more watched in shelters, or on televisions powered by generators in their wrecked homes. "We wear this patch on our jersey the rest of the year to represent you," Hinch told the crowd in an address before Game 1. "Stay strong, be strong, and we appreciate every one of you."

On September 3, Correa finally returned from the disabled list. The Astros won again. On September 4, in Seattle, they won once more, behind $7^2/_3$ innings of two-run ball from Keuchel.

Verlander made his Astros debut on September 5. With his new slider and old fastball, he struck out seven Mariners over six innings, allowing just one earned run in another win for Houston. Verlander won all five of his September starts for his new team, yielding a total of four earned runs for an ERA of 1.06. "He is the most prepared pitcher I've ever been around," marveled even Carlos Beltrán, who had shared clubhouses with hundreds of them.

As recently as two seconds before the onset of September, the Astros had been adrift. Now, restocked and replenished and with a new rallying cry—Houston Strong—they were virtually unstoppable. They finished out the season by going 21–8, winning 10 of their 12 games in Minute Maid Park. Their last victory was their 101st of the year. In a three-game series against the Rangers near the end of the month, just four weeks after their in-state rival had deepened their demoralization in Florida, they outscored Texas by a total of 37–7, winning each game by at least nine runs. As October's playoffs approached, they were often not just beating teams. They were blowing them out.

Jeff Luhnow couldn't help but reflect on the untold thousands of decisions he and his front office had made that culminated with his August 31 scramble around Los Angeles. Not every decision had proven correct, but each of them had mattered, and each could have catalyzed a chain reaction that could have resulted in a very different September. Luck played its role. Luhnow likely would not have ended up with Justin Verlander had the Orioles not pulled out of the Zach Britton trade. But had he succumbed to calls from the fans, the media, rival general managers, and even Dallas Keuchel to loosen his grip on his top prospects in July in order to keep up with the Cubs and Dodgers and Yankees, he likely wouldn't have ended up with Verlander, at least not at the moment the Astros needed him most. You could only make each decision once.

"It's amazing how these things work out," Luhnow said. "Even though the month of August was painful, and we went into a tailspin, I don't think there could have been a better outcome had we made a move earlier."

As Verlander completed a September that fell into the 99th

percentile of the Nerd Cave's projected outcomes, and as the Astros shifted their sights to the playoffs, Luhnow also often thought of one of the last things Al Avila had said to him in the final hour of August 31: "Justin Verlander's going to get you to the World Series, and you're going to win it." That was the Astros' plan, best laid as it was.

9

THE SERIES

Sig Mejdal hated the World Series. He loved it, of course. It was the whole point, the simulated goal when he had spent his boyhood flicking the spinners of All-Star Baseball, the real one as he endlessly tweaked his models during all those late nights above his fraternity brother's garage. Intellectually, though, he hated it. Baseball wasn't a game like basketball, in which the best team—the Golden State Warriors, say—could reliably defeat almost any opponent at least 80 percent of the time. Baseball excellence could be judged only over the long term, and yet its annual champion, the club that history would remember, was decided after a series of no more than seven games. Any major league team could beat any opponent four times out of seven. "I wish it was a 162-game series, instead of seven," Sig said. "But it's seven. In every game, you have somewhere between a forty-two to fifty-eight percent chance of winning. Which is very close to a fifty percent chance. Which is a coin toss. The World Series is a coin toss competition."

That was especially true against an opponent like the Los Angeles Dodgers, who had just as much talent as the Astros did, and significantly more resources. The Dodgers won a league-best 104 games during the 2017 regular season behind a league-high payroll of $265 million, more than 70 percent above the Astros' $150 million. They had lost just one game in the playoffs' first two rounds, rolling through J.D. Martinez's Diamondbacks and then through the defending World Series champions, Theo Epstein's Cubs. The Dodgers also had all the Astros' analytical firepower. Their team president, the former Wall Street analyst Andrew Friedman, had previously turned the low-budget Tampa Bay Rays into a consistent contender. Their general manager, an economics PhD named Farhan Zaidi, had spent a decade apprenticing under Billy Beane in Oakland. Their own Nerd Cave was so large that it occupied the room in Dodger Stadium that had formerly served as the visitors' clubhouse. So they could not only find and develop previously undervalued assets—like leadoff man Chris Taylor, a castoff who had, like Martinez, trained with Craig Wallenbrock and Robert Van Scoyoc and become a slugger—but simply pay for appropriately valued ones. Clayton Kershaw, their ace, made more than $35 million in 2017 by himself.

In a short series, few of those macroeconomic advantages were significant. While the organizations had selected players who might succeed when it mattered most, and equipped them with every tool to do so, the outcome was now in the hands of the players themselves. That was why Jeff Luhnow stayed calm, almost Zen-like, no matter what was happening on the field. "You've done everything you can do as a GM," he said. "The decisions you make during the postseason are not going to impact the outcome too much. You just have to sit back and watch it, and appreciate it for what it is."

Once the future Sig had devoted his career to predicting finally arrived, he tried to intellectualize the experience, too. He calculated the Astros' chance of winning each game and then the resulting probability that they would win the series. That was mostly an attempt to distract himself from his emotions as he watched the playoffs. "It's excruciating," he said. "I'm a human being who wants to make good decisions, not Mr. Spock." One thing Sig didn't need to gauge was his heart rate. He could feel the organ pounding in his chest all October long. *Is this how somebody has a heart attack?* he asked himself. When he sat in the stands, and not in the Astros' front office's private box, concerned fans watched, horrified, as Sig chewed on the terry-cloth rally towels the clubs distributed to spectators. "Is he all right?" they whispered to the placid Luhnow.

That was relative. Not really, but he was doing better than he would have been had the Astros not reached the World Series at all, as had nearly happened.

//////////

SIG'S TOWELS STAYED RELATIVELY DRY during the Astros' best-of-five American League Divisional Series against the Boston Red Sox, during which they continued their dominant play from September. José Altuve began October by slugging three home runs in Game 1 alone, an 8–2 rout, and the Astros won Game 2 by the same lopsided score. Though they lost Game 3—the winning pitcher was one the Red Sox had acquired from the Cardinals three years before, a diminutive fireballer named Joe Kelly—the Astros then closed out a three-games-to-one series victory just four days after it started. That clinching win was due to a contribution from a now unlikely source: Carlos Beltrán, who had finished the regular season batting a career-low .231, with just 14 homers and 51 RBIs. By October, the 40-year-old had become not just a designated hitter, but a part-time one. Thirteen years after his record-setting first postseason with Houston, he started most games of his second one on the bench—or, usually, watching video in the clubhouse—waiting for a chance to pinch hit. He made the most of one of those opportunities in the top of the ninth inning of Game 4, lacing a curveball from Red Sox closer Craig Kimbrel to deep left to drive in the series-winning run. "I just knew he was going to have a big hit for us in the postseason," Jeff Luhnow said of that double.

At first, the American League Championship Series appeared as if it might be as smooth a ride. Behind stellar home starts from Dallas Keuchel and Justin Verlander, the Astros earned a pair of 2–1 victories over the Yankees to take another two-games-to-none series lead. Over Verlander's first three postseason appearances against the Red Sox and Yankees, two as a starter and one from the bullpen, he continued the renaissance he had begun in his final days in Detroit and carried through the end of the regular season in Houston. He won all three outings, with a 2.04 ERA and 16 strikeouts in $17^2/_3$ innings.

In New York, though, the Astros went cold. The Yankees pummeled them for three straight games, outscoring them 19–5. Aaron Judge slugged two homers and by himself drove in more runs, six, than the Astros scored. Minutes after the third of those losses, a 5–0 shutout that put them one loss from elimination, Beltrán entered the visitors' clubhouse at Yankee Stadium and encountered something he never before had after any of his team's 171 games in 2017, even after the 65 that had turned out to be losses: silence.

Though there were no boxing belts to be awarded, after every other defeat Beltrán's teammates had sat in their lockers and faced the room, chattering in English and Spanish and Spanglish, ready to reverse their fortunes the next night. Now he saw 24 hunched backs. "Close the doors," he told the clubhouse attendant.

Beltrán stood in front of his locker and addressed the team. "Guys, this is simple," he said, in a calm and measured voice, as each of his teammates turned around. "The first two games, we took care of business at home. When we came here, I know nobody, not even myself, was expecting to lose three games in a row. But in order for the Yankees to survive the series, this was what they needed to do. Now we go home. We're going to play in front of our crowd. We took the first two games of the series there. We can do it again. We're a good team. And we're going to finish them off at home."

Immediately, the Astros stood up and began packing for Houston. Verlander took care of Game 6, firing seven shutout innings in what would end up a 7–1 romp. "I literally love Justin Verlander," José Altuve gushed to a national audience on Fox afterward, incubating a cottage industry of internet memes and T-shirts that bore the quote.

Game 7 was tighter. By the top of the fifth inning, the Astros held the slimmest of leads, 1–0, and the Yankees were definitively threatening it. New York had Aaron Hicks on first and Greg Bird on third, with one out, when Todd Frazier hit a bouncing ball toward Alex Bregman, the 23-year-old third baseman.

Bregman, though, didn't give a shit that he was playing in his first postseason. He didn't give a shit that he was only 23. He didn't give a shit about pressure. After suffering the embarrassment of failing to sign Brady Aiken, the Astros had turned their focus to Bregman in part because of his skills, but also because their scouts had reported that he really, truly didn't give a shit about anything but winning baseball games. Two and a half years later, he still didn't.

As Bregman charged in from third and Bird began sprinting for home, Sig, sweating in the front office's box, immediately calculated the play's probabilities. The mathematically correct play was to throw to first base. Though it would mean conceding the tying run, it was the safe throw, one with a near 100 percent chance of leading to an out.

But there was another option. Bregman could go home. That would mean delivering a pinpoint throw over Bird's shoulder to the catcher, Brian McCann, and also that McCann would successfully apply a tag and then hold on to the ball. Bregman would essentially have to throw the ball into a cup from 60 feet away. No human being could reliably make a throw like that even while standing still, and Bregman was running in at full speed. Such a throw's chances of success were, maybe, 25 percent. And if it didn't work, then the Yankees would be liable to blow the game open, with two men on, the game tied, and still one out. Sig awaited the throw to first. Then he screamed.

"Pulled out the inner Peyton Manning, and dropped a dime," Bregman explained later, as his teammates doused him with expensive champagne, his reward for nailing the improbable, game-changing throw that Sig had both imagined and feared. "Hey, I felt like I had to go for it. It's Game Seven. You can't hold anything back. Everyone in this clubhouse has big balls." The Yankees never did score that night. Lance McCullers, pitching out of the bullpen, finished off the 4–0 victory by throwing 24 straight curveballs to New York's fastball-hunting sluggers.

The Astros had done precisely what Beltrán promised them they would. They went home, they scored 11 runs and allowed just one, and they beat the Yankees. In the seven-game series, Beltrán had just one hit in 12 at-bats. Even so, the Astros knew they would probably not have advanced past the ALCS without him.

//////////////

It was an hour and a half before the first pitch of Game 2 of the 2017 World Series, and a voice cut through the 100-degree heat on the field at Dodger Stadium, above the din of the slowly arriving fans. *"I be-lieve I can hit,"* it warbled, tremulously riffing on the R&B singer R. Kelly's most inspirational anthem. *"I be-lieve I can hit."*

The voice belonged to George Springer, who stood on the first-base side of home plate, ready to take his first batting practice cuts of the day. During the regular season, Springer had continued to follow an improvement curve that appeared impossible five years earlier, when he indiscriminately whiffed his way through the lower minors. He struck out 111 times—three fewer, in 140 games, than he had in 78 games as a rookie. His strikeout rate of one per 5.7 at-bats put him not just far below Adam Dunn territory, but better than the league median. For A.J. Hinch, there was only one place in the order to bat a player like that, who could ignite an offense with his power and speed and no longer threatened to dampen it with his strikeouts: first. Springer batted leadoff in every game he started.

From the top of the lineup, against the Red Sox, he hit .412, with two doubles and a home run. But against the Yankees in the ALCS, the old George Springer, the one who played too fast, returned. In 26 at-bats from the top of the order, he had just three singles, and he struck out seven times.

The previous night, in Game 1 of the World Series against the Dodgers and the best pitcher of his generation, his slump had deepened. Kershaw, Los Angeles' three-time Cy Young winner, rang up two strikes against Springer in each of his three at-bats against him. Then, each time, Kershaw threw a low fastball, and Springer hacked above it, hitting only hot air. Leading off the ninth inning, Springer could only watch a fifth cutter in a row from Dodgers closer Kenley Jansen sail by him. It was his first four-strikeout game of the season.

Even as Springer struggled that night, Dallas Keuchel matched Kershaw pitch for pitch, until there were two outs in the bottom of the sixth. Before that, each starter had allowed only a solo home run. Then Dodgers third baseman Justin Turner hit a two-run shot off Keuchel. "They had two big swings," said Hinch. "We had one." The Astros lost 3–1 in two hours and 28 minutes, the quickest World Series game in a quarter century.

They needed more big swings, at least successful swings, especially from the very top of the lineup. For many experts outside the Astros' clubhouse, drawing upon eight straight games of evidence, there was above all one thing for the club to do to get them: move Springer out of the leadoff position for Game 2.

One of those experts sat on a sofa in a steamy, faux-wood-paneled trailer parked just beyond Dodger Stadium's center-field wall. If there was anyone who knew about the pressures of hitting in late October, it was David Ortiz. Over three World Series with the Red Sox, all of them wins, Ortiz batted .455, and he was twice named MVP. Now, a year into his retirement, Ortiz had become a rookie member of Fox Sports' pre- and postgame playoff shows. As they planned the beats of their Game 2 shows, and with no cameras nearby, the other panelists—including Frank Thomas, Keith Hernandez, and Alex Rodriguez, Ortiz's longtime rival when Rodriguez played for the Yankees—debated what Hinch should do about Springer. Ortiz, quiet until then, stood up and walked to the center of the room.

"Guys, every man in baseball is replaceable," he said. "You try to win the fucking World Series. You do whatever you need to win the World Series. A-Rod, I remember what Joe Torre once did to Roger Clemens in the second or third inning of the ALCS. He *took him out*. Springer is struggling badly. He's not even hitting his pitch. That is baseball. You gotta keep the line moving. It happened to you, it happened to everyone in baseball. Why not to him? Move him. Somewhere else. He's not helping me as a leadoff man."

Sweat started to bead on his temples, and his voice rose to a shout. "He's trying to hit the ball out of the stadium with *every swing*. All right, let him hit the ball out of the stadium. Meanwhile, *I need someone on base!*"

The only sound in the room was the air conditioner's futile hum. Everyone was thinking the same thing, which was that this must be exactly the type of speech Big Papi had delivered hundreds of times, before big games, at the center of the home clubhouse in Fenway Park. No one, not even Rodriguez, could muster a retort to the king of the postseason walk-off.

The night before, though, Hinch, the Stanford psychology major, had sent a text message to his floundering leadoff hitter. *It's not about the 0-for-4 or the strikeouts,* it read. *It's about you going out and having fun and enjoying the best time of your baseball life, because you never know if you're going to get back here.*

The final say as far as the lineup, as always, belonged to the manager. For Hinch to move Springer down, he would have had to believe a few things. He would have had to believe that the last eight games had more predictive value than the nearly 800 before them, during which Springer had gradually transformed himself from an incorrigible 22-year-old free-swinger in Lancaster to a disciplined

28-year-old All-Star in Houston. He would have had to believe that Springer wasn't just experiencing a small-sample-size slump, consisting of 27 poor outcomes, but that he had fundamentally changed as a hitter. He would, in other words, have had to believe that because he had hit on 16 against a 7 a bunch of times in a row and busted, the next time, he ought to refuse another card.

None of the Astros believed any of those things. Hinch didn't, either.

The next afternoon, not long after Big Papi's soliloquy, Hinch announced his lineup. "George Springer has had way more good days than bad days, and way more good stretches than bad stretches," he explained. "So I'm going to continue to encourage him. He's going to lead off."

When he was done warbling his own version of R. Kelly's paean to possibility, Springer stepped into the cage. "I'm not going to swing hard today," he told Dave Hudgens, the Astros' hitting coach, after he'd nearly driven the ball out of Dodger Stadium with a few easy cuts. "I'm not going to swing hard today," Springer repeated to himself.

Rich Hill, the 37-year-old southpaw for the Dodgers who would start Game 2 against Verlander, owned exactly the type of pitch to prolong Springer's slump: a looping curveball that spun at a rate of nearly 2,800 revolutions per minute. Hill had ridden the pitch to an unlikely comeback from independent ball into the majors when was in his mid-30s, and then, the previous winter, to a three-year, $48 million free agent contract with Los Angeles. To begin the top of the first, Hill threw Springer four straight fastballs, running the count to two balls and two strikes. Everyone knew what he would throw next and, based upon Springer's recent history, what the result was likely to be.

Hill's first curve arrived down and in, darting toward Springer's feet. Springer held off. The next curve tailed in to catch the outside border of home plate. With a controlled swing, Springer flicked it foul. With his seventh pitch, Hill tried a cut fastball, up and away.

Springer held off again. As he trotted to first base, he suppressed a grin. It was only a walk, but what mattered was how the pitches he'd faced had looked to him: slow and manageable again, as they had all year long, right up until Game 1 of the ALCS. And if the game felt slow, then Springer's ability to consistently hit the ball was no longer a matter of belief.

"That walk," Springer said, "changed everything."

//////////

JUSTIN VERLANDER SPENT the second half of Game 2 doing what he always did when he was nervous. It was the same thing he had done in his living room during the waning minutes of August 31, when he and Kate Upton were trying to decide whether to leave Detroit. He paced.

He had allowed just two hits in six innings against the Dodgers, but they were damaging: a solo homer by Joc Pederson in the fifth, and then a two-run bomb by Corey Seager in the sixth. He left the game trailing 3–1. For the first time since he had come to Houston, the box score would not list a *W* next to his name. The Astros were unlikely to emerge with a win, either. The Dodgers were a difficult team against whom to mount a late comeback, due particularly to the looming presence of Jansen, the All-Star closer. In 2017, the Dodgers had finished the eighth inning with a lead in 98 games. They went on to win all 98 of them.

So Verlander paced, his eyes glued to the television in the training room at Dodger Stadium as he watched his teammates try to climb from the hole, shallow but daunting, in which he had put them. He kept at it even after Carlos Correa's eighth-inning single drew the Astros within one run, and even after Marwin González's ninth-inning solo shot off Jansen tied the game at 3–3. When González blasted Jansen's 94-mile-per-hour cutter to center field, even Luhnow lost his Zen-like calm. He leapt from his seat in the Astros' field box, in sync with Sig.

Leading off the top of the tenth, Altuve drove a 97-mile-per-hour fastball from Dodgers reliever Josh Fields over the wall in left center. Two pitches later, Correa lifted a curve from Fields to almost the same spot in the bleachers. In the training room, Verlander heard the fans groan and the old stadium rumble a split second before he saw the reason for it on TV. With the Astros now leading 5–3, Verlander finally stood still, but soon his pacing grew more frantic than ever. The Dodgers tied the game in the bottom of the tenth, on a leadoff homer by Yasiel Puig and a two-out single by Kike Hernández. Verlander experienced a sinking feeling he'd had before.

José Altuve hit .310 with seven home runs in the playoffs.

"It felt like a punch in the gut for me, and I knew that everyone else was feeling the exact same way," he said. Five years earlier, in 2012, his Tigers lost a close Game 2 to the Giants after having dropped Game 1, and they couldn't recover. They were swept. Though he was no longer on the mound, this time he was going to do something to avert a similar fate.

During the break before the top of the 11th, Verlander, wearing a sleeveless undershirt, stormed out of the trainer's room, through the tunnel and up into the entrance of the Astros' dugout. He had a message for his teammates. "Look where we are!" he shouted down the bench. "If somebody were to tell you that right now we're in Game Two of the World Series, and it's a tie ball game, if you didn't just get punched in the gut you'd say, 'Hell yeah, let's go win this thing.' *So let's go win this thing!*"

By the end of Game 2, Sig's rally towel nearly had a hole gnawed through it, but George Springer was four hours into his resurgence. After that first-inning walk, he'd singled and doubled. As he stepped into the box against Dodgers reliever Brandon McCarthy with no outs and a man on second in the top of the 11th, two things resonated in his mind. One was Verlander's speech. The other was his rediscovered mantra: *Don't swing hard.*

On McCarthy's fourth pitch to him—a low slider—he didn't. The ball exited his bat at 101.5 miles per hour, softer than he'd struck both his single and his double. But he hit this one in the air. And, 389 feet later, it landed in the stands in right center, to give the Astros a 7–5 lead.

The Dodgers would respond with a solo shot, by Charlie Culberson, in the bottom of the frame, but Springer's bomb proved the difference. He had delivered Houston its first victory in a World Series game since Roy Hofheinz had founded the club 56 years earlier. That was just trivia. What mattered was that the series was tied. As Sig discarded his saliva-soaked towel, he calculated the odds. A two-games-to-none deficit would have given the Astros just a 19 percent chance of winning the series. Of the 52 teams who had ever fallen behind two games to none in the World Series, just 10 had come back to win a ring. But a one-one tie? That brought it back to fifty-fifty. And now they were headed home.

///////////

ALTHOUGH CARLOS BELTRÁN WOULD NOT make the starting lineup for Game 3 of the World Series, as he hadn't for Game 1 or Game 2, he still devoted his time leading up to it to studying one Dodger in particular: Yu Darvish, the scheduled starter. Beltrán knew Darvish well. He had spent two months the previous year as Darvish's teammate with the Rangers, and had seen firsthand how devastating his arsenal could be. In particular, Darvish threw a biting slider that complemented his 94-mile-per-hour fastball and against which hitters batted just .151 in 2016 and .177 during 2017's regular season.

The Astros knew Darvish, too, though they wished they didn't. On April 2, 2013, in the first outing of his second season in the United States after signing a six-year, $56 million contract to come over from Japan, Darvish came one out from throwing a perfect game against Houston. Even though they regularly faced Darvish thereafter, as an American League West foe, they couldn't figure him out. Before the Dodgers acquired his services at the 2017 trade deadline, Darvish made two starts against the otherwise ascendant Astros in which, over 12 innings, he'd allowed eight hits and four runs.

Darvish would throw 49 pitches to the Astros in Game 3. He tried to be unpredictable, delivering 25 fastballs, 23 sliders and cutters, and one changeup. Usually, Darvish's pitches were among the most difficult in baseball for opposing hitters to make contact with, even to hit foul. During the regular season, they'd missed completely on more than 26 percent of their swings against him. In Game 3, the Astros swung at 25 of Darvish's pitches and missed just twice—a whiff rate of eight percent. Darvish would record only five outs in Game 3. By the time he left, in the bottom of the second, he had allowed six hits and a walk, as well as more runs—four—than the Astros, with Lance McCullers on the mound, would need to emerge with a 5–3 win. Darvish didn't understand. There was no doubt that the Astros' hitters were talented. On this night, it was almost as if they *knew* what was coming.

In fact, they did.

As Beltrán had absorbed video before the game of his former teammate's recent starts, he thought he noticed something. He no longer had to deal with screeching videotape, as he had when he had once found Bartolo Colón's tells. All he had to do was click a button on a computer. There it was again. And again.

When Darvish planned to throw his fastball, Beltrán observed, he regripped the baseball as he brought it to his glove, rotating it in his palm to find the proper seams with his fingers. When he intended to throw a slider, or a cutter, which broke similarly, he didn't adjust his grip; he already had the proper one. Beltrán knew when Darvish was going to throw his breaking ball, and when he wasn't, every single time. Quietly, he went around the clubhouse, informing all his teammates of his findings. Darvish is tipping, he told them quietly. Look at his fingers and wrist when he comes into his set position. If they wiggle, it's a fastball. If they don't, it's a slider or a cutter. Trust me.

Beltrán still had more work to do, in a way that even he couldn't have anticipated. Yuli Gurriel had begun the Astros' scoring with a long home run to left field. As Houston's second-inning onslaught continued, Beltrán was watching video in the clubhouse when the team's Spanish-language translator rushed in. "We have a problem," the translator said. "Look at this."

The international broadcast had captured Gurriel's reaction when he returned to the Astros' bench. *"Chinito,"* he appeared to say, as he smiled and nodded his head. Then, with some 15.7 million viewers watching across the nation, he pressed his fingers to the corner of his eyes and pulled out.

Yes, Beltrán thought. *We have a problem.*

Instantly, discussion of what appeared to be a racist gesture by Gurriel came to dominate social media, along with calls for an immediate suspension, including from the leading national baseball columnist and Fox on-field reporter Ken Rosenthal. The Astros' public relations staff encouraged Beltrán to wait until after the game to discuss the matter with the first baseman. "No, he should know now," Beltrán said. "Let him think through the innings we have left, and about what he wants to say after that." Beltrán knew that Gurriel would immediately step into a media firestorm, its flames licking at him in a language he didn't understand, and he wanted him to have the rest of the game to prepare for it.

In the dugout, Gurriel explained to Beltrán that in the heat of the moment, and with his vocabulary still limited to a few English words, he was trying to communicate to his teammates how thrilled he was that he had homered off a pitcher against whom he'd never before had success. In Cuba, *Chinito* was not considered an objectionable phrase by which to refer to an Asian person, and he had unthinkingly pulled at his eyes in an attempt to describe who he was talking about. He insisted that he was not trying to mock Darvish.

"If it's in your heart that you did not mean to offend the guy," Beltrán counseled Gurriel, "you should say that."

After the game, few reporters were interested in asking about the Astros' victory, or their two-games-to-one lead in the series. They crowded around Gurriel's locker. "It caught me by surprise," he said through a translator. "I didn't try to offend anybody. I was kind of shocked when people told me I had. I feel bad and apologize if he got offended over there. It was not my intention."

Meanwhile, Beltrán was texting Darvish, his old friend from the Rangers. "You know I wouldn't stand up for anybody if I didn't think he was a good person," he wrote. "Yuli's a great guy. He made a mistake. He understands that he made a mistake, and he apologizes."

That was enough for Darvish. "No one is perfect," the pitcher wrote on Twitter that night. "That includes both you and I. What he had done today isn't right, but I believe we should put our effort into learning rather than to accuse him. If we can take something from this, that is a giant step for mankind. Since we are living in such a wonderful world, let's stay positive and move forward instead of focusing on anger. I'm counting on everyone's big love."

Citing both Gurriel's remorse and Darvish's response, commissioner Rob Manfred announced that he would not suspend Gurriel during the World Series, but would instead dock him five games at the beginning of the next season. In one day, Beltrán had given his lineup the key to unlocking Yu Darvish, and then successfully de-fused a potentially explosive racial incident, the shock waves from which could have extended through the rest of the series. It wasn't a bad evening of work for a player who didn't even play.

///////////

IN THE SIXTH INNING of a scoreless Game 4 against the Dodgers, the Astros faced an identical threat to the one they had seen exactly a week earlier in Game 7 of the ALCS: men on first and third, with one out. Once again, the batter, Chris Taylor, hit a bouncer to Alex Breg-man. Once again, Bregman charged it. Once again, Sig screamed. And once again, Bregman nailed the baserunner at home. Although the Astros would lose the game 6–2, after a five-run ninth-inning implosion by relievers Ken Giles and Joe Musgrove, the game con-firmed that Alex Bregman still didn't give a shit, even though it was the World Series.

Sig had developed a theory—a hypothesis, to be exact—about undersized ballplayers, after so many years of watching Jed Lowrie and José Altuve, and now Alex Bregman. Most players with their skills but traditional pro bodies had lived their entire lives without having ever been told no and often without suffering any setbacks. So, when faced with the prospect of failing at a critical moment, they didn't know how to handle it, because they'd never had to do so before. Nothing was easy for a small player, and nothing was given to him. Bregman had lived on the brink of baseball failure all his life, and he no longer feared it. "He's probably already been failure-proofed," Sig said. That was what the scouts meant when they said Alex Bregman, allegedly six feet tall, didn't give a shit.

"One of the reasons I have this opportunity," Bregman said, "is because I'm a winner." It was the sort of thing that many players said winkingly. Bregman wasn't joking.

Game 5 featured the same starting pitchers as Game 1, Kershaw and Keuchel. That was where the similarities ended. While Game 1 was a surgical pitcher's duel, a matchup of Cy Young winners at their best, Game 5 was a bloodbath from the start. The Dodgers knocked out Keuchel in the fourth inning, having scored four runs against him. "It was a weird feeling," Keuchel said. "I just gave up four runs in Game Five of the World Series, and I'm sitting there trying to be pissed. But I couldn't be pissed, because I knew it didn't matter that we were down four runs against Clayton Kershaw." Kershaw left the game an inning later, after yielding six runs. The clubs traded blow after blow thereafter, scoring a total of 24 runs between them until, by the end of the ninth inning, they found themselves back where they had started: tied.

Seven of those runs had been driven in by José Altuve and Carlos Correa. Unlike George Springer, neither Altuve nor Correa had experienced any jitters beneath October's klieg lights, and they still didn't in Game 5. Altuve hit a three-run homer in the fifth and ripped an RBI double in the seventh. Correa nearly matched his output, with an RBI double in the fourth and a two-run homer in the seventh, despite having nursed a secret for the previous two weeks: He had injured his thumb so badly during the celebration after Game 2 of the ALCS that the digit became pocked with needle marks from repeated painkilling injections. "I look like a drug addict," he said, but someone who played every night of his childhood, no matter how tired or injured he was, wasn't about to miss an inning of the World Series.

The score remained 12–12 in the bottom of the 10th, and a game that was already more than five hours old seemed certain to continue much deeper into the night. Nobody in Minute Maid Park had use for their seats any longer, Jeff Luhnow included. Jansen, the Dodgers' seventh pitcher of the evening, recorded two quick outs in his second inning of work, but after that he hit McCann with a pitch and walked Springer. Then Alex Bregman stepped to the plate.

Brian McCann had many strengths, but foot speed was not one of them. Statcast measured the average sprint speed of 465 big leaguers in 2017. McCann ranked 464th. Meanwhile, the 24-year-old Derek

Fisher—the last man on the Astros' bench, one of the highly regarded prospects whom Luhnow had refused to trade—ranked 15th. It required little advanced statistical analysis for Hinch to decide to pinch run for McCann with Fisher.

Fisher didn't stand on second base for long. The previous evening, Bregman had hit a long ninth-inning home run off Jansen, one that came too late to affect the game's result. Now his approach was different. "I'm going to stay on top of his cutter," Bregman told Hinch. Of course, as Hinch said, "It's one thing to talk about it and another thing to do it."

With his first pitch to Bregman, Jansen threw the cutter he was looking for, down and away. Bregman stayed on top of it. He drove it to left. Fisher raced around third and slid into home. The Astros not only won their last game in Houston of the year, but were headed back to Los Angeles with a three-games-to-two lead and, Sig knew, a 68 percent chance of taking the series.

As Bregman rounded first, his teammates mobbed him. They began ripping the shirt from his body. That was fine by him. One of the many things about which he definitely didn't give a shit, especially now, was his jersey.

////////////

"I CAN'T SAY I'M SURPRISED the baseball gods said, 'OK, here we go, we're going to Game Seven,'" Justin Verlander conceded after Game 6. In Game 2, Verlander had failed to record a win for the first time as an Astro, and now he had earned another new result: a loss. He hadn't necessarily deserved it. He had begun the game with five shutout innings, but in the sixth the Dodgers scraped together two runs on a single, a hit by pitch, a blooped double down the line, and a sacrifice fly. As they had in Game 1 precisely a week before, the Astros got just one big swing, this time a third-inning home run by Springer. They lost by the same score, 3–1. Sig immediately calculated the Astros' odds of winning Game 7, which were now one and the same as the odds that they would win the series. "Forty-two percent chance tomorrow," he said, factoring in the Dodgers' home-field advantage and the looming threat of Yu Darvish. "The excruciating coin toss competition continues."

This time the coin was unevenly weighted. The probabilities suggested that the Dodgers held a slight edge, but they couldn't account for the fact that Carlos Beltrán had disarmed Darvish of his greatest weapon.

After the first pitch of Game 7, the Astros could tell that, at some point in the previous five days, Darvish and the Dodgers had figured out the same thing that Beltrán had. The pitch was a 96-mile-per-hour fastball to Springer, and as he brought the ball to his glove, Darvish's wrist and fingers moved less than they had in Game 3. But the wiggle was still there. Even more damaging, to Darvish, was that he had to think about not tipping before each pitch instead of simply throwing it. As Dallas Keuchel would say, "When you start thinking about stuff other than pitching, you're screwed."

Darvish's third pitch to Springer was a low slider. Springer turned on it and drove it down the left-field line for a leadoff double. He flashed two thumbs to the Astros' bench. Springer scored the game's first run after Darvish's next pitch, when Dodgers first baseman Cody Bellinger scooped up a Bregman grounder and threw it into the dugout. Two pitches later, Darvish tried another slider. Base stealers like to run on off-speed pitches, as they arrive slower than fastballs and are more difficult for catchers to receive. Bregman, on second base, got a suspiciously large jump. He swiped third without a throw. Two pitches after that, Altuve got a piece of another slider, grounding it to first and allowing Bregman to cross home for a 2–0 first-inning lead.

The lead was 3–0 with two outs in the top of the second when, with a man on third base, Springer stepped to the plate for his second at-bat of the evening. Darvish had already thrown 41 pitches to nine Astros, and had induced just one swing and miss. Now he faced a hitter who was nothing like the one who struck out four straight times in Game 1. Springer had reached base in nine of his previous 10 plate appearances. He had homered in three straight games, and in four in the series overall. Dodgers manager Dave Roberts had Brandon Morrow, his shutdown setup man, warming in the bullpen, but he opted to keep Darvish on the mound.

Darvish's fifth pitch to Springer was a slider. This time, it worked. Springer swung through it. The count was full. Then Darvish tried a fastball. It came in at 96 miles per hour over the middle of the plate.

World Series MVP George Springer (No. 4) exults with Carlos Correa after Springer's Game 7 home run off Yu Darvish.

In the history of the World Series, only two players, the Hall of Famers Lou Gehrig and Reggie Jackson, had homered in four straight games. Just two, Jackson and Chase Utley, had hit five home runs in a single series. On Darvish's 47th and last pitch of the evening, Springer turned those duos into triumvirates. "The pain is going to stay with me awhile," Darvish said of what he was feeling as he trudged off the mound with a 5–0 deficit, in the process becoming the second pitcher ever to start two World Series games and fail to reach the third inning in either.

José Altuve, meanwhile, was feeling something else. Long ago, back in Maracay, he had learned never to allow himself to peer into the future. Nothing was guaranteed to anyone, especially a baseball player who was five foot five. The moment, and what you did with it, was what mattered. Altuve hadn't even permitted himself to assume what had become a lock a month earlier: that after a regular season in which he had batted .346, with 24 home runs, 81 RBIs, and 32 steals, he would win the American League's Most Valuable Player Award over a rival, the Yankees' Aaron Judge, who stood 14 inches taller than Altuve and outweighed him by 117 pounds. Now, though, with a 5–0 lead in Game 7 of the World Series, Altuve couldn't help himself. He began counting outs.

Three hours later, Altuve stationed himself in shallow right field. The Astros, now leading 5–1, with two outs in the bottom of the ninth, had shifted against Corey Seager. Bregman played where Correa generally did, at shortstop, and Correa stood in Altuve's usual spot. As the pitcher, Charlie Morton, prepared to deliver an inside, 97-mile-per-hour fastball to Seager, Altuve pounded his glove with his fist and bent his knees.

///////////

Carlos Correa hadn't asked Carlos Beltrán only about hitting in 2017. He also asked him about love, particularly that which Correa felt for Daniella Rodriguez, the former Miss Texas USA who didn't care if a motel room smelled like piss. Correa heard the way Beltrán talked about his wife, Jessica, and their three children. Although Correa was only 23, he knew he wanted that for himself.

"Are you happy?" Beltrán asked Correa.

"Yes," Correa said

"Are you guys connecting?"

"Yes."

"Does she understand your job? The travel, the things you gotta go through?"

"Yes."

"Then there's nothing else to talk about."

Correa hatched a plan, and he enlisted the help of Fox's Ken Rosenthal before Game 6. It was predicated on the Astros' winning one of the series' final two games.

At 8:57 p.m. in Los Angeles—10:57 p.m. in Houston—on November 1, 2017, Seager hit the ground ball for which Luhnow and Sig had been planning for six years, for which Correa had been hoping for 23, and for which Houston had been waiting for 56. The Dodgers' shortstop hit it exactly where the Astros' data indicated he might, to the shifted Altuve in shallow right. *Don't miss it*, Altuve said to himself. He didn't. He picked it up, as he had thousands of times before. He threw to first base, as he had thousands of times before. This time, it was the final out of the World Series.

None of the Astros could remember exactly what he did over the next few minutes. Altuve ran toward Correa, who picked him up and lifted him high in the air. The club gathered on a stage that was rolled out behind the pitcher's mound at Dodger Stadium. They took turns raising the World Series trophy, and Springer accepted the series' MVP Award. Then, for Correa at least, everything came into focus. He and Rosenthal put their plan into action on national TV.

"You dreamed of this your whole life, this feeling," Rosenthal said. "Is it everything you thought it would be?"

"It's everything and more, man," Correa said. "It's one of the biggest steps of my life, one of the biggest accomplishments of my life. And right now, I'm about to take another big step in my life."

The shortstop reached into his back pocket and turned to Rodriguez. "Daniella Rodriguez, you've made me the happiest man in the world," he said. Then he dropped to one knee. "Will you marry me?"

"Oh my God!" Rodriguez said. She put her hands on Correa's cheeks and began to weep.

After Fox's cameras cut away to a dumbfounded Big Papi, Correa found someone else to embrace. He bent down to pull him into a bear hug that lasted several minutes. Correa buried his face into the man's sun-scorched neck, and now he cried himself. *"Lo hicimos,"* he whispered into Carlos Sr.'s ear. *We did it.*

Carlos Correa hugs his father, as Justin Verlander embraces Kate Upton.

As the reality of their victory set in, the thoughts of each of the people who had collaborated to produce it shifted back to the road that had led to it. The result mattered, of course. It was why, two days later, more than 750,000 Houstonians—some of whose houses were still powered by generators, and some of whom no longer had houses at all—would line 20 downtown blocks for the Astros' first-ever championship parade. What mattered more, and what they would really always remember, was how they got there.

"Even when the heat was on, I told Jeff Luhnow, 'I'll stick to the plan,'" said Jim Crane on the field at Dodger Stadium. "'The plan, the plan, work the plan.' And that's what he did." Crane wore a checked light blue sports coat and the grin of an owner whose franchise had not only just won the World Series, but had more than doubled in value in just six years. The Astros were now worth $1.65 billion, according to *Forbes*.

The Astros rush the field immediately after clinching on November 1, 2017.

Jim Crane gazes at the result of the Astros' process.

"It only took me twenty years to get to this position," said a red-eyed Carlos Beltrán, the poker shark among blackjack mavens. "It's a blessing. Now I could go either way." In reality, he knew where his career was headed. In his arms he carried his young son, who kept tugging on his ear. Two weeks later, he announced his retirement. Not long after that, he interviewed to become the manager of the Yankees. Although he didn't get the job, there was little doubt that, one day soon, he would be a skipper.

As José Altuve threw to Yuli Gurriel to secure the final out of Game 7, Jeff Luhnow, sitting in the front row of the Astros' front office's box on the mezzanine level of Dodger Stadium, held his own son on his knee. He carried the now three-year-old Henry down the stairs, through the stands, out onto the field, and up onto the stage for the trophy presentation. "I don't know if he will remember it," Luhnow said. "But he was there." Not half an hour later, with Henry safely in the hands of his mother, Gina, Luhnow's mind had already flipped from the result to that which had always given his work meaning: the process. He walked off the field with his arm around Justin Verlander, who had agreed to come to Houston not just for 2017, but for 2018 and 2019, too. "This is one," Luhnow told his still new ace. "We have two more to go."

Verlander's mind had shifted ahead to a nearer future. His wedding to Kate Upton was to occur three days later. When they had planned the event, the odds of the only thing that could have interfered with it—a World Series Game 7 for the Tigers—had seemed long. Now, while the couple was still in Los Angeles, their guests had already begun arriving in Italy. "Your wedding's so pretty," attendees at a welcome event that evening had texted them. "Wish you were here."

Sig, his monthlong grimace replaced with a wry smile, kept to the periphery of the celebration, with Arati by his side. He stood on the wrong side of the metal barricades that ringed the stage, and then in the hallway outside the clubhouse where the players lit cigars and doused one another with champagne. Some of the players high-fived him as they ran past. Most didn't look at him at all. That was fine.

Our world celebrates outcomes. Sig did, too. "Winning is fun," he said. "Getting a World Series ring for doing math is fun." The Dodgers scored precisely as many runs in the series, 34, as the Astros, but the Astros' runs were better distributed, so now they were the champions. But Sig contemplated a different series, that of the decisions—thousands of them, made by thousands of people—that had combined to lead to this moment, which was never assured. What was life, if not a string of decisions? And why would anyone not want to do his best to make better ones? That was the only thing he and Jeff Luhnow had set out to do in St. Louis a dozen years earlier. They never thought they could always beat life's dealer. "If anybody tells you they have an idea of what the future looks like, don't believe them," Sig said. "The future is a lot weirder than we imagine. The future is a lot weirder than we *can* imagine. If you think you've got it figured out, just wait. You will be wrong."

What Luhnow and Sig had always believed was that they could give themselves a better chance of being right more often than they were not. That chance was what they would continue to pursue.

"No more points needed," said Sig, happy but weary. "This season, anyway."

ASTROWORLD

As the Astros surged through the early months of the summer of 2017, and then swooned in August, Sig Mejdal was not in Houston to observe it. Instead, he was becoming familiar with the backroads and drive-thrus of the Northeast. He had traded in the usual Nerd Cave uniform of khakis and polo shirts for a different one. It read VALLEYCATS across the chest, in bold red script.

Jeff Luhnow had assigned Sig to spend June through August wearing a baseball jersey for the first time since his final Little League season with the Papagallos in San Jose 36 years earlier. He sat on the bench with the Tri-City ValleyCats, the Single-A affiliate of the Astros who played in the New York–Penn League and called the old industrial city of Troy, New York, home. Sig rode the ValleyCats' bus as far north as Vermont, as far west as Ohio, and as far south as West Virginia. The ValleyCats had a roster filled with players who could barely legally drink, and many who couldn't. The oldest of them was 24, the youngest 18.

Sig mostly stuck with the coaching staff, men who were just a decade or two his junior, not three. The ValleyCats' manager was Morgan Ensberg, who had been the Astros' third baseman in the mid-2000s. One night, after a long bus trip, Sig found himself in the same bar in Troy as many of the team's players. It was awkward, like when Sig was an undergraduate at UC-Davis and saw one of his professors out of the classroom. Now he was the professor.

As last call approached, Sig realized that one of the players to whom he had sheepishly waved earlier could use his help. The player hadn't been drinking, but he'd drawn the attention of the Napoleonic bouncer anyway. The bouncer accused him of making too much noise as he played *Big Buck Hunter*, the arcade game in which participants slay digital wildlife with neon plastic rifles. The bouncer stormed over and pulled the game's plug. The player turned the faux rifle on the bouncer and clicked the trigger. That was Sig's cue. As the bouncer geared up for the challenge he had been aiming for all night—that of taking down a much larger, professional athlete—Sig intervened. He guided the player outside, then returned to confront the bouncer, who seemed as if he'd be just as willing to maul a middle-aged data scientist. But it was Sig who landed the first and final shot. It wasn't with his fist.

"You need to be nicer to your patrons!" he told the bouncer.

Luhnow did not send Sig to Troy in order to stave off barroom brawls. Sig did that for free. He was officially there to advise Ensberg and the players

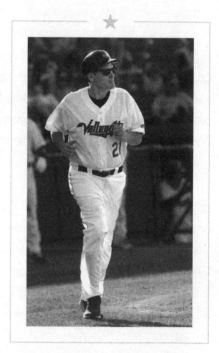

Sig Mejdal in uniform with the Tri-City ValleyCats in June 2017.

on how to incorporate data into their infield positioning and pitch selection, to coach first base, and mostly to make observations and recommendations under the auspices of his new job title with the Astros, another one that nobody had ever heard before. He was no longer their Director of Decision Sciences. He was now the Special Assistant to the GM, Process Improvement. The number he wore on his back was 21. Blackjack.

//////////

By 2017, THE ASTROS' rivals had caught on to many of the techniques and strategies that had once represented a competitive advantage as they laid the foundation for a World Series champion. Every club, even the Tigers, had a growing analytics department, stocked with engineers and data whizzes, that could help it synthesize all sources of predictive information to nail drafts and properly value players based upon their future performances. Two winters earlier, the Brewers had hired David Stearns, Luhnow's top assistant, to be their 30-year-old general manager, occasioning the promotion of Mike Elias to take Stearns's place. "Sometimes we can't help but think back to the good old days, when we were alone at the buffet," Sig said. The Astros' winning records, starting in 2015, meant that their first picks would for the foreseeable future fall into what used to be Cardinals territory, and the improved sophistication of the clubs selecting ahead of them meant there were ever-fewer overlooked diamonds to be mined.

Every club ran defensive shifts. Major league hitters faced more than 26,000 of them in 2017, a near-fourfold increase from 2013, when Luhnow and Stearns had introduced the concept to a skeptical Dallas Keuchel. And more clubs than ever had embraced the usefulness of losing, as a way of stockpiling resources to be deployed in a distant future when they were ready to win. "You could find yourself competing with more teams for the number one pick than you would for the World Series," said Jerry Dipoto, the general manager of the Seattle Mariners. As the 2018 season approached, at least eight teams, representing a quarter of the league, harbored no intention of participating in that October's playoffs. Over the winter, none of them had committed more than $20 million to signing free agents, and two, the Braves and the Pirates, hadn't added a single one.

That strategy couldn't possibly work out for all of them as it had for the Astros. At least a few of those eight were committing themselves to another decade of losing and empty stadiums, after which they would have to rebuild once more. There is only one first-overall pick each year, and, eventually, only one World Series ring. The Astros had no desire to ever again enter that sort of demolition derby, and also no need to. They hadn't spent all those seasons in baseball limbo, or somewhere worse, for a single shot at a championship. If their 162–324 record between 2011 and 2013 represented the nadir, then 2017 alone was never meant to represent the summit—merely the first peak in a dense range.

Of the 25 players on his World Series roster, Luhnow had inherited three, drafted four, traded for nine, and signed nine as free agents, with the idea of assembling a roster that could not just win once but could keep doing it. The Astros' four most important hitters, the first four of their World Series lineup—George Springer, Alex Bregman, José Altuve, and Carlos Correa—were 28 years old or younger. Bregman and Correa were just 23. Springer wasn't due to reach free agency until 2021, Correa until 2022, and Bregman until 2023. In March 2018, Luhnow locked in Altuve for even longer than that. He signed the reigning American League MVP to a five-year, $151 million contract extension that would run through 2024. Starting in 2020, the second baseman would, by himself, earn each season as much as the entirety of the Astros' 2013 Opening Day roster.

None of their pitchers was immediately going anywhere, either. Keuchel would be the first to be eligible to test free agency, after 2018, but Lance McCullers would remain the Astros' property until three years after that. Luhnow also had succession plans in place in the form of the top prospects that Elias, now in charge of both the domestic and international scouting departments, and Kevin Gold-stein continued to provide, and with whom Luhnow had steadfastly refused to part, even for Justin Verlander.

Luhnow had prepared his organization for the future in other ways. The process that he and Sig had invented in St. Louis, and then refined and expanded in Houston, had worked, and had provided his Audi a new vanity license plate: ws 112, in honor of the Astros' total number of victories in 2017. But Luhnow had never believed that it represented an ultimate answer to winning in perpetuity.

For one thing, the process was fundamentally backward-looking, and therefore static. Sig's projections had brilliantly harnessed all sources of information—hard and soft, human and statistical—to predict the future. But there was another level beyond that, a world of innovation that would allow the Astros to stay ahead of competi-tors who had gotten wise to the techniques that had turned them into champions. To reach it required figuring out how to exploit their information to enable players to attain a level of success that their past performances suggested was beyond them, to give each small slap hitter with a growth mindset the best chance of becoming José Altuve, and each soft-tossing control artist the greatest odds of be-coming Dallas Keuchel. It was one thing to predict the future. It was another to consistently change it.

Though the specifics of Sig's minor league assignment were top secret, that was the process he was tasked with figuring out how to improve. He wasn't trying to do it by himself.

///////////

BRANDON TAUBMAN GRADUATED FROM CORNELL with a bachelor's in economics in 2007. Like many Ivy Leaguers, he went into bank-ing, and became an expert in valuing the complex financial instru-ments known as derivatives, first at Ernst & Young and then at Barclays. As a five-foot-seven Long Islander, Taubman had long be-fore transitioned from playing baseball to watching it, but he remained connected to the game via the modern version of All-Star Baseball: daily fantasy, in which websites like DraftKings and FanDuel allowed players to select their own lineups each night, and to risk and win real money. With a friend, Taubman used his financial training to design a system that entered hundreds of lineups a day to exploit overlooked but predictive factors like weather forecasts. They won 58 percent of the time, a significant margin over the break-even point of 53 percent. In 2013, Taubman responded to a job posting for an analyst position that would pay him much less than he made at Barclays, or even via daily fantasy. While almost all of the other 499 applicants for the position held advanced degrees, Jeff Luhnow plucked Taubman's name from the slush pile.

Taubman began as an economist, helping Stearns in areas like contract valuations. Over the years, his responsibilities grew. Luhnow promoted him almost every season, until, in September 2017, when he was 31, he became the Astros' senior director of baseball operations, research, and innovation.

Sig's own promotion, to special assistant, had meant that Mike Fast, the former semiconductor engineer and *Baseball Prospectus* writer, took over the Nerd Cave. By the fall of 2017, the Nerd Cave had expanded to house a staff of nine, and Fast's early expertise in player tracking technology, like PITCHf/x and TrackMan, had become more relevant than ever. Before Luhnow gave Fast his first job in baseball, Fast's prowess had allowed him to essentially discover the value of pitch framing—how a catcher's ability to receive a borderline pitch, and to subtly deceive a home plate umpire into calling a strike on what was actually a ball, could by itself provide or cost a team several dozen runs a year. With the Astros, Fast's analytical skills had revealed the underlying value of Collin McHugh, and more recently Charlie Morton.

Entering 2017, Morton was a 33-year-old journeyman with a 46–71 record and a career ERA of 4.54. He also had a mid-90s fastball, a sinker he threw too frequently, and, like McHugh, a curveball that he didn't throw often enough. Despite his unimpressive statistical résumé, Taubman and Fast lobbied Luhnow to sign Morton to a two-year, $14 million free agent contract before the 2017 season. The frequency with which Morton threw his sinker declined from 63 percent to 41 percent, and his curveball rate increased from 24 percent to 28 percent. Morton went 14–7, with a 3.62 ERA, then closed out the World Series.

In the months after their championship, the Astros focused their efforts on acquiring another pitcher whom they thought their analytical resources could help. The Pirates had picked Gerrit Cole, out of UCLA, first overall in 2011. Four years after that, he had gone 19–8, with a 2.60 ERA, and finished fourth in the National League Cy Young voting. His outcomes had deteriorated in the next two seasons: He went a combined 19–22, with an ERA of 4.12. There was nothing wrong with his arm. He was just 27, and could still throw his fastball more than 100 miles per hour. Curiously, by 2017 he had begun to throw his sinking fastball more often than his slider, though his slider was the better pitch. While opponents hit .360 against his sinker, and swung at and missed it just seven percent of the time, they batted .268 against his slider and whiffed on nearly 34 percent of them. In January 2018, at Taubman's and Fast's urging, the Astros acquired two years of Cole's services in exchange for four minor leaguers, none of them ranked among their top prospects, who still included the pitchers Forrest Whitley and Francis Martes and the outfielders Derek Fisher and Kyle Tucker. It was a safe bet that in Houston, Cole—a potential third ace in the rotation, behind Justin Verlander and Dallas Keuchel—would be throwing many more sliders.

Meanwhile, the Astros had hundreds of players already in their system whom they could help rapidly improve without their having to sacrifice prospects or millions of dollars to give them the opportunity. Baseball technologies had exploded in the six years since Luhnow and Sig had arrived in Houston, and Jim Crane, listening to his analysts, had made early investments in at least three of them. There was TrackMan, which the Astros had used for years before it became formally adopted by the league as Statcast. There was Blast Motion, a disc containing an accelerometer and gyroscope that could be attached to a player's bat and measure its velocity and angle as it moved through space. And there were high-speed video cameras that could record every one of a player's actions in both games and training in fine detail, and break them down to the thousandth of a second.

The Astros installed each technology not just on the major league level, but in each of their minor league parks, even in Troy. Sig and Fast folded the data they collected into the Nerd Cave's algorithms, rendering their predictions ever more accurate, but the technologies were useful in other ways. Had the Astros attached a Blast Motion sensor to the knob of J.D. Martinez's bat during spring training of 2014, the club's executives wouldn't have had to rely on just his word and a small sample of plate appearances to decide whether his revamped swing was real. They would have seen it. Realizing they hadn't seen it only accelerated their technological investments, and boosted their resolve not to miss such a development again.

In concert, the technologies were even more powerful. TrackMan data, combined with high-speed video, could allow the club's analysts to detect if changes in a pitcher's delivery or pitches suggested that he could be on the cusp of sustaining a long-term injury that might be avoided, or even if he was fatiguing during a given game before he could bring himself to admit it to A.J. Hinch.

The technologies could also be used to provide the Astros' players, on all organizational levels, with immediately measurable goals. It was one thing for a hitting coach, relying on experience alone, to suggest that a player might try to change his swing in order to hit the ball in the air more often. It was another to present the player with hard evidence in a format that was easier to understand, for anyone who was not himself a data scientist, than graphs or plotted points: Here is TrackMan data that demonstrates that balls hit with a launch angle of 19 to 26 degrees have the best chance of turning into home runs or extra base hits. Here is Blast Motion data that captures what your typical swing looks like now. And here is high-speed video, overlaid with digestible data visualizations, that shows you what your best swings look like against every type of pitch, so you can repeat them more often than not.

After 2017, the Astros' front office had an advantage besides their early adoption of technology: a track record. They once had to coax players like Dallas Keuchel into trusting that their methods would not only work, but would be individually beneficial. Over the years, Luhnow had largely ceded that job to an executive named Pete Putila, who was an intern when Luhnow arrived in 2011 and whom he had kept around because of both his skills and his genial bedside manner. Now Putila was the director of player development, and one of the only staffers who remained from the pre-Luhnow days, in part because the West Virginia graduate was so good at translating data-driven suggestions to players throughout the organization and at persuading them to give the suggestions a try. After 2017, that job became easier for Putila, and for everyone in the front office. Their rings did much of the talking. That José Altuve and Carlos Correa were using the same tools did much more to convince young players to buy into them than the promises of dorks in khakis and polos.

The Astros' success also had another result. It earned them the admiration, sometimes begrudging, of longtime baseball men who had once viewed them as know-it-all outsiders. "I think they've unlocked a lot of things on the hitting side, and are more advanced in that area than anyone else," said one rival general manager. "They're ahead of the game in terms of offensive information. I do hear from some baseball operations people who say, 'I want them to lose so fucking bad, because they're arrogant.' But Jeff Luhnow's not paid to win popularity contests. He's paid to fucking deliver. And he's doing that."

Even some player agents, frustrated by the Astros' general refusal to pay their clients a dollar more than their valuations suggested they were worth, had come to appreciate them. "You can tell that they really believe in what they're doing," one agent said. "They have a system, and it was not an accident that it worked. Exactly what they thought would happen, happened. I think Jeff Luhnow is a great general manager. I may not want to go on vacation with him—but I'd work for him."

///////////

AFTER THREE MONTHS on the ValleyCats' bus, Sig returned to his fraternity brother's garage, and then endured the most wonderful and horrible October of his 51 years. The process had worked, and yet the process continued. There were so many ways in which it could be improved, which even the most forward thinking of organizations had not yet begun to address. Perhaps they could try a new type of defensive shift, in which they turned one of their infielders into an outfielder against particularly extreme fly-ball hitters. Perhaps they could, one day, install a uniformed analyst to work side by side with the manager in the dugout—not just with Morgan Ensberg in Tri-City, but with Hinch in Houston.

They could certainly improve the food. In the lowest levels of the minor leagues, the postgame clubhouse spread was often a loaf of Wonder Bread, a tub of peanut butter, and a jar of jelly. The meal money, $25 per day, was only generous enough for players to order from fast-food value menus, if they ordered at all. Many of the Latin American players went without, instead sending their per diems home to their families in the Dominican Republic or Venezuela. And yet, somehow, they were still expected to develop into world-class athletes.

They had even further to go in understanding clubhouse chemistry. The Astros gave $16 million to Carlos Beltrán for reasons beyond his ability to hit home runs, but they had no way of predicting that without him, they would likely not have won a World Series in which he didn't have a hit. Kate Bezrukova and Chester Spell, the professors who conducted some of the first academic research into the effect of chemistry on a club's performance, had expanded their work for one of Sig's former employers: NASA. They were studying how factors like narcissism and aggression could impact the efficiency of a group of a half dozen high-performing people who might one day be locked together in a shuttle the size of a one-bedroom apartment for more than a year, the time it would take to successfully complete a mission to Mars. Their techniques, they believed, could be applied to a baseball clubhouse. It would require the installation of cameras to analyze every interaction between players, both conversational and nonverbal, and biometric devices to record their stress responses, like their heart rates and cortisol levels. But it could be done.

There was always more data to be collected and harnessed. That underscored the inadequacy of the data you already had. Were the Astros run by computer, they would probably never have drafted a high school shortstop out of Puerto Rico, or retained a five-foot-five second baseman, or signed a 40-year-old free agent, or traded for an aging pitcher who made $20 million a year. And, if not for the intuition of a single person, the Cardinals' owner Bill DeWitt Jr., and the timely publication of a book called *Moneyball*, the men who made those calls would have likely remained in Silicon Valley and at NASA. Data could help guide best practices, but it was unwise to confuse those with perfect practices. If people who denied the power of data could no longer compete, neither could those who believed that data alone provided an answer, not a tool. "All models are wrong," the British statistician George E. P. Box once wrote. "But some are useful."

As the data landscape flattened—as every organization gained access to the same set of numbers and technologies—then the new edge might come from those sources that were virtually impossible to quantify and to incorporate into statistical models. There would, in other words, always be a place for human intelligence alongside the artificial kind, and not just in baseball. There would always be a role for gut feels.

I joined *Sports Illustrated* as a temporary reporter 14 years ago. One of my first assignments was to interview a champion bloodhound who worked out every day on a treadmill. *SI* has been my professional home ever since, so the relationship is at least semi-permanent by now, and the subjects I write about have become more forthcoming, for the most part. *Astroball* was born in the magazine's pages, and dozens of my colleagues contributed to it, particularly Taylor Ballantyne, Mark Bechtel, Steve Cannella, Albert Chen, Richard Demak, Adam Duerson, Max Fucci, Maggie Gray, Hank Hersch, Ryan Hunt, Ted Keith, Terry McDonell, Gabe Miller, Stephen Skalocky, Emma Span, Tom Verducci, Grant Wahl, and Jon Wertheim—and, yes, even Alan Shipnuck. It is impossible for a falsehood to slip past Sarah Kwak, who fact-checked every word of *Astroball,* or for an evocative image to evade Abby Nicolas, who found its photos. This book would not exist without Chris Stone, who will always nurture a writer's ideas, however far-fetched.

Sports Illustrated's library might be the world's best sports archive and is now housed in the New-York Historical Society, where I spent hours poring over yellowed clips and documents that chronicled Judge Roy Hofheinz's founding of the Astros and the concurrent rise of Houston. In order to gain an outside perspective on the modern Astros' innovations, I consulted with many people in baseball, journalism, and academia, especially the professors Kate Bezrukova and Chester Spell. The MLB Network's Chris Arnowich, Doug Jaclin, Micah Karg, Brian Kenny, and Chris Russo were early and consistent supporters of my assertions about the Astros.

The majority of my reporting came via interviews with members of the Astros organization. Over the past five years I have spoken with at least 46 of them, several for hours on end over more than half a dozen sessions. Carlos Beltrán, Carlos Correa, Mike Elias, Dallas Keuchel, Jeff Luhnow, J.D. Martinez, Sig Mejdal, George Springer, and Justin Verlander were particularly generous with their time and insight. That they won the World Series was also quite helpful.

Chris Parris-Lamb immediately grasped my vision for *Astroball* and continually worked with me to sharpen and refine it along the way. He is an agent who not only sells a writer's work, but cares about making it better. That is true of everyone at The Gernert Company, especially Sarah Bolling and Jack Gernert, as well as Steven Fisher and Christopher Reid of Underground Films.

No publishing timeline, apparently, is too short for the team at Crown, and it was remarkable to watch it spring into action to get this book made. Craig Adams, Tammy Blake, Tricia Boczkowski, Julie Cepler, Jon Darga, Melissa Esner, Ellen Folan, Kevin Garcia, Andrea Lau, Ivy McFadden, Kathleen Quinlan, Annsley Rosner, and Molly Stern all believed that *Astroball* would be worth the effort. Kevin Doughten, my editor and friend, dropped everything to tirelessly shape *Astroball*'s narrative into what it has become, and deserves several weeks of Superchunk concerts.

I'm fortunate to have friends who perfectly complement one another as far as their talents and peculiarities—a group without fault lines. In particular, Rachel Blitzer, Matt McCarthy, and John Phillips formed an ideal daily sounding board, both endlessly patient and endlessly opinionated as far as even the most seemingly inconsequential elements of this book go, such as whether it was a good idea to use an epigraph from a 90-year-old horror story about an aquatic monster. (A minority of one won that debate.) Charlie Finch, the novelist, essayist, and critic, is the best friend any writer could have.

I wrote the first words of *Astroball* in the home of Serra and George Goldman, as George watched over my shoulder and asked what blackjack was. Billy and Marie Goldman were never far from my mind as I worked on it every day thereafter, and will remain as such even though I've now typed its last period. While most of its members are lucky enough not to have to know exactly what an OPS is, the rest of my family has also always avidly read and supported me anyway: Lyn and Glenn Reiter; Diana Reiter and Sean, Eve, and Lily Mersten; Julie Reiter; Susan Goldman; and Danny, Corinne, Olivia, Noa, Everly, and Aidan Goldman. Henry Rodin is my most attentive and encouraging reader of all.

The central lesson I took from the Astros has been the importance of focusing on processes over outcomes. As it turns out, the process of writing a book in a single winter is harder on an author's wife and children than it is on the author. Alice, Madeleine, and Celia Reiter put as much into *Astroball* as I did, and will always have that which resides just above my gut—my heart.

Page numbers in *italics* indicate photographs.

BEN REITER is a senior writer for *Sports Illustrated*, which he joined in 2004. He has written 23 cover stories for the magazine and has also contributed to *Time* and *The Village Voice*, among other publications. He frequently appears on radio and television stations across the United States and around the world, and is a regular commentator on the MLB Network. Reiter is a graduate of Yale and Cambridge. He lives in New York City with his family. *Astroball* is his first book.